The Seminary
Protestant and Catholic

The Seminary
Protestant and
Catholic

by *WALTER D. WAGONER*

Sheed and Ward : : New York

To my colleagues for eleven years in
The Fund for Theological Education

YORKE ALLEN, JR., BENJAMIN E. MAYS,
NATHAN M. PUSEY, CHARLES L. TAYLOR,
HENRY P. VAN DUSEN

Acknowledgments

"An Innocent Abroad" might be the best way to paraphrase the title of this book. The stumbling and bumping about which besets a well-intentioned Protestant who goes forth to explore the Roman Catholic Church can be as humorous as it is exasperating. Without the constant guidance and map-reading by Catholic friends along the way, I would have wandered forever in circles. Even so, and despite the embarrassing number of hours and days of courtesy offered by these friends, I finally had to make the interpretations and to pass the judgments. Many of those Catholics who have so endeared themselves to me must now stretch charity to the limit as they read a sentence here or a paragraph there which appears to them to be quixotic or just plain wrong. But it is far better, I hope, to take the risk of writing a Protestant diary than a Catholic interlinear translation.

I am particularly grateful to the Board of Directors of The Fund for Theological Education for the study-leave granted me to pursue this inquiry: full-time for almost six months, plus more than a year's additional work part-time. Those in the Princeton office: Mr. C. Shelby Rooks, Miss Edith Colton, Mrs. Robert Green, have been quick to help and to cover my tracks. Mrs. Christopher Meadows has been the most cooperative typist imaginable.

I am more pleased than I can say that the prominent Catholic publishing house of Sheed and Ward, through the derring-do of Mr. Philip Scharper, has ventured to issue this volume. The graciousness of Father Roland Murphy's Foreword is a kudo which I greatly cherish.

It would be hopeless to indicate the exact contribution of the many, many persons, both here and abroad, who were so generous and helpful to me in preparing this book. There is no adequate way to express my appreciation. I can only hope that the book itself will seem to them worth all the trouble they took with me and my queries. Because I feel that the reader will want some idea of the thoroughness of my investigation in the interest of this book, I have listed the many people to whom I am so grateful in Appendix 5. I should also like to say that some of the material in Chapter 2 was used in the Jones Lectureship for 1966, Austin Presbyterian Theological Seminary.

A Catholic Foreword

The *Decree on Priestly Formation* (conveniently reproduced in this book) did not catch the headlines accorded to several other decrees and constitutions of Vatican Council II. Yet there is widespread agreement that this document is of supreme importance, for it deals with the future of the Church: the preparation for the spiritual leadership which can be expected from the clergy. The renewal in the Church would be seriously impaired if the training of priests did not correspond to the spirit of the *aggiornamento*. Its very importance perhaps accounts for the disappointment which some have found in the Decree. However, it is at least a promising document; windows have been opened here as in so many other areas. The way is opened to a much-needed adaptation of current seminary life and studies to the kind of training called for by the American situation. The key role of the national episcopal conference, which will have authority to promulgate specific recommendations for the general implementation of the Decree, is at once obvious. But at this writing it is not yet apparent what direction American seminary life will take under the aegis of the episcopal conference.

The Decree places emphasis on both the spiritual and the intellectual formation of the seminarian according to the new directions of Vatican II. This means a liturgical and pastoral orientation, a sensitivity to the Word of God, a nurturing in faith and love, in maturity and responsibility. These ideals are seen in a new light in virtue of the spirit of Vatican II, and new methods of actualizing them must be reached. The intellectual formation receives a number of new emphasis: the role of biblical study and the historical development of theological thought (as opposed to the static theory that has characterized theological manuals over the past years). Even such a detail as the recognition of seminar and discussion (in contrast to the overworked lecture method) is very welcome. The passivity which has character-ized the theological process, and the irrelevancy of some of it, must go. A decidedly pastoral slant will not sacrifice, but complement intellectual training and integrity.

Where can the Church turn for help in bringing the theory of the Decree into reality? In America itself forth-right critics, both clerical and lay, have contributed serious and worthy suggestions for a renewal of seminary life. Now we have the sincere attempt of a Protestant clergyman to share his reaction with us. The impetus of the ecumenical movement has made inevitable such books as this one. Protestants have examined the conciliar statements of Vati-can II and have shared their critical judgments with Catho-lics. The *Decree on Priestly Formation* must necessarily remain abstract to those Americans who do not have first-hand contact with seminary life. What is the ethos that in-forms the training of seminarians? The answer to such a question helps explain the Church to Catholics and Protestants alike. It is particularly fitting that a Protestant educator such as Walter Wagoner should have taken pains to investigate this area. He presents a challenge, friendly to Catholic and Protestant alike, based on his observations at many Catholic seminaries and on his own committed involvement in Protestant seminary education.

His book is not a scientific analytical study of Catholic seminary life. Many such studies of various aspects of seminary training are still needed, and at many points in this book their lack is deeply felt. But one may not simply wait for them; one must prepare for them, and this book does precisely that by its urgent presentation of various issues. We lack a detailed study of Catholic seminary life from the point of view of academic theology (something in the style of *The Advancement of Theological Education* by Niebuhr, Williams and Gustafson, alluded to in this work). I feel that this book points up the necessity of such a study. It remains important that Catholics listen to the voices of their separated brethren. *The Seminary: Protestant and Catholic* is a lively and moving story of the emphasis in seminary training, as a Protestant has been able to share it and to witness it. It is worth noting that the author turns freely from the Catholic to the Protestant situation for parallels and contrasts. Such give and take makes possible mutual impovement. Mr. Wagoner is not so much proposing solutions as challenging assumptions and accepted ways. Herein lies the value of the book. Surely no other Protestant educator has attained such first-hand knowledge of the total seminary scene, and the openness and sincerity of his appreciation calls forth our gratitude and contributes to the sharpness of our own vision.

One important aspect of the ecumenical movement is the interchange between Protestant and Catholic seminarians.

Both priests and ministers have had to overcome their respective prejudices, often enough in common work for civil rights and social improvement. This mutual understanding and respect is indeed welcome, but it should reach back into seminary life. There have been many contacts between seminarians of various faiths in recent years—perhaps none more successful than the long vigils at the Lincoln Monument in Washington, D.C., before the civil rights bill was made law in 1964. But this is not enough; there is nothing like the experience of living together and studying together, as I can say from my own experience at Pittsburgh Theological Seminary (Presbyterian) and at Yale University Divinity School. The ecumenical movement needs such a development, if the lingering mistrust is to be utterly dispelled. This book can lead both Protestant and Catholic reader to that goal. In this alone it could count its success, but happily it also serves to remind both groups of the strengths and weaknesses of the respective seminary systems. The impressionistic, gad-fly quality of Mr. Wagoner's analysis will prompt all seminary teachers to ask more pertinent and more important questions.

I personally hope that many of the points raised by the author will soon be outdated by the *aggiornamento* which has begun in many seminaries and which is to be implemented by the national episcopal conference. There are already many happy signs of a move away from regimentation and isolation, and a new professionalism can be expected to appear in academic life. As the Church deepens its realization as the People of God, and the voice of the laity comes to be heard in the land, the seminary system is bound to be enriched. However, a caution is perhaps in order. The current unrest in Catholic seminaries over personalistic issues and social involvement should not cause one to lose sight of the basic requirements of theological training. The activism which has been manifested in the first reaction to justified criticisms was perhaps to be expected. With it often goes a devaluation of hard-nosed application to study—and often in the name of relevance. No one can deny that sensitivity to modern issues should operate in the selection and emphasis given to various theological problems; the Vatican II *Decree on Priestly Formation* wisely underscored the value of an historical approach to theology. But there is a trend to the easy solution, to the *merely* kerygmatic, to the neglect of a taxing, historical analysis of sources (not to mention the dearth if not the death of the knowledge of biblical languages in both Protestant and Catholic seminaries—and this despite the recommendations of the Vatican II decree). The famous theologians of Vatican II are quoted generously in seminary "bull-sessions" (the Catholic counterparts of Niebuhr and Barth—and now Bonhoeffer— who themselves form the staple of many a discussion in Protestant seminaries). But how seriously are their theological works studied and judged? How deep is the penetration into the sources on which their theological studies are based? The present ferment relative to seminary life must be extended equally to straight theological interests. Otherwise America will not develop first-class theologians among its Catholic clergy. No one can truly plead that this emphasis is only for future professional teachers of theology. America has had more than its share of "practical" clergy (a term which should not be made synonymous with untheological). Present and future needs call for a clergy that is theologically-minded; then they will be able to speak to the practical, to the pastoral, and to the secular city. The idealism and generosity of Catholic seminarians leads one to believe that they will successfully meet this challenge.

On the other hand, what about the seminary faculties? Drastic changes are in order. Specialization on the part of faculty members in various areas of theology is perhaps the greatest need. In too many seminaries sabbaticals for research opportunity are simply unheard of, and teaching loads often preclude the research that must accompany teaching. And here there is the opportunity of having trained teachers from the laity engage in the education of seminarians. The recent discussions of American Catholic intellectual achievement never came to rest on seminarians and theologians for the life of the Church.

The issues discussed by Mr. Wagoner are only the beginning of a long road that Catholic seminaries will have to travel. They will succeed in the up-dating because the Spirit that animated the Ecumenical Council will also, one feels confident, stay with the Church to carry through the work to the end.

Roland E. Murphy, O. Carm.

A Protestant Preface:
Catholicism as Catharsis

In the writing of this book I have kept alongside my typewriter the words of Cardinal Newman to Lord Acton, apropos of an unruly Catholic critic of their Church:

> He will always be very clever, amusing, brilliant and suggestive. He will always be flicking his whip at Bishops, patting them in tender places, throwing stones at Sacred Congregations, and, as he rides along the high road, discharging pea-shooters at Cardinals who happen by bad luck to look out the window.[1]

Monitored by the taste of Newman, I hope that these pages have been spared that grossness and angularity which tempts Protestants who write about the Roman Catholic Church.

For eleven years my own work for The Fund for Theological Education has preoccupied me with the problems and opportunities of Protestant theological education, particularly the identification of better human beings for the ordained and teaching ministries.[2] This personal interest has led me to search the highways and byways of Catholic seminary life in order to find fresh insight.

No one can study the Roman Catholic Church objectively and sympathetically without seeing more clearly the distant battlements and flags of the City of God. The Roman Catholic community preserves in an incalculably precious way the signs of the Presence of God: majestic worship, the disciplined community serving the living Christ, an unrelenting concern for good theology, a host of dedicated apostles.

The contemporary Protestant should be filled with genuine gratitude and awe at the Catholic accomplishment. The Protestant, even of the most ecumenical sophistication, may not know how Catholic riches are to be added to Protestant poverty, or vice versa; but he knows very well that he must no longer regard Catholicism with the one eye of the Reformation, but with the full vision of deep thanksgiving and critical reflection.

When I, a Protestant clergyman, find gracious and open welcome to Catholic seminaries, the religious world has circled many times in its orbit since the sixteenth century. And the truth of this becomes ever more vivid when I sleep in the Bishop's room in one seminary, in the Cardinal's room at another, and when, on the same day, I rise to pray with Dominican monks at five and stay up until midnight drinking beer with same.

Protestants and Catholics alike find it a great relief to share each other's strengths and weaknesses as human beings, as imperfect servants of Christ. We have wasted so much psychic energy in defensive polemics and outmoded posturing that we have had little power left with which to do common service to Christ.

A study of Roman Catholic theological education reveals the continuing need for demythologizing. When those in each of our camps who live by slogans, by pejorative prejudice, and by what must be called the "vested interest of opposition" are discounted, those who remain will find that in theological education, as in so many other areas, they share the same problems and opportunities. This is what W. A. Visser't Hooft has called, more generally, the ecumenical challenge of pro-existence, rather than simply co-existence.

The pre-ecumenical response to a common problem would have been to say, "My solution is better than yours," or "Our problem is not as bad as yours." The only adequate response, however, is this: "What insights may we share that will enable each of us to do better what separately we are doing so inadequately?" Name almost any area of theological education—curriculum, field work, identification of potential seminarians, financing, devotional life—and the deficiencies are so challenging that only the most Tridentine Catholic or the most doctrinaire Protestant theological educator will wish to avoid taking counsel together.

Thus, the two overarching purposes of this study have been, first, to ascertain which areas of Roman Catholic theological education may offer strength and assistance to Protestant theological education and, secondly, to mark out those areas of Roman Catholic theological education which are being most debated by Catholics. Each purpose enlightens the other. It is astounding beyond words that a critique of this type has been so long in coming. It is the first serious critique of American Catholic theological education done by an American Protestant.[3] When one considers the enormous influence of theological education on the life and future of the Church, it is galling and appalling that we have neglected each other's riches for so long. Would that a more competent person had written this book. But what great good luck to have been able to do so!

This study tries hard to observe certain ground rules, the chief of which is that no Protestant has the right to criticize a Catholic or Catholic theological education for attempting to be Catholic. For example, what gratuitous insults would be implied if a seminary *ratio studiorum* were criticized because it made the Eucharist central, or taught a non-Protestant view of ordination, or made strong claims for the Papacy. Conversely, this study has attempted to criticize Roman Catholic theological seminaries on educational grounds. And here, as anyone knows who has been following Catholic literature, Catholics themselves have been stridently vocal. There are few subjects in the following pages which have not come from pens wielded by aroused Catholic laymen. Indeed, those within the Catholic household of faith have the right to express themselves at a higher decible level than do I. The amazing amount of bold Catholic self-criticism is all the more acidic for having been bottled up so long. While it has been an enormous help in exposing the Catholic mind, and thus making this study much easier, it also made it more difficult to keep some issues in perspective. The natural Protestant impulse is to sympathize with those Catholics who are saying things about Catholicism which Protestants like to hear. This is no guarantee, however, of fairness, and it may distort one's reading of normative Catholicism.

Catholicism's vision of its mission in the world is most vividly seen, if one must pick out the clearest single vantage point, in those communities of study and prayer which prepare men for the priesthood. Here the teachings of the Church are carefully explicated; here it is that the standards of the Church are lovingly cultivated. The quintessence of Roman Catholicism is seen and savoured in the ideals and actualities of seminary life. What the Church holds highest and dearest it painstakingly seeks to embody in the education and formation of its priests. This book thus concentrates on seminaries and seminarians, not primarily as ends in themselves, but much more as a rewarding way for Catholic and Protestant alike to look critically and appreciatively at the Roman Catholic Church and all that it means for human society.

The priest occupies such a unique role in Catholic soteriology, much more central than in Protestantism, that his education, character, and presence is absolutely crucial to the life of the Roman Catholic Church. And this crucial role explains the importance of seminary education. To catch this high priority in all its fullness, it is worth remembering an incident (by no means an accident) of the visit of Pope Paul VI to the United States and to the United Nations in October, 1965. This was the first visit of an incumbent pontiff in the history of the United States, and millions of persons were listening to and watching his celebration of the Mass at Yankee Stadium. His homily on that occasion, *the most solemn and formal address given specifically to the faithful in the course of that brief visit,* concluded with a plea for support of a new archdiocesan seminary for New York City, to which the Pope presented a stone from St. Peter's Basilica. To some it must have seemed that one of the great prophetic moments in American Catholic history ended with a camouflaged fund drive. It must be allowed, however, that whatever courtesy the Pope wished to show to his host, Cardinal Spellman, he saw nothing at all incongruous, felt no twinge of dénouement, in finishing his talk with words of encouragement for the building of yet another Catholic seminary in a state which already has eighty.

Since seminaries are the instrumentalities by which men

are prepared for ordination, and since the priesthood is related so directly to the destiny of the health of the Church
and the soul of the individual Catholic, Catholics not only
must be excused the high-pitched criticism of seminaries
now aboard in all lands; it must, indeed, be expected of
them. It is only natural for Catholics to deal severely with
priestly education and formation. It is to the credit of that
Church that there is such a ruthless analysis underway, even
though large segments of officialdom still wish to play it
safe.

It was only a handful of years ago that the study and
visitation reflected in this book might have been characterized as spying out enemy territory. The spy would have written down in his little black book all the faults and weaknesses
discernible, then return to his office to warm himself by the
dying embers of jealous pride. The spied-upon, in turn,
might have been guarding nervously all chinks in the
armour, determined to make a good impression. These instincts linger in our psyches, conditioned as we are by
history. But the old desire to gossip about Catholic faults,
to whisper conspiratorially about "Rome," leaves a dead
taste in the mouth. Those instincts have been subordinated
not so much by the desire to be academically objective, but
by the deadliest of all of God's traps: one falls in love with
fellow Christians. To say this is not irenicism fluttering its
wings like an ecumenical peacock; it is a sure testimony that
acquaintance leads to friendship, friendship to respect and
candor, and that, in turn, to deep and critical affection.
Months of Catholic hospitality, hours of conversation, days
of reading Catholic literature, nights under the roofs of
Catholic seminaries—all this inexorably works a redemptive
magic. For me it has been nothing short of a conversion. The
most marked result of this study has been a marrow-deep conviction that the Protestant-Catholic wall of partition has

been broken and that no amount of valid disagreement will be permitted to build it up again.

There is one assumption which I have tested and found valid in the course of this study and visitation: no matter how strongly one is convinced of the truth of one's theological position, it is highly desirable to be perfectly open, not defensive, about these convicitions with those who differ. It will not hurt my Protestantism to be exposed to the best in Catholicism any more than to be exposed to the best in the secular circles of society. If anything is lost, it is dross; and it is replaced by a better conviction. I would say the same to Catholics. Nothing is gained—nothing—by hiding behind ecclesiastical fortresses.

I fail completely to understand those who worry that either *aggiornamento* or ecumenical involvement is a threat to their Church. I see more charity and promise in these new developments than heresy or danger.

Fortunately for me and for the reader, the publication within the last year of several fine books, dealing in detail with Catholic seminaries, has made it unnecessary to duplicate their contribution.[4] It is one of the most remarkable, healthy, and healthful—almost volcanic—eruptions of self-criticism in the annals of any institution. It is healthy because the volcano, in this case, is not spewing forth ashes with which to bury some magnificent Herculaneum of the church; rather, it is raining down good, rich topsoil over fields which had become rather dry and barren. So now is the time when gardeners and landscape artists must get to work. And those who wish mighty shade trees will have to wait. All in all, there is a lively sense of fresh beginning.

The reader will look in vain for a tidy unity to this book. It is really intended as a series of essays and asides which are strung along the thread of seminary education. Both Protestant bias and educational conviction are cheek by jowl.

The most concerned reader, Protestant or Catholic, will not find everything to be of equal interest. It is a book written for both sides of the ecumenical street; yet it is not a nicely balanced affair which nervously seeks to give "equal time" to both sides on each issue. Anything, however, which smells of over-ripe generalization should, by the charity of the reader, be forgiven as personal whimsy gone out of bounds.

It must be recognized that the title of this volume is to be taken only in the broadest sense. There is no attempt here to describe or analyze in minute detail the intramural structure, curriculum, and community life of Protestant seminaries. Indeed, an uninformed reader may not get enough feel of the warp and woof of Protestant theological education. Essentially, this book faces in the opposite direction: it is a critique and evaluation of Roman Catholic theological education by a Protestant and with just enough reference to Protestant seminaries to reveal the assumptions and background of the critic. There very much needs to be a comparable volume written by a Roman Catholic, with perspectives reversed.

The chapters and sub-headings represent categorical divisions which are inherently a bit forced. The Catholic Church is too complex to be easily pinned and labeled. But some handles had to be offered to the reader. What I really hope the reader will do is to look up now and again from the pages, gaze a few years ahead, and try to figure out what all this means for the future of both the Catholic and Protestant churches.

These pages are ecumenically presumptuous. When my wife and our children and I quarrel as a family, with fingers pointed 'round the clan, we are quick to take umbrage at an outsider's criticisms—even when he repeats our own words. The family circle closes in self-defense. Likewise, it is yet an unresolved question as to whether the majority of Catholics and Protestants really consider themselves to be one family, welcoming or at least tolerating mutual criticism, or whether the smaller circles drawn by historical god-fathers will continue to divide. These chapters are a small bet that history can be surmounted.

My own instinct is that Protestants and Catholics have more family feeling than we care to admit. It might get out of hand, all of this kinship to Christ. If it did, then our careful rationalizations, shibboleths, and defensive architecture would be an embarrassment. The war paint would run down our cheeks and we would look silly. Deep inside of my Protestant psyche is an hegelian demon. He flits about in Catholic minds, too. He would make religious ideologists of each of us. An ideologist lives by categories, systems, slogans, epithets, and thin-lipped judgments. And with an ideology it is almost impossible to be a lover. Thus, I suppose it is that this book is finally to be explained as a cry for exorcism.

Walter D. Wagoner

PRINCETON, NEW JERSEY

Notes

[1] Jean Guitton, *The Church and the Laity* (New York: Alba House, 1964), p. 25.

[2] This fund is supported by the Sealantic Fund, by the Rockefeller Brothers, and by the Booth Ferris Foundation.

[3] An indispensable companion volume and one of broader range is: Yorke Allen, Jr., *A Seminary Survey* (New York: Harper & Row, 1960). Part II (pp. 293–498) of this work describes in detail the nature of Catholic major seminaries in Africa, Asia, and Latin America.

[4] See Bibliography, Appendix IV, pp. 249 ff.

Contents

THE SEMINARY
Protestant and Catholic

1

The Roman Epicenter

Seminaries and the Holy See

It is appropriate to begin in Rome. Without the Roman angle of vision the American Catholic seminaries appear out of focus. Furthermore, it is necessary to indicate the formal and canonical influence of the Holy See (particularly the Sacred Congregation of Seminaries and Universities of Study[1]) on Catholic seminaries and to describe that powerful complex of universities, institutes, and seminaries (The Roman Athenaea) in which Catholic seminarians, graduate students, priests, and faculty from around the world gather to worship and to study.[2]

The "presence" of Rome in American seminary life is felt with a seismographic sensitivity both because of the waves of influence which emanate from the formal and hierarchical authority of the Holy See and because so many seminary teachers have studied in Rome.

The Holy See may be defined as the combined authority of the Papacy and the Roman Curia. The Roman Curia consists of the Sacred Congregations, Tribunals, and Offices.[3] A sacred Congregation is an administrative unity of the Church, sharing the jurisdiction of the Pope by his delegated authority. The Pope possesses the final authority. The titular head of each Congregation is a cardinal, with much of the administrative supervision being done through a Secretary or Prefect—often an archbishop.

All Catholic seminaries are related, in this hierarchical plan of organization, to a Congregation. When one traces the chain of command, or the working influence, from a given seminary back to Rome, one ends up, insofar as most issues are concerned, in one of three curial centers: the Sacred Congregation of Seminaries and Universities of Studies; the Sacred Congregation of the Propagation of the Faith; the Sacred Congregation of the Affairs of Religious.

The Congregation for the Propagation of the Faith supervises those seminaries which educate priests for missionary apostolates (e.g., Maryknoll) ; the Congregation of Religious has authority over seminaries which prepare men for the Orders (e.g., St. Meinrad). It is the S.C.S.U.S., however, which must occupy center stage in this account. This congregation has canonical jurisdiction over all other seminaries, including diocesan seminaries operated by religious, over all Catholic pontifical universities, faculties, and institutes of instruction. The S.C.S.U.S. is a relative newcomer, having been created in 1915 by a *Motu Proprio*[4] of Benedict XV. Actually, however, it has a long history of related predecessor organizations going as far back as the *Congregatio pro Universitate Studii Romani* created by Sixtus V in 1588.

S.C.S.U.S., the Congregation for Propaganda, and the Congregation of Religious work closely together on seminary matters in a mutually reciprocal and interpenetrating fashion. Many S.C.S.U.S. rulings, for example, will also be issued by the other two Congregations, with or without a suitable amendment. The magazine, *Seminarium,* published by S.C.S.U.S., is well worth reading. Its influence, however, does not seem to be extensive in the United States.

This very sketchy organizational background need not be elaborated here. What does deserve underscoring is the fact that all Catholic seminaries are in a system of hierarchical obedience which ends and begins in these Congregations under the Pope.[5] The actual influence of the S.C.S.U.S. on any given American seminary is not easily discernible. Yet, it is always in the background.

S.C.S.U.S. is not a bureaucratic policeman forever knocking and peeping. At this writing, it is one of the more conservative curial centers.[6] It does require triennial reports from every seminary. These are demanding and detailed reports which contain information on curriculum, faculty, library holdings, physical equipment, spiritual formation, and the like. It is an ecclesiastical version of a report to an American accrediting agency.

Because S.C.S.U.S. is formally responsible for the curriculums of the seminaries under its purview, until quite recently it was informed even of textbook changes. More and more seminaries, however, are restive under this type of minute scrutiny, and one gets the distinct impression that seminary administrators tell S.C.S.U.S. no more than is necessary and as little of that as possible.[7] Happily, the *Decree on Priestly Training* permits consciences to be stretched further and further. Actually, of course, the S.C.S.U.S. is instrumentally dependent on the cooperation of bishops. Bishops who want to give maximum educational autonomy to rectors and faculties can do so; those who like to "go by the book" may play it safe. The one area in which seminaries, or any other area of the church, must be obedient is that of faith and morals as defined dogmatically. *Sedes Sapientiae,* for example, over the signature of Pope Pius XII in 1956, is relentless:

The professors of philosophy and theology, therefore, must be fully aware that they do not carry on their work in their own right and person, but exclusively in the name and authority of the Supreme Magisterium, and that they perform this ministry under the watchful eye and guidance of this same Magisterium.

It is of the very nature of the Roman Catholic Church that one feels that watchful eye. Yet even in dogmatic matters, while there is, of course, no yielding on the central claims (an unblinking eye), the last six years have witnessed a permissive invasion of seminary classrooms and libraries of other ideas, philosophies, and world views which for centuries had been sealed out. Dogma, presented with as much fervor and logic as ever, at last has a chance to be taught in a context more corresponding to the world outside the seminary and outside the Curia.

Catholic obedience requires that the S.C.S.U.S. be respected. Its *de facto* authority varies a great deal, often depending on the independence of this rector or that bishop. There is nothing comparable to it within Protestantism, for Catholic seminaries are very much anchored in this international matrix of common tradition, Roman authority, and local responsibility. The Vatican II *Decree on Priestly Training* will, of course, give more—much more —initiative to national episcopacies. But even then, S.C.S.U.S. has the power of approval and veto. The curial view *from* Rome naturally sees its empire of seminaries as one which ought to be in constant filial obedience to the curial understanding of theological education. The view of Rome from the office of an American seminary rector is more apt to see the S.C.S.U.S. as a mixed blessing.

It will interest a Protestant seminary administrator to note that his opposite number at a Catholic seminary must be sensitive not only to the wishes of his faculty, the criticism of his students, and the quarterbacking of his graduates, but also to the thinking in Rome, directives from S.C.S.U.S., the desires of his bishop, and that long, long tradition of seminary life which began at Trent.

The Influence of the Roman Athenaea [8]

In evaluating the Roman impact on American Catholic seminaries, and through them on American Catholicism, one tries to judge the personal and scholarly influence of these schools on the hundreds of seminarians who study there for one or more years of major theology and on the hundreds of priests who labor there each year for doctorates and other advanced degrees.

Rome is far more than a foreign university center for these men. It is the seat of the Church, the repository of centuries of Catholic hopes and fears. These men come not only as scholars and students but as pilgrims to the chief shrine of the Church. Protestants have no single city which sings with such overtones for all the sons of the Reformation.

More so than Paris or Louvain, more so by far than any university or city in the United States, Rome is the place where most of the American Catholic seminary teachers have done their graduate study. It is undoubtedly true that not one medium or large Catholic seminary in the United States is without a core of teachers who have studied in Rome for two or three years. No other center of theological study can match the influence of Rome. Rome, then, in addition to its historical and spiritual meaning for the Catholic scholar *qua* Catholic, is also the academic graduate center with the most impressive and direct influence on the minds and academic styles of Catholic seminary teaching in the United States.

Prolonged study in Rome naturally forms American Catholic scholars not in a neat mold, but very much with distinctive characteristics and tendencies.

First: the chanceries and the episcopacies of the United States, ordinariates which have such firm control of diocesan seminaries, are filled with priests who have a Roman educational background which has emphasized Canon Law and the juridical mentality. These men, admirable and capable as they may be, do not readily experiment in educational affairs, nor do they have an affinity for the critical appraisal and evaluation of theological education. Like career-minded Annapolis graduates, they prefer a "taut ship" run by the book.

Second: graduate doctoral work in Rome is carried on under assumptions and ground rules which are foreign to Protestants, but which Protestants must sympathetically try to understand, even if agreement is not possible. That is: *the Roman Athenaea are completely a part of the Church.* As a faculty member of the Pontifical Angelicum University said in an interview: "Rome is the best place to study. In other places the students could ruin their faith, under clever professors teaching errors or false ideas. The theology taught to Roman Catholics should be Roman Catholic theology." Michael Cardinal Browne of Ireland, also in an interview, made the same point: "Ecclesiastical universities, directly destined for theological investigation and teaching and for those branches of science connected with theology, cannot fairly be compared with secular universities. . . . the Catholic university is based on a hierarchy of studies."

The point here is that the Catholic understanding of graduate theological study, even at the doctoral level, generally assumes that such study is to be carried on within the dogmatic assumptions and limitations of the Church's teaching. The Roman Athenaea are not graduate universities in the sense, let us say, that the graduate faculties at Stanford are, nor, for that matter—even at a specialized graduate-theological faculty—are they graduate universities like Yale Divinity School. When the typical Protestant graduate student thinks of a theological faculty, he does not see the same model as the Catholic.[9] The Protestant, particularly at the doctoral level, regards as a true university one with a wide diversity of opinion, academic freedom, faculty autonomy, and a lively sense of being an open-ended community. In Rome the Catholic schools are typical and normative in working under an entirely different set of principles: a hierarchy of studies, a definite commitment to the dogmatic bases of the Church, and a hierarchy of administrative control. This is not to say that non-Catholic ideas are not presented. At the Angelicum, for example, there is a Dominican Father who specializes in Protestant theology. Nor is there intention here to give the impression that on most matters there is not a vast amount of difference of opinion within the Catholic community. But it has to be made quite clear to Protestants that Catholic graduate theological study, just as at all levels of seminary study, is very much within the teaching authority of the Church. Protestant seminaries and graduate faculties, on the contrary, carry on their work more at arm's length from the Church, at much more of a critical distance. All of this does mean that the vast majority of Catholic seminary teachers in the United States have never studied in what many Protestants and most secular scholars would define as a true university.

There is in Rome, then, no university graduate faculty of theology in the sense of Oxford, or Harvard, or Marburg. This is a great pity, for Rome would be an exhilarating place for such a faculty. The University of Rome, while it has a few courses in comparative religion and one or two other cognate fields, even now has a lingering legacy of the secular, anti-clerical tradition of the nineteenth-century *risorgimento*.[10]

Third: doctoral work at the Athenaea is of a most uneven quality. Since there are so many students from so many parts of the world, it is difficult to teach at much more than the level of the common denominator. The faculties have more variety, up and down the scale of scholastic standards, than would be true at the better graduate faculties in the United States, Germany, Canada, or England. One cannot assume that each doctorate from the Roman schools means all that it should. In some cases—for example, at the Pontifical Biblical Institute—a doctorate is indicative of first-class scholarship. Catholics themselves who have studied in Rome report a conflicting variety of scholarly experiences. It is not special pleading to say that, as a case study of the differences in systems, a doctoral dissertation on the same aspect of Thomas Aquinas—one written at Rome and one at Yale—would differ substantially. The dissertation written and defended at Yale by a student with no more or less personal competence than the student at Rome would be critically examined by a committee composed, let us say, of an agnostic linguistic philosopher, a Lutheran existentialist, a Jewish metaphysician, and a Catholic canon lawyer. It stands to reason that such a dissertation ought to be a better one than if it had been done in Rome This is not to say that the work of a Roman school is always cheap and easy. Not so. It is but to repeat that Roman Catholic scholarship, by definition and intention, takes place behind a theological *cordon sanitaire*. This situation makes it very difficult for the Catholic scholarly community to develop the style of dialogue, the give and take of various ideas, which is so characteristic of the great graduate schools.

Fourth: studies in Rome are carried on in an entirely clerical atmosphere. There are very few lay scholars at the Athenaea. It is a priestly domain, which means that it is a celibate community. In Italy, especially, this situation means many rules and regulations, permissions and confinements. It is always astounding to have grown men say that they cannot go to the opera or that they must be in "behind the walls" by 10 P.M. It seems a great pity that visiting seminarians and priests are so restricted in availing themselves of the cultural opportunities of Rome.

Fifth: study in Rome simultaneously latinizes and broadens, narrows and expands, the world perspective of the students. Each person intensely feels the historical Roman tradition, the Latin mentality, and the rather narrow, juridically-oriented viewpoint of the Italian Catholic community. At the same time, each visitor lives with hundreds of men from all around the world and cannot help but appreciate the catholicity of the Church. It could be an even more catholic experience if the scores of national colleges and dormitories could be more internationalized.

Speaking of the Latin mentality, the Italian cultural heritage plays a subtle and powerful part in the formation of the Roman Catholic mind. There is a lingering caeseropapism, a baroque triumphalism which infects everything:

The Perennial Baroque: what happened to Italy is what usually happens to old ladies who were once famous beauties. Just as they relinquish only reluctantly the gestures, curls, witticisms and fashions of their sunset years, Italy still clings to the manner and ideals of the two centuries which followed the coronation of Charles V . . . pointlessly complicated, capricious, eccentric, over-ornate. Life was codified, hierarchies organized, orthodoxy defended, much outward show, religious life was regimented, the spiritual hegemony of the Church was utilized to keep the people docile . . . conformism and opulence . . . all this endures today . . . the Church is a world in itself, the most labyrinthine and complicated of all human organizations. From the outside, to the stranger, it looks monolithic. Inside it is an entanglement of factions politely and almost imperceptibly fighting each other for the greater glory of God: the Pope and his private advisers against the Curia, the Curia against the Bishops, liberal against conservative bishops, all bishops against the lower clergy, the religious orders against the priests, the religious orders among themselves, all tenaciously struggling for supremacy.[11]

Those five traits which we have touched upon are among the more obvious consequences of study in Rome. Each of them has a subtle cumulative effect on Catholic seminaries everywhere. Furthermore, these characteristics of Rome must be understood if one is to comprehend why certain Catholic seminaries are now trying to throw off much of the Italian (as distinguished from Catholic) tradition.

The observer of the Roman scene is also struck by the same aggravating logistical situation which he finds among seminaries in the United States: not enough cooperation among the various schools: insufficient common planning; too much waste and duplication. The alternative to the present situation is not some unthinking leveling of the various traditions represented by the constituent faculty resources, but more reciprocal-trade agreements on courses of study, a much better coordination of library holdings and purchases: in short, the implementation of plans which will make *more open, understandable, and available* the scholarly riches which are in Rome. The old principle of *cuius regio eius religio* is very active still among the Roman schools. These various empires have every right, of course, to separate and distinctive communal-religious lives, but graduate scholarship demands a maximum of cooperation. One example of what can be done is the cooperation of several of the major schools in editing a forthcoming study of "The Theology of Vatican II."

In 1962 the Rector of the Pontifical Salesian Atheneum, Fr. Alfonso M. Stickler, S.D.B., proposed the creation of a *"Pontificia Universitas Romana"*—a merging at certain levels, under one administration, of many of the faculties now under separate jurisdiction. He was eager to strengthen the impact of Roman Catholic scholarship, and this plan was offered as one possible way of so doing. In essence, he was proposing a return to the medieval notion of a *Studium Generale*, which would permit diversity within unity. He advocated the opening of such a university to all qualified students, not merely clerics, as a step toward the formation in Rome of an elite faculty and student body. The details of Fr. Stickler's proposal[12] need not concern us here, but the proposal itself was a heartening one, even though it met vigorous opposition and has for the time being not succeeded. It is an eminently worthwhile strategy. A case can be made that such a centralizing would permit more control by the conservatives. Perhaps so, but the present uncoordinated situation surely needs major surgery.

One must comment inevitably on the common use of Latin as the means of instruction in Rome. Rome is one of the very few places left in the Catholic scholarly world where the bulk of lecturing is in Latin. Latin has the obvious advantage of binding together students from diverse national backgrounds. Facility in that tongue has been one of the main factors behind the development of Rome as a community of international scholarship. Will the growth of the vernacular as the lecture and liturgical language of national seminary systems force another language to the fore in Rome—perhaps Italian?[13] To what extent will the weakening of Latin also weaken the Roman Athenaea?

A more probing question concerns the ability of Latin to keep up with the "meaning" requirements of modern theology. The nuances and development of contemporary theological language in whatever vernacular are hardly capable of being translated with accuracy into Latin. At Vatican II, for example, the contemporary philosophical usages of "existential" simply were beyond the reach of preparatory commissions wrestling with theological and philosophical matters which had to be translated into Latin before a vote could be taken. To what extent, then, does the use of Latin in Rome both weaken and aid scholarship there?

After what has been said about the nature of the Roman schools, in contrast to the German, English, and American types of graduate theological education, it may be naive and even unfair to venture the following comment, for one should not ask an orange to be an apple. But the heavy concentration of dogmatically controlled Catholic scholarship in the Roman milieu does appear to be narrowly religious. Let us stretch the paradox by saying that Roman Catholic theological education is too religious and not catholic enough. Any religious community, especially one with the strength that is Rome's, can easily become too pre-occupied with its own history, dogma, hagiography and cultus. Graduate study in biology, or physics, or mathematics is properly expected to stay with the formal limits of the respective discipline. No one writes a doctoral dissertation for a physics faculty on the "Morality Implicit in the Poems of Robert Frost." But Christianity, as phenomenon and as faith, is so intertwined with the humanities, the social sciences, the arts, that the theological education of Christian clergy must not be narrowly conceived. A Christian seminary and a Christian scholarship which is *overly* engrossed with ecclesiology, soteriology, and *heilsgeschicte,* may end up fostering a false dichotomy between the realm of the church and the realm of the created order. Not only St. Theresa and Abelard, not only Calvin and Jonathan Edwards, not only transubstantiation and concelebration but Wittgenstein, Harlem, and class structure in Brazil fall within the proper scope of seminary education. Of course seminaries are not to turn out dilettantes and theological water-bugs scooting about forever on the surface of life. Nor, at the other extreme (and the question is whether scholarship in Rome, *in toto,* is at the other extreme) should Catholic seminary scholars be narcissistically and exclusively involved with matters Roman Catholic. Is there enough attention being given within the Roman Athenaea to the theological and Christian implications of the secular world?[14]

Thus, there is one grim fate which the Catholic scholarly community in Rome does not deserve and yet may inherit. Namely, the fate of becoming less catholic (in the cognate sense) religiously and less a fine academic community than many other places which have had no comparable history or tradition.

One thing is certainly clear. When a Protestant stands in the City of Rome he will, if there be any sense of perspective and appreciation in him at all, know full well that the Catholic scholarly community there has such a powerful influence over the Catholic Church that it must be supported in every way; that Protestantism will in turn be strengthened by availing itself of these resources; that the Catholic Church must, as *Mater et Magistra* of its own, do everything possible to raise the level of its Roman schools. Everyone truly and faithfully committed to the Body of Christ will rejoice when Catholic learning thrives at its best. That is why one hopes for the Roman Athenaea a fuller realization of its potential and the shunning of a petty destiny. To urge that more Catholic scholars study elsewhere than in Rome, or to do graduate work *both* in Rome *and* elsewhere, in no way depreciates the Roman contribution. Let the Roman schools seek for a maximum of effectiveness, a maximum of openness to non-Catholics. At the same time the Roman magnet should not be the only field of force pulling Catholic scholars. These are not self-contradictory statements, for the Catholic Church can use the academic diet of Rome while at the same time encouraging its scholars to eat at many other tables as well.

Applied directly to the American scene, the inference is that at this moment in the intellectual history of the Catholic Church in the United States the imbalance caused by the heavy traffic to Rome for graduate study ought to be rectified by encouraging more American Catholic seminarians and teachers to do their study at the better schools in the United States and elsewhere.[15]

Does the powerful influence of "Rome and all that" inhibit the proper development of a vigorous indigenous American Catholic theology? Each nation has its own color to add to the theological spectrum. One suspects that the American Catholic community is underplaying its own native intellectual abilities. Any movement of American Catholic scholarship, not away from or around Rome, but through Rome and in and out into the best secular American and European university life will bring a welcome freshening of attitude and a more truly catholic maturity.

There is still another key issue to be driven home, writing now as a non-Catholic[16] to Catholics. Rome is the perfect illustration of what can be found almost anywhere in the world where there are significant numbers of Catholics: far too many outstanding Catholic scholars, far too many remarkable human beings who are tucked away in academic hot houses, walled away from the scholarly and human intercourse which they should enjoy and from which "the rest of us out there" could so much profit. How often one comes away from some Catholic school, or seminary, or community, or from an Order of Land-locked Fathers—saying to oneself, "Why, oh why, do we not know each other?" So anything which can be done to open up Catholic academe to the world, to lure Catholics into the open air markets of the world's intellectual economy, the better it will be.

An Ecumenical Center in Rome

The City of Rome has an ecumenical potential which is absolutely unique. The vistas and possibilities opened up by Vatican II clearly reveal the need for "scholarly and ecumenical ambassadors to the Holy See." It is under the rubric of genuine ecumenical advance, in one of the great nerve centers of Christianity, that a plea is entered here for an Ecumenical Study Center in Rome. Ecumenical centers and activities elsewhere cannot possibly fill this vacuum. Centers such as Strasbourg, Notre Dame, Benzheim, Bossey, Salamanca, for all of their merit, cannot overcome the absence of such a center in Rome itself. At the present time in Rome it is only the small Waldensian community and seminary which can be said to have even a beach-head.

At all costs a strategy must be worked out which will avoid the establishment in Rome of separate or even joint offices and delegations by various churches. The worst possible strategy at the moment would be for the Anglicans or the Methodists or the Orthodox, et al. individually to set up offices for the purpose of study and of maintaining contact with the Holy See. Unilateral missions of this sort not only would embarrass and exhaust Roman Catholic courtesy, they would contradict the central accomplishments of twentieth century ecumenical history. But unless an Ecumenical Center is established, the vacuum is so obvious that such missions would be inevitable.

The Center proposed here is one which would have support and representation from a wide spectrum of churches—generally speaking, those now included in the World Council of Churches. The Center needs to be autonomously and corporately organized, subject finally to its own Board of Directors. This independence would give it the necessary advantage of not being regarded as an official spokesman for any ecclesiological position. Its Board of Directors should include, *ex officio,* men and women from many churches and nationalities: persons publicly identified as responsible ecumenical statesmen. Roman Catholicism, through the Secretariat on Christian Unity, should be invited to have members on the Board, either as full voting members or as Honorary Consultants. It is essential that such a Center begin and continue with the welcome of the Holy See.

Such a Center, in its initial and exploratory stages at least, probably should be related closely to the Waldensian Faculty, Library, Church, and Bookstore, near the Piazza Cavour, only a few minutes walk from St. Peter's. Here an office could be maintained, and here meeting rooms and research facilities are available. The functions of the Center would include:

1) Maintaining a small staff who would over the years cultivate a wide circle of acquaintances in Rome, at the Athenaea, and at the Vatican, and who would make themselves knowledgeable in various Catholic matters, become familiar with the City of Rome and its cultural and academic facilities.

2) Provide study facilities for visiting faculty and graduate students. In a fashion somewhat comparable to the American Academy in Rome[17] these Fellows would have

many opportunities for both intra- and extra-mural social and intellectual life. The Center should have endowed funds with which to underwrite at least partial fellowships for a representative group of faculty and graduate Fellows.

3) The Center should own or control a few apartments and lodgings.

4) Sponsoring a year-round variety of meetings, colloquia, discussions, seminars, lecture courses, informal social gatherings. These activities would involve both Roman and non-Roman Christians.

5) Running special summer programs for visiting tourists, both lay and clerical.

6) Maintaining its own library, in collaboration with the Waldensian library (the only significant Protestant library in Italy). The Waldensian librarians and the staff of the Center can be of invaluable help in guiding scholars to the rich collections of the Roman Athenaea, Vatican Library, etc.

Such are but a few of the more obvious services which this Center could provide. The core of the Center would be, then, in three general areas: first, scholarship, particularly with regard to bolstering Protestant weaknesses in patristics, Catholic church history, and contemporary Catholic life in the Holy See; secondly, special short-term educational programs for visitors from all churches (there is every evidence to suggest that the Roman Catholic faculty, seminarians, and officials in Rome would find this a welcome service) ; thirdly, the slow formation of personal friendships. This subtle but pervasive influence is of inestimable influence on the future of the ecumenical movement—in a way quite comparable to the personal friendships formed in the 20's and 30's by men and women who later became colleagues in the World Council of Churches.

In a world of rapidly maturing Christian ecumenicity, this Ecumenical Center in Rome would be as welcome as it is necessary.

Notes

1 The exact title is *Congregatio De Seminariis et Studiorum Universitatibus:* hereinafter abbreviated as S.C.S.U.S.

2 This chapter, as well as the appendix on "Rome for the Protestant Scholar," could never have been written without the invaluable aid of the Rev. Thurlow Weed, Federation of Evangelical Churches in Italy.

3 The *Sacred Congregations* are: Holy Office, Consistorial, Oriental Church, Propagation of the Faith, Rites, Ceremonial, Extraordinary Ecclesiastical Affairs, Seminaries and Universities, Affairs of Religious, St. Peter's Basilica, Sacraments, Council.

The *Offices* are: Apostolic Chancery, Apostolic Datary, Apostolic Camera, Secretariat of State, Briefs and Letters.

The *Tribunals* are: Sacred Penitentiary, Apostolic Signatura, Roman Rota.

4 See especially Canons 256, 1376, and 1377. Anyone desiring to sample the authority of these Congregations *vis à vis* seminaries can do no better than read the Apostolic Constitution *Deus Scientiarum Dominus* of Pius XI, 1931. This is a major directive of the S.C.S.U.S. for diocesan seminaries. A comparable document for religious is *Sedes Sapientiae*. Supplementing and superseding each of them is The Decree on Priestly Training of Vatican II.

5 It should be perfectly clear, especially after Vatican II, that the Roman Catholic Church is not a monolithic organization of pure vertical and hierarchical dimensions. It is imperialistic in attitude, autocephalic in practice, and extremely diversified in opinions on non-dogmatic matters.

6 It has been generally interpreted that the Pro-Prefect of the S.C.S.U.S., Archbishop Garrone, will wield a vigorous broom in sweeping out much dust.

7 Typical of many critical remarks about the extreme conservatism of S.C.S.U.S. is this: "One of the most serious objections to that

academic system which is imposed upon all eccleciastical faculties all over the world by the S.C.S.U.S. is its uniformity, inflexibility, and curial centralization. The whole system is firmly founded on the Italian situation and mentality, which is, so far as clerics are concerned, a very particular one."—Fr. Peter Fransen, S.J., *Theology and the University*. p. 96.

[8] For a descriptive analysis of these various schools, see our Appendix on the Roman Athenaea and Libraries, pp. 203 ff.

[9] Most Protestant seminary teachers have received their doctorates from six of the outstanding American *secular* universities: Harvard, Union-Columbia, Yale, Chicago, Vanderbilt, Duke. This difference in Protestant faculty doctoral background, *vis à vis* Catholic seminary faculties, is a matter of real significance and one which will be referred to several times in these pages.

[10] Wm. Purdy wryly notes that "when the newly-ordained Father John Baptist Montini (Pope Paul VI) began his post-graduate course in Rome, he simultaneously enrolled for a course in Italian literature at the Sapienza [the predecessor of the University of Rome]: his superiors soon told him with little circumlocution that he was wasting his time, and he abandoned the course in favour of part-time work at the Vatican Secretariat of State." *Clergy Review*, April, 1964, p. 205.

[11] Luigi Barzini, *The Italians* (New York: Bantam Books, Athenaeum Publishers, 1964), p. 230 ff. and *passim*.

[12] See his article in *Seminarium*, S.C.S.U.S., Vatican City, October-November, 1962, pp. 651–670.

[13] Even now—at the North American College, for example—some seminarians need the help of a *Repitor* to review in English what had been heard in Latin an hour previously at the Gregorian.

[14] In American Protestant theological circles just the opposite needs to be asked: "Are you paying enough attention to Roman Catholicism, to pre-reformation and patristic history, to liturgical life, etc.?"

[15] Professor Oscar Cullmann, commenting on a first draft of this chapter, emphatically retorted: "And make sure that American Protestant theologians don't depend so heavily on Germany!"

[16] The adjective "non-Catholic" is an unfortunate one; a Catholic would not like to speak of himself as a "non-Protestant"—but we limp with this usage.

[17] The closest reciprocal relationships could be maintained with the American Academy.

2

The Catholic Seminary
as Theological Oratory

Prayer as Priority

There is nothing more impressive in Catholic theological education than the seriousness with which it seeks to form the future priest in his spiritual and devotional life. Speaking on the four hundredth anniversary of the Council of Trent, Pope Paul VI had this to say:

For Catholic doctrine teaches us that no one can fulfill all the precepts of the natural law or acquire the fullness of virtue without the healing grace of our Saviour. From this fundamental principle there follows an important corollary for clerical training. The candidate's formation as a human being must proceed apace with his formation as a Christian and a priest. In this way his natural energies will be fortified and purified by prayer, sacramental grace, and the supernatural virtues; and the supernatural virtues in turn will be sustained and supported by the natural energies.[1]

23

That is a fine illustration of the main objective of Catholic seminary life. It is an altogether representative quotation, for no matter where one goes in Catholic seminary circles, no matter what one reads in seminary literature, the same goal is assiduously sought. This priority of spiritual formation in Christ is held up high for all to see in the fourth chapter of Vatican II's *Decree on Priestly Training:*

The spiritual training should be closely connected with the doctrinal and pastoral, and, with the special help of the spiritual director, should be imparted in such a way that the students might learn to live in an intimate and unceasing union with the Father through His Son Jesus Christ in the Holy Spirit. Conformed to Christ the Priest through their sacred ordination, they should be accustomed to adhere to Him as friends, in an intimate companionship, their whole life through. They should so live His paschal mystery themselves that they can initiate into it the flock committed to them.

A seminary, then, is the school where the priest-to-be is helped to live the Easter mystery in a continuing familiarity with the Father; it is the place where the seminarian seeks for Christ, meditates on God's Word—a quest which is sustained by the holy mysteries of the Church, especially the Eucharist.

There is not the slightest evidence that the Roman Catholic Church will change its conviction that the formation of the seminarian in Christ is the absolutely central purpose of the seminary years. This goal is so self-evident to the Catholic teacher and student as to be beyond question. The Catholic is completely baffled by a Protestant version of seminary education which puts any other goal in first place. Spiritual formation and education for the priesthood are completely co-terminous in the Catholic mind. *The seminary is not primarily the intellectual center of the Church's life; it is primarily that place, those years, wherein the seminarians are helped to devotional and spiritual maturity.* To niggle at that assumption would seem to the Catholic educator as foolish as asking if a boat were meant to float.

What does the Catholic Church mean by the word "spiritual"? There is no brief answer. The above quotation from the *Decree on Priestly Training* is as good as any other short one. Fr. Louis Bouyer, whose writings on the spiritual life command wide attention within the Catholic community, offers this helpful definition:

Christian spirituality is that life in which our most personal, most interiorized relationship with God himself in His transcendent reality is fully recognized and cultivated . . . a Christian spiritual life is not one dominated simply by the ineradicable, indestructible *idea* on the part of the Christian that God is a person. This life flows from the *fact* that God has revealed Himself to us as a person. No Christian spirituality worthy of the name can exist where the conviction has been weakened that God, in Christ, has made Himself known to us by His own words, His own acts, as Some One . . . God not only has spoken to us, but He continues to speak to us in His Christ by and in the Church. . . . Protestantism tends to produce a spirituality which springs entirely from the co-presence and mutual relationship between the Person of God revealed in the Christ of the Gospels and the individual person of the believer. But for Catholicism there is no fully authentic Christian spirituality without the realization of an equal co-presence of our fellow believers with Christ and ourselves, in the Church . . . it might be said that, in Protestantism, everything goes on, or seems to go on, as if the Incarnation had ended with the Ascension of the Savior.[2]

A prime characteristic of one way by which spirituality is given life and meaning in Catholic seminary years is the organic union of theology *as a rational science* with theology *as a prayerful expression of one's faith and devotion.* In large part this is due to the historical influence of monasticism. Monasticism regarded theology as handmaiden to prayer and as a means to personal sanctification. Not even the most sterile extremes of scholasticism ever intentionally tried to divorce prayer and learning, faith and its expression.

Dom Jean Leclercq in his superb *The Love of Learning and the Desire for God*[3] contrasts St. Bernard's sermons and Peter Lombard's *Sentences* as illustrating two modes of religious understanding: the spiritual theology seeking a deeply personal knowledge of God, and the scholastic theology which seeks to explicate the mysteries of God. They are complementary, not in essential opposition.[3]

As Dom Leclercq maintains in another one of his writings, the object of a theological education is to create a unity of theology and devotional life:

Theology is an activity of the intelligence which takes for granted, which envelops, a certain interior experience which is absolutely inseparable from it . . . the contemplative and devotional life gives to theology not truth, but the tones of vigor and conviction. The intelligence searches out the truth.[4]

Another way of illustrating this Catholic priority is seen in this quite typical excerpt from the *Constitution on the Sacred Liturgy* of Vatican II (paragraph 16):

The study of sacred liturgy is to be ranked among the compulsory and major courses. . . . Moreover, other professors, while striving to expound the mystery of Christ and the history of salvation from the angle proper to each of their own subjects, must nevertheless do so in a way which will clearly bring out the connection between their subjects and the liturgy, as also the unity which underlies all priestly training.

The Catholic conscience on such matters as the spiritual life keeps reminding everyone—its own seminarians and priests most of all—that those who give up prayer must fall back on law or activism. The seminary schedule is therefore fully anchored on the pedagogical axiom that no study or any form of field-work apostolate is to be divorced from a steady reflection on its spiritual meaning.

Catholic seminary education seeks always to fuse theology and prayer, one illuminating the other: each interpenetrating, and all within a community of the Church. Likewise, pastoral activity must originate in the interior life: "God should be cultivated separately, in Himself, outside of action, through the spiritual exercises, of which the most important is mental prayer."[5]

These priorities, these theoretical goals, are built into the daily habit patterns of seminary students. Here is an aspect of character formation which can too easily be dismissed by Protestants as mere routine. It often is routine: and, when it is, it can kill the spirit. On the positive side, however, this intense habit formation has much to suggest to Protestantism. Fr. Henri Nouwe of Utrecht remarked to the writer, "You probably have no idea how a priest can become almost physically ill if he omits crucial and daily acts of devotion." It will not do for Protestants to dismiss the influence of habit in devotional life as so much reflex piety.[6]

There is, then, a formal pattern of devotional discipline in the daily schedule at all Catholic seminaries. The tendency recently in the United States is to make it more flexible and open, with more initiative being expected of the student rather than mere administrative coercion. Nevertheless, Catholic wisdom dictates that there must be some minimal schedule of performance and expectation in the devotional practices of the seminary. It looks about like this: the seminarian rises in the morning, says a short Morning Prayer (self-examination, resolution, and adoration—usually based on a Scripture text). Those acts are a necessary prelude to Holy Mass, the most important spiritual action of the day. The Mass is to be followed closely and attentively in the Missal. To Mass the student brings his morning resolutions and intentions. At midday there is usually a time set aside for Particular Examen, an opportunity to recall the early morning resolutions and to hear a Scripture reading. Most seminarians visit the Blessed Sacrament at least twice a day, spending a few minutes, quietly seated in the sanctuary, inwardly voicing acts of adoration, thanksgiving, and petition. In addition to these types of devotional rule, there are the regular disciplines of Rosary, Spiritual Reading, and Confession. There may be, especially in the seminaries operated by monastic communities, a beautiful pattern of chanted Offices. Catholic seminary schedules insist on brief periods of community Silence during the day and often during meals. Finally, seminary life is punctuated monthly by a Day of Recollection—a day set aside for more intensive sustained prayer, meditation, contrition. There is also the *Annual Retreat* (usually of a week's duration) with systematic bible study and meditation, visiting preacher (retreat master), silence, discussion, and reading. There are special retreats throughout the seminary years in preparation for each of the stages leading to ordination.

Such is the plain and telling outline of Catholic seminary spiritual formation. The outline does not mention what are often the most persuasive and influential forces: the lives and example of fellow students, faculty, and spiritual directors.

The Catholic spiritual life should not be romanticized to sound like a choir of angels on perfect pitch. Catholic seminarians often find such devotional discipline tiring and chafing. There is no doubt but that a seminary rector can impose a schedule which is a challenge to Simon Stylites and a West Point plebe—overdone in austerity and severity.[7] A few seminary administrators are spiritual martinets operating a "boot camp" for God. For the moment, however, all concerned with this key dimension of seminary education must give the Church of Rome its full due for setting high standards and for reminding all Christians that in the Christian life the most important graces come only with prayer and fasting.

Comparing the actual daily timetable of two typical seminaries—one Catholic and one Protestant—will reveal something of the difference in the approach to the spiritual and academic formation of the students.

In 1965–66, St. John's Seminary, Brookline, Mass., the seminary of the Archdiocese of Boston, observed the following daily schedule:

5:45 A.M.	Rising
6:00	Lauds and Meditation
6:35	Community Mass
7:20	Retire to rooms
7:35	Breakfast,[8] Recreation until
8:10	Retire to rooms
8:30	Class
9:20	Class
10:10	Class
11:00	Class
11:45	Recreation
12:00 P.M.	Visit to Blessed Sacrament and Examen
12:15	Dinner,[8] Recreation until
1:15– 5:40	Study
(1:30– 2:30	Recreation for Theology Community
(2:30– 3:30	Recreation for Philosophy Community
5:40	Visit to Blessed Sacrament and Spiritual Reading
6:00	Supper,[8] Recreation until
7:00– 9:30	Study
9:30–10:00	Recreation
10:00	Compline
11:00	Lights out

In the same school year at Union Theological Seminary, New York City—one of the world's outstanding non-denominational, university-related Protestant seminaries—a student day looked something like this.

——	There is no set rising time or bed time.
8:00	Breakfast
8:30	Chapel (voluntary)
9:00–12:30	Classes and study
12:30– 1:00	Luncheon
1:00– 6:00	No set schedule: combination of leisure, study, field-work preparation, classes, physical exercise—widely differing from person to person.
6:00– 7:00	Dinner hour
7:00–12:00	Largely study, but may be varied with a party, watching television, many special lectures and discussions, interest groups, night on the town, etc.
10:30–11:00	Worship (voluntary)

It must be emphasized that there is no such thing as a typical day at a seminary such as Union. There is a bewildering variety of individual schedules. Beyond a few housekeeping and big-city security regulations, there are no rules which bind the student. Meals are cafeteria style, with no communal pattern to them. Class attendance follows the customary graduate-school pattern: although attendance is not taken, most students go to class because the teaching is excellent. The average B.D. student probably spends no more than 16–18 hours per week in class.

Chapel attendance is not monitored in any way whatsoever. About one-fourth of the seminarians attend morning chapel. Very few members of the faculty regularly worship at morning chapel.

Weekends are wide open. Virtually everyone does field work or is employed in some remunerative job. Nothing much is scheduled on Saturday or Sunday.

One prominent Union student leader described life at Union in these words:

Union is very much like the world, apart from relative unity of commitment to some form of ministry of Jesus Christ. The chapel is not central to most of us, regardless of how much we may talk about the necessity of some sort of authentic worship. Darn few students partake in any self-styled personal religious discipline. Action is more prominent than prayer; Harvey Cox is more closely studied than St. Paul. Retreats are relatively infrequent as opposed to the protests of *ad hoc* social and political action groups. Union students are on the go, trying to juggle an incredible number of outside or extra-curricular commitments together with a respectable amount of required academic assignments. To this extent, Union is very much like the world outside[9]

The contrast of schedules is not intended to be invidious in either direction. The St. John's timetable reflects a highly organized celibate community, concentrating on a spiritual formation which is largely sacramental and communal. It allows very little room for outside activities, for independent study. It is even closer to a preparatory school life than it is to undergraduate college. It is, indeed, closer to West Point, in that the student is viewed primarily as one "under orders."

The Union Seminary schedule, contrariwise, scarcely differs from that of a graduate student in the English Department at Columbia University across the street. The seminarians come and go under very few rules; they are expected to be motivated for graduate study. They make use of the cultural attractions of New York City as their purses and self-devised timetables will permit. Family obligations consume much time, with some of the married students often engaged in outside remunerative employment which may or may not have direct relationship to the educational goals of the seminary. The Union student spends far more time in independent study than does his St. John's counterpart—and far less time in devotional discipline.

The contrast between St. John's and Union obviously is symptomatic of radically differing views about the nature of the ordained ministry.

The lesson for each tradition is not some mathematical compromise whereby Union would set aside *x* number of hours for devotional life, while St. John's would release *y* number of hours for intellectual and cultural pursuits. There is no such formula-solution. Each community can only take thought about the essential nature of the church and the ministry, *vis à vis* the needs of the world, and keep devising and revising seminary programs which incorporate such convictions.

It is necessary to reiterate, especially for the Protestant, how essential it is fully to grasp the depth and scope of Catholic seminary spiritual formation. It is not pious catalogue or public-relations talk. It exists not only in manuals of devotion, papal encyclicals, and *monita* from the Holy See; it is formally implemented, day in day out, in the public community life of the seminary. And it is expected to be a part of the student's private life. As a rough guess, the Catholic seminarian probably spends five times as much of his daily schedule on spiritual exercises as does his Protestant equivalent. This proves nothing, of course, but it does demonstrate what Catholic seminaries are about; and, unless one is a docetist, it stands to reason that bodily and institutional routine does have a direct relationship to spiritual growth.

Whatever the Catholic seminary, diocesan or religious, there are certain aspects of spiritual formation which are held in common:

1. *An overruling intention, and participation by the faculty.* Rector, faculty, and students alike fully accept and wish to implement the spiritual formation of the future priest as the primary function of the seminary. The faculty will permit nothing to interfere with this.

2. *The seminary is a school of prayer.* Whatever the form, public or private, all Catholic seminaries are praying communities. The concept of spirituality may be more broadly defined than it is presently, but it may not be defined so as to eliminate prayer.

However, although all must prize highly the human and natural training of the religious clergy, there can be no doubt that the supernatural sanctification of the soul holds first place in the whole program of formation.[10]

3. *There is communal discipline.* There is a structure, a routine, a program in which everyone shares. This liturgical rhythm is increasingly biblical in nature, always centered around the Eucharist. Week in and month out, a very powerful communal habit of worship is formed. Each person sustains and is sustained. This reflex is grounded in the fact that the spiritual life is always an act of the Church, not a convocation of individuals.

4. *It takes time.* For six or seven years the Catholic seminarian is formed in the patterns, reflexes, habits of spiritual training. It is highly questionable whether the Protestant pattern of a wide-open three-year B.D. curriculum, on top of a generally non-spiritual undergraduate four years, is capable of doing the main task of theological education.

5. *It takes competent supervision.* A *laissez-faire* attitude toward spiritual formation assumes too much from human nature, just as it implies that wisdom and experience in these matters cannot be imparted. All seminaries have

spiritual directors whose work is supplemented by other members of the faculty and who take a personal interest in the spiritual maturation of the students.

If Protestant seminaries had as rigorous a standard of moral and spiritual requirements for graduation as do the Catholic seminaries, Protestant seminary attrition would be much, much higher. If Catholic seminaries would exercise as much care as the better Protestant seminaries in the academic and psychological testing of candidates for admission, the Catholic attrition rate would be much, much lower. In between those two generalizations is the space on which representatives of both communities should take counsel together.

Faculty Judgment and Ordination

"It is possible to define the work of the seminary as the happy elimination of the unfit." That unsentimental phrase introduces another aspect of Catholic theological education, faculty judgment of seminarians, about which Protestants have much to learn to their profit. The subject is best introduced by a quotation from the Most Rev. John F. Whealon:

For priests engaged in seminary work, one of the most important and most practical documents published is the letter dated September 27, 1960, sent from the Sacred Congregation of Seminaries and Universities to the Bishops of the world on the occasion of the Third Centenary Year of the Death of St. Vincent de Paul. This letter was a forceful reminder that a seminary is, in addition to being an institution for the training of soul and mind, a court of judgment in which the faculty, like a Supreme Court, sits in judgment concerning the fitness of each candidate for priestly studies. It said, in part:

The Church has the strict obligation to seek the signs of a true vocation in all who feel themselves called to the sanctuary. She must make sure, at the same time, that they have the qualities which will enable them worthily and efficiently to fulfill their office. We know that whenever God lays on men such exalted duties and responsibilities, he gives to those so chosen sufficient graces to enable them to carry them out worthily. The candidate puts himself forward for the judgment of the superiors. It is for the superiors to judge and act accordingly.

This scrutiny begins from the time a student first enters the seminary. It ends either with his ordination or with his dismissal as soon as it becomes apparent that he is unsuitable. Each superior in a seminary has his own particular sphere, but each, by reason of his sacred trust, has a twofold office. He is to be an educator in the daily task of making a new man out of each of these entrusted to his charge: and he is to be a judge, as to whether they are corresponding to the graces they have received, as to their progress or otherwise, as to the evidence of further physical and spiritual development, and as to their resistance to or inability to profit by the work of formation. It is a task which is heavy and full of difficulties but it is a task which cannot be shirked. The superiors, in their actions, must be guided by the light of God, to Whom all hearts are open, and Whom all hearts obey.

These solemn words remind us that every seminary professor, and especially the rector, is a judge. This obligation to render judgment on seminarians is shown likewise in the liturgy of ordination. In the liturgy of the priesthood ordination, a ritual but realistic dialogue takes place between the ordaining prelate and the seminary rector prior to the ordination ceremony. *"Scis illos dignos esse?"* interrogates the Bishop, fully mindful of the prohibition of St. Paul and of the Church that he should not "impose hands lightly" on any candidate. And the seminary rector, equally mindful of *his* responsibility and with a special prayer for one or two in the class, says in words that even the vernacular could hardly make clearer: *"Quantum humana fragilitas nosse sinit, et scio et testificor ipsos dignos esse ad hujus onus officii."*[11]

How many teachers and administrators in Protestant seminaries can honestly say that careful and sustained faculty scrutiny of seminarians is provided? How often are students admitted and permitted to graduate largely on the basis of academic performance, but without sufficient attention being paid to their personal and Christian maturation? With regard to the requirements for ordination, a seminary is not comparable to a law school or to a graduate school; it has *sui generis* responsibilities for these qualities of mind and heart which are required for the pastoral ministries.

The Catholic seminaries themselves cannot maintain uniformly high standards, especially when there are so many seminaries. But let the Protestant be grateful that the Catholic system keeps alive crucial criteria for ordination, implemented throughout the seminary years.

The Catholic criteria are not in all cases the same as those which Protestants would emphasize. Bishop Whealon lists the following: aptitude for priesthood; honesty and openness of character; spirit of charity; respect for authority; mental maturity; good judgment; willingness to work; sociability; personal habits; physical health.[12] Any faculty would vary somewhat in its choice of criteria, or in their rank order. But no faculty should be without criteria.

Protestant seminaries have their reasons for avoiding the systematic faculty review of each student's character and spiritual stature, the chief of which is probably a seminary job-definition which sees itself more as a graduate school of religion than as Christian community. Christian *koinonia* is not a noticeable achievement of American Protestant seminary life; and it is only in *koinonia* that love, judgment, justice, and mutual concern for the health of each other and the Church is felt. The Catholic faculty is apt to be more assiduous and surgically painful in its judgments about students just because of its intense *koinonia* and consequently high ordination standards.

Catholic faculty judgments, *in camera,* are usually made four times yearly.[18] Then there is a final faculty decision as to each student's fitness for ordination. It is in the context of ordination that the faculty votes are taken. Both Protestantism and Catholicism recognize that ordination is a multistep process which includes interior call or conviction, education, judgment of the Church, as well as the act of ordination. Granted that this agreement is quite apparent, it is discouraging to have to report that far too many Protestant seminary faculties, while giving good stewardship in the husbanding of academic talent, simply do not take seriously enough the spiritual and personality maturation of the seminarians. Of course, the Catholic seminary, with its unity of faith, is an organic part of the Church to a much more significant degree than many Protestant seminaries feel themselves to be—even some of the denominational seminaries. Given such a diffuse sense of relation to the Church, it is only natural that neither the Protestant faculty nor the student body feels the seminary years to be a carefully scrutinized part of the whole ordination process.

Voltaire thought his age sought virtue without principle; it may just be that more Protestant seminaries than one would like to count are gnostic communities, little concerned with Christ's Body. If so, it is one of the oldest heresies and deviations in Christian history. It is one which does not come wilfully, but by lack of personal disciplines and by an idolatry of the intellectual life which, in its pride, will not be obedient to Christ.

There is still another matter, related to the final months of seminary, in which Catholic practice has something to teach Protestants: the final steps prior to ordination. No Protestant self-flagellation is in order; but there can be no doubt about the indifferent, even sloppy, protocol and preparation which too often afflict the ordination procedures of many Protestant denominations.

Catholic practice affords two reminders. The first is the Catholic practice of a retreat for ordinands. This permits a final time of quiet and concentrated contemplation of the step about to be taken; it permits prayer and discussion; it occasions a soul-searching. Protestant seminarians tend to take a more casual, even perfunctory, path. There are some churches which even have the final ordination examination on the same day as the Ordination Service! While no generalization is possible about all the Protestant practices, yet most of the Protestant churches could add to the dignity and meaning of ordination by devising their own forms of retreat and by developing more rigorous and systematic examination procedures prior to ordination.

The second Catholic contribution is less specific. It is that atmosphere of expectation, of solemnity, of uniqueness which attends the sacrament of Holy Orders. To be sure, the Catholic concept of indelible orders, plus the role of the priest in Catholic soteriology, contributes a dimension which most Protestant ordination services cannot attain. This is no excuse, however, for that pedestrian quality which threatens many Protestant ordination procedures. Some Protestant seminarians give evidence of being more excited over receiving a graduate degree from the seminary than at the prospect of being ordained. This may be because the ordained ministry is regarded more as a function than as an office in the Body of Christ. No *sotto voce* plea is here made for pomp and circumstance. Rather, this is a plea for an up-grading in Protestant ordination practices commensurate with the proper authority, dignity, and sacrificial servanthood of the sacramental ministry.[14]

The Spiritual Director

A distinctive and most revealing aspect of Catholic seminaries is to be found in the role of the Spiritual Director. It is distinctive when contrasted to Protestant seminaries, and it is revealing in what it declares about the Catholic methodology of spiritual formation.

Spiritual Directors or their equivalents are to be found in all Catholic seminaries. Their presence and function is rooted in a long tradition and required by Roman directive. Depending on the size and organization of the seminary, the work of the Spiritual Director may be part-time or full-time, with or without collateral teaching responsibilities.

Each student must consult the Spiritual Director regularly during the school year. This varies from once or twice a month to no more than four times per year. Everyone on the faculty, of course, takes an interest in the spiritual formation of the seminarians. A student may, indeed, select almost any member of the faculty to be his special "Father-in-God," but the Spiritual Director of the seminary must be satisfied that each student is receiving the proper attention. No matter what the variety of pattern in a given seminary, no student goes without such personal guidance.

Ordinarily the Director does not serve as academic advisor, nor does he sit in any kind of disciplinary jurisdiction over the seminarians. Some seminaries do not permit the Director to serve as confessor.

When spiritual directors talk and write about their duties, they assume a rather precise definition of spirituality of the type presented previously in this chapter: the systematic search for personal holiness, in community, according to the counsels of perfection and the means of grace. This quest relies not only on the liturgical and sacramental acts of the Church, but also on a regular appropriation of that monumental Catholic tradition of Christian literature, lives of the saints, spiritual exercises, and the like. In short, there is a content, a subject matter, to spirituality. It is definable both as a historical corpus and as the living presence of Christ in His Church. The Spiritual Director is a priest specially qualified to help the seminarian with the study of, and prayerful immersion in, this realm of spiritual treasure. Writes Fr. William C. Bier, S.J.:

Neophytes in the spiritual life, as minor seminarians certainly are, need someone to introduce them to the ways of the spirit, to teach each of them the meaning of responsiveness to the promptings of the Holy Spirit within them, and to set their feet firmly on the road to spiritual perfection.[15]

The Spiritual Director prays with his students, inquires after their formation, suggests readings, interprets the experience of the Church in matters of the interior life, and, by personal example, seeks to discipline them in search of Christian virtue and obedience. Fr. Bier goes on to say:

The Spiritual Director is an expert in the spiritual life. He is competent to offer instruction in this area, which he does in his spiritual conferences [lectures to the entire student body], and in the advice which he imparts in his private conferences, guiding them in the development of the spiritual life as an individual growth within each of them.

It is interesting to note that Fr. Bier is Chairman of the Psychology Department at Fordham University, interesting because the psychology of spiritual formation cannot escape notice. It appears that much of the prevailing Catholic psychology of the spiritual life is a rationalistic first cousin to the faculty psychology which divides man into thinking, feeling, and willing components. On the surface, at least, the psychological assumptions of spiritual directing do not reveal much of the dynamic complexity of man. Generalizations are very tricky here, but most writing about spiritual directing very quickly makes the point that the Spiritual Director is not a personal counselor concerned with the deeper problems of maturation, identity, etc. This is not to say that the Spiritual Director has no knowledge of psychodynamics; it is rather to observe that the spiritual life of the student is conceived of as being *different enough* from personality dynamics to warrant a status of its own, with distinct faculty responsibilities, in much the same way as French is different from English, though with cognate relationships. Spiritual Directors are often quite eager not to become too much involved in the "non-spiritual" problems of their advisees. This substantive and psychological separation is, as will be shortly noted, quite different from the operating assumptions at most Protestant seminaries.

Dean Kevin O'Rourke, O.P., of the Aquinas Institute, Dubuque, Iowa, makes this separation clear and with the same logic as Fr. Bier:

While it is true that some few individuals have attained outstanding sanctity without a spiritual director, the general rule is that those who reach any notable degree of holiness do so with the counsel and guidance of a competent spiritual director . . . to put it another way, the first principles of counselling are from human knowledge, while the first principles of spiritual direction are from faith, or divine knowledge. Both arts require a recognition of the principles basic to the other, but the distinction of the two must also be maintained.[16]

In the language of Catholic theology, both Fr. Bier and Fr. O'Rourke are equating the function of the Spiritual Director in the Mystical Body with that of the rational instrument of the Holy Spirit, the principal cause of the soul's sanctification.

It now remains to indicate again, particularly to the Protestant, that the high priority accorded spiritual direction in Catholic seminaries is an *implemented* priority. The Spiritual Director is another example of the Catholic conviction that living in Christ is not achieved by happenstance or by the random and peripheral attention of a non-disciplined community.

What evaluative comments does the Catholic Spiritual Director elicit from a Protestant? The first is that, given the high status of the Spiritual Director in Catholic theory, there seems to be a distressing variety of what can only be called professional competence. It does not appear that any minimal standards must be met for appointment as Spiritual Director. Some are very impressive persons with extraordinary minds and hearts; others are priests who have been appointed to fill a vacant faculty slot, but who have no particular stature for this work. There is variety of competence in any field of discipline, but this particular area of work seems to have such a wide variety that one wonders if the Church takes preparation for these responsibilities as seriously as the definition of the office demands. There are, of course, seminaries and institutes in the United States and elsewhere—Rome, for example—where special training is given to Spiritual Directors. The question raised here, however, is whether the traditions of spiritual directing do not require more specialization.

A more important comment revolves around the methodology of spiritual formation implied in the role of the Director. Is it true that the quest for charity, for the inspirited life, can be so neatly or formally separated from the holistic understanding of personal growth? Can prayer and rectitude, for example, possibly be separated out, like curds and whey, from the hundred and one problems flesh is heir to? Human behavior, motivation, and development is so complex that too narrow a definition of spiritual directing seems highly suspect.[17]

Is there a place within Protestant theological education for a Spiritual Director? There is. In any adequate faculty there ought to be at least one person who is steeped in this tradition, whose presence reminds both faculty and students that no definition of secular or worldly Christianity can omit the prayerful discipline and means of grace. Most Protestant theological faculties would be rightly suspicious if entire reliance should be placed on such a Director. It will never work that way because spiritual maturity does not come in that way alone. Christian maturity, personal and/or spiritual—however one defines it—is the end result of a gathering of many influences and disciplines: academic, practical, communal. But just as no faculty should be without a New Testament teacher, no faculty should be without one or more persons of proven competence who are charged to keep alive the vast and saving heritage of spirituality.

The Belgian Experiments

There is a great deal of insight into spiritual formation and theological education, particularly in their relation to apostolic activity, to be gained by a brief look at two seminaries in Belgium. The lively imagination exercised by Cardinal Suenens of Malines and his associates has been chiefly responsible for encouraging *avant-garde* experimentation at Louvain and at Namur. Cardinal Suenens, incidentally, is an outstanding example of what a bishop can do on his own initiative to make progress without checking every jot and tittle with Rome. In that sense, he has been acting for some time according to a strategy only recently and formally sanctioned by the *Decree on Priestly Training,* that is, designing seminary education in keeping with local and national insights and conditions.

The first of these Belgian seminaries worth close scrutiny is Le Séminaire Jean XXIII à Louvain. Under the vigorous leadership of Fr. Hermann Servotte (whose many accomplishments include a Master's degree in English Literature from Yale University) this new and small seminary is only three miles from the University of Louvain, the largest Catholic university in Europe. The seminary thus has a healthy relationship to a major cultural center. The program and curriculum at this seminary may be the most pioneering of any Catholic seminary in the world. It contains most of the features advocated by the more progressive Catholic advocates of seminary reform. In physical plant the seminary departs from the prevailing military-barracks style of most seminaries, sub-dividing the students in groups of six or seven in small houses, each with a priest-master. Meals are taken by priests and students together, without the old-style faculty assembling at a separate hier-archical high-table. Families and friends are encouraged to come to the campus and are invited occasionally to meals. The atmosphere is intended to be much more in-formal, home-like, less regimented, and leaning more in the direction of freedom.

The assumptions behind the planning of Le Séminaire Jean XXIII clearly disavow a perpetuation of the monastic pattern: men being fitted for the secular clergy are not to be regarded as religious living in an order; spiritual and educational formation is aimed at developing a priest able to move about in the world of the present, not the past.

"Il s'ensuit que dans la formation religieuse au séminaire on portera l'attention plus que par le passé sur l'apostolat conquérant. Au séminaire Jean XXIII on veillera spéciale-ment à cela."

The seminary will try to do everything feasible to develop a community dynamic, *"la vie en communauté."* This means more than merely a collection of bodies going through the same routine at the same time; it is intended to create dialogue, group- and self-criticism, to encourage seminars and forums, to get away from too many formal lectures without opportunity for questions. Living in small groups will make for much conversation concerning the week's work in and outside the seminary. Each seminarian will be encouraged to do considerable visitation of parishes, work with youth groups, in hospitals, in the business world. In short, each seminarian will gain a realistic knowledge of what parish life will be like, will hear the questions that are really being asked by people, and will not be satisfied simply to know the answers given deductively from some Scholastic system. The system of spiritual directors will be maintained, but the seminarians will be encouraged and expected to develop a style and a pace of individual spiritual life which is not so dependent on community bell-ringing. The seminary at Louvain attempts to keep the central fea-tures of Catholic worship life—Mass, the liturgy, breviary, etc.—but, at the same time, aims to give the seminarian more responsibility for developing a spiritual discipline which will be his own when he leaves the school. There is no apparent diminution of the intention, the expectation, and the seriousness with which Catholic seminaries have al-ways regarded spiritual formation. The Protestant eye is taken by the deliberate way in which the John XXIII faculty is making the liturgy and the personal devotional life *as biblical as possible!* *"On pourrait ainsi retarder la messe* *jusqu'au soir et organiser, le matin, une prière communautaire inspirée par la Bible . . . en recherchant communautairement une forme adéquate \pour la prière biblique."*

Finally, this seminary experiment is notable for its unequivocal movement away from too heavy a dose of Scholastic philosophy during the first two years and toward a first-year curriculum which consists of "Introduction to Holy Scripture, Particularly the New Testament," "The Mission of the Church," "The Mission of the Priest in the Church," and a course on "The Faith." The traditional philosophy instruction is moved to the latter years of instruction. Also, this seminary has much more instruction in sociology, anthropology, and psychology than is usually found in major theologates. The faculty makes the wise assumption that a first-year student, particularly, is not a miniature priest, but an inquiring layman, and that his needs must be spoken to at the most relevant personal level during the first year. It is the best curriculum, in the opinion of this writer, now existent in a Catholic major seminary.

One can only admire the work-camp with which the seminary year opens. It is a mixture of manual labor on a work of charity—building a school, for example, or some other useful task—plus shared companionship and common prayer life. It does much to set the right style for what is to come.

The second Belgian seminary we would single out for study is an hour's distance from Louvain, at Namur on the Meuse River. There, at the foreign-missionary seminary— Scholasticate of the Missions of Scheut— is a parallel type of program. This reformed curriculum at the Scheut seminary is five years older than the experiment at Le Séminaire Jean XXIII, but both bear the Cardinal Suenens imprint and particularly reflect his book, *The Church in the State of Mission.* At Scheut the faculty, themselves products of the classical, more monastic type of seminary education, took not a little convincing about the advisability of such changes in seminary life. In one of the reports of the faculty there is this sentence: "Certainly at the beginning, the whole body of professors was not made up of enthusiasts. It required a good deal of reflection, of prayer, and even *the encouragement of obedience* to vanquish the last hesitations."[18] Such "encouragement," alas, is not among the armory of weapons which a Protestant seminary dean takes to a faculty meeting!

The Scheut Seminary has a highly developed system of student-faculty teams: ten students and one faculty per team. These teams form the pedagogical basis for the spiritual, intellectual and apostolic formation of the seminarians. Since the team format has necessitated radical changes in the former seminary timetable, the faculty has gone to great lengths to insure that the teamwork be carried out in a climate of prayer and of thoughtful reflection. "This atmosphere will give to the team meetings their distinctive soul, without which they will quickly degenerate into mere study circles or business meetings . . . it is necessary to pray in teams if one wants to work in teams, for it is necessary to implant the conviction that apostolic action grows from prayer and must constantly be reformed there."

Each team has a student president, the faculty member serving as spiritual director. In addition to the student teams is a "Directing Team" of faculty. This faculty team gives an immense amount of time to the supervision of the student teams' apostolic activities (field-work), *and there is probably no other seminary in either Protestantism or Catholicism where field-work is so closely supervised and so carefully correlated with spiritual formation.* The teams have a required formal meeting at least once a week to discuss, pray, and reflect upon their activities. Between meetings the student members of the teams—always in pairs—involve themselves, outside of class hours, in such activities as hospital visitation, Catholic youth work, visiting the boatmen on the Meuse, working with retreatants, editing a mission review, visiting military camps, pastoral visiting of families, helping with parochial-school catechetics, and sharing in Catholic youth movement summer vacation activities.

Fr. Edmund E. Veillesse is Spirtual Director at Scheut. In conversation at Namur he was greatly concerned to relate how this type of team apostolate has increased remarkably the motivation of the seminarians because they now see more clearly the relation between prayer, study, and pastoral care. Again and again he emphasized the point which, *vis à vis* spiritual formation, is so crucial for the Protestant seminary faculty to understand: professors are no spectators to the spiritual and devotional life of students; they must always be united in seeing that the entire community is in a state of mission and spiritual preparedness.[19]

Both the Louvain and the Namur seminary experiments are encouraging re-definitions of the older Catholic concept of spirituality; the intention now is to involve the student in the world of the laity, to correlate prayer and action, to make curriculum more relevant, to treat the student as a mature person, and to increase faculty-student rapport.

A Protestant Appraisal of Catholic Spiritual Formation

An appropriate word from an outstanding ecumenical leader, Bishop Stephen Neil of the Church of England, is a good starting point for an examination of the Protestant conscience in matters spiritual and devotional:[20]

It is none of my business to pry into the intimate lives of my friends. Yet, inevitably the question does from time to time arise. As far as I can judge, among the young ministers, those who regularly set apart a time each day for the development of the inner life, for prayer and meditation, are very few. Some feel no need for such an inner life; others know that they should have it, but have found no inner spring of self-discipline to overcome the natural human reluctance to be burdened, and no method which will serve as wings to the spirit. If this is true of ministers, I judge it to be still more true of students. They are deeply concerned with the academic aspects of theology, and prepared to discuss problems to all hours of the night. Yet they do not find it easy to discover the way back from the critical dissection of the scriptures to hearing the voice of God in the Bible; and the life of prayer is, to most of them, a sealed book. Any suggestion that prayer and meditation are essential is likely to be brushed aside as either "catholicizing" or "pietistic," words of deepest condemnation today. To take part in a brief public service of worship is something that may reasonably be expected of a theological student residing in an institution; can more be rightly demanded? Many students would answer emphatically, No. I would judge that the great majority of theological students set aside no time at all in any regular fashion for the care and nurture of the inner life of the Spirit.

Once again, this is not the whole story. Students who have, for instance, visited Taizé have come back startled and deeply impressed by the quiet, deep, unemotional, interior life of the brethren, have become aware of a need, and have then found it difficult to know how to translate something of this spirit into their own everyday life, heavily burdened as it is by all the demands of the academic vocation. There is a new interest in retreats and in the use of silence. But these things are signs of a possible movement rather than a movement itself.

Bishop Neil's stethoscopic diagnosis of the poor health of Protestant spirituality coincides with the evaluations of many qualified observers making the "grand rounds" of Protestant seminaries. The seminaries are, after all, *the* place to listen to this particular heartbeat. Seminaries may warn away those who lobby for a hundred and one special courses by which they intend the seminary to save the Church a hundred dire fates; but the spiritual life they may not shrug off and still claim any justification for existing.

A brisk finger-pointing indictment of Protestant seminaries, telling them to study Catholic seminaries and "do likewise," gets nowhere. There is more than enough for Protestants to ponder as they look at the spiritual formation in Catholic seminaries, but, first, there has to be an understanding of the Protestant "predicament." This is a predicament made up of both reasons and excuses.

Protestant seminaries are, with few exceptions, not communities knit together by a coherent confessional basis, by a uniform theology and Christology, or by a sustaining liturgical tradition. In this regard they both cause and reflect the Protestant ministry and Protestant church membership: many denominations have as high as a fifty per cent mobility of both membership and ministry (i.e., members change denomination when moving from one city to another, and ministers often are ordained in churches in which they were not raised). Furthermore, Protestantism has never had either the dogmatic theological basis of Rome or any pan-Protestant eucharistic liturgy. These factors alone are shattering to seminary attempts to build a spiritual household.

Diverse Protestant approaches to the Bible, plus the wide range of current hermeneutical battles going on in seminaries, do not provide a common stance for public devotions. The confusing theological alarums and cries of the seminary forum scarcely make for spiritual development. If God is dead, if Christ is only some sort of existential referrent, and if the supernatural categories are outmoded language forms, then *who* is going to worship *what,* and *how?* Protestant theology is very exciting, adventuresome, and much more explorative than Catholic theology. The Protestant principle of ruthless self-criticism, plus a soupçon of skepticism, makes for heady theological study, but it certainly complicates worship. The answer is not easy. Protestantism will never be anchored to rigid belief-patterns simply in order to permit worship. Without a deep devotional life, however, Protestantism can and will become a very thin porridge.

The situation of married Protestant seminarians is another complicating factor. This "diaper diaspora" does not make things easier. Theoretically, if there were manageable housing arrangements, student family life could be a source of a very deep and meaningful communal and spiritual cohesion. At the moment, however, housing logistics need to be solved, a chaplaincy to families established, and a much greater discipline expected.

Twentieth-century Protestant seminaries are the homes, or refuges, of many scholars who have been so quick to flee the worst excesses of old Protestant *pietism* of the ego-centric, saccharine, non-theological bosom of Jesus type that they have suddenly discovered that most of their spiritual baggage was lost in the flight.[21] Not sustained by a liturgical movement, these Protestants concentrate more and more on being scholars of religion. Protestant seminaries thus are always tempted to become graduate schools of religion. The academic level of the better Protestant seminaries is very high, much more so than the Catholic average. Write that sentence backwards: the "better" Protestant seminaries are those which have high academic standards. "Spiritual and devotional" considerations seldom enter into the use of the adjective "better," so far as this writer can tell.

Professor Roland Murphy, O.Carm.,[22] the distinguished Catholic biblical scholar who has taught at several Protestant seminaries, has this to offer as a comment on the problem of spiritual life in such schools:

Another severe responsibility placed upon the students is the "imitation of Christ." While this flows naturally from one's Baptism, and the priesthood of all believers, what does a student for the Protestant ministry propose seriously to do about it? Merely from the viewpoint of the spiritual needs of the faithful to whom he ministers, is he not bound to a familiarity with prayer and the experience of God? Otherwise, how can he expect to exercise a ministry different from that of a psychological therapist or a social worker?

One wonders if the extremes of Pietism have not dangerously influenced the development of the spiritual life as an ideal among Protestant clergy. Why cannot piety be approached in terms of a virile service of God, of true Christian nurture, in both an academic and practical manner? Yale Divinity School has its daily chapel service, and also various denominational services, as well as informal "ecumenical worship," based upon the Taizé liturgy. In the pluralistic society of Yale Divinity School this is welcome and productive of much spiritual life. Freedom of worship seems to correspond to freedom of theological opinion. But there should be a corresponding emphasis on the study of worship and the spiritual life as there is on systematics or other disciplines. Is the problem of "holiness" faced squarely by the student body? Or is the reality of the Spirit and his activity a category simply unspoken and, in a sense, not subject to discussion?[23]

Protestants have noticed such criticisms. They have taken seriously—with a sincere *mea culpa*—the Catholic examples concerning the need of discipline, routine, competent supervision, faculty participation, adequate time, and the other elements in Catholic practice which have a transfer value for Protestants. What reservation now remains for Protestants to voice?

Foremost, there is a deep distrust of any concept of the spiritual life which, in formal theological fashion, defines "spiritual" too narrowly. A compartmentalized, packaged approach to "spiritual" not only seems to violate the complicated picture of human psychology, but to do injustice to the doctrine of creation. Psychologically, the human in quest of the Divine finds himself in a search which involves his whole being, his motivations, his family and environmental influences, his intellectual questions, his unconscious psyche. It is neither easy nor possible to separate "spiritual growth" from "personal maturation," and that is why the very word "formation" is suspect. It sounds a bit as if the "spirit" of a man were equivalent to an arm or a leg—the Church, through the Spiritual Director, being the sculptor. Further, since the Holy Spirit works in His graciousness throughout all of creation, it would seem healthy and sane to define man's spiritual growth in such a way as to give due credit to all that is of good report in all of life; that is, spiritual development is going to come from social action, from an openness to the arts, from exposure to the whole range of secular contributions in literature, companionship, and the very stuff of ordinary daily living in our urban, scientific world. This is worldly holiness or holy worldliness.[24]

The Protestant is very much concerned with openness, with spontaneity, with freedom, and with initiative in the quest for Christian maturity. He will jealously repudiate any tendency to tidy things up, divide into neat categories, turn quest into law, or buy some theological simplicism in order to protect piety.

But the time has now come to recognize as sub-Christian any theological position which (in the name of demythologization, or existentialism, or linguistic analysis) effectively undercuts the personal obedience to God and the consequent response to Him of person-in-community. Protestants have a magnificent opportunity to beg, borrow, steal, and jointly share the Catholic vision and experience of the spiritual life and to do so without a literal imitation which does violence to Protestant theological integrity. Catholics also have the opportunity in a moment of expanding ecumenicity to gain refreshing insights from Protestantism.

But the conclusion here ventured is not intended as a nicely balanced bit of irenic me-tooism. It appears that in the realm of spiritual and devotional life, broadly understood, it may be much easier to modify the Catholic tradition than to reinvigorate the Protestant. Harshly stated: *if the sixteenth-century Reformation be in any way defined as a return to the Bible and as a cleansing and strengthening of spiritual life, there is more than enough evidence available at the seminary level to conclude that, on both counts, Protestantism may be falling well behind the best in contemporary Roman Catholic theological education.*

Notes

1 The Apostolic Letter, *Summi Dei Verbum,* November, 1963.

2 *Introduction to Spirituality* (Collegeville: Liturgical Press, 1961), pp. 4 ff.

3 A Mentor Omega book, published by New American Library, New York, 1962. See pp. 13 ff.

4 "Theology and Prayer," in *Encounter* (Indianapolis: Christian Theological Seminary), 1963, 24, 3, pp. 349–364 .

5 See "The Seminary and Prayer," in *Clergy Review,* April, 1964.

6 "Formation of the Seminarians toward a Diocesan Spirituality," by Rev. Sergius Wroblewski, O.F.M., in *National Catholic Educational Association Bulletin* (hereinafter: *NCEAB*), August, 1962, p. 75.

7 The military figure, applied to spiritual and moral discipline, was used by the late Fr. J. Cyril Dukehart, S.S., of the National Catholic Educational Association. In the *National Catholic Educational Association Bulletin* (1960, p. 5), he wrote: "Unlike most of the professional schools (law, medicine, etc.), which give only knowledge, the seminary aims at training the will. Like West Point and the Naval Academy, it subjects the student to a system of discipline by which he may gradually acquire habits becoming his profession. In the priest, holiness of life is more essential than professional science."

8 At most Catholic seminaries, silence is observed during meals, with a student reading from the Bible, devotional work, or even a secular novel. All meals and all classes begin and end with a prayer.

9 The average student at Union Theological Seminary is married, as are sixty per cent of B.D. students.

10 *Sedes Sapientiae,* Pius XII. See also *The Twentieth-Century Popes and the Priesthood,* by Louis S. Secondo, T.O.R., Rome, 1957.

11 "Judging the Character of Seminarians," in *NCEAB*, August, 1962, pp. 103 ff.

12 Aptitude for the priesthood is the key criterion; it is basically a powerful desire to acquire a deep awareness of the supernatural, of Christ as priest and victim.

13 The ever present danger in the Catholic system of faculty judgment is that it may create docile students who cravenly will do anything to pass muster. Perhaps some of the judges should be outside the power structure.

14 There is an in-group esprit, a subtle but extremely pervasive, almost caste-like sense of belonging which is characteristic of Catholic priests and which is not nearly so intense among Protestant ministers, even of the same denomination. It is what Fr. Thomas Corbishley, S.J., in his *Ronald Knox, the Priest* (London & New York: Sheed and Ward, 1964, p. 30) terms "the freemasonry of the Catholic priesthood . . . for all the superficial differences and disagreements which are often more present to the consciousness of the laity than they are to the minds of those who are supposed to be responsible for them, no priest, whatever his background or personal qualities, ever fails to realize that these are insignificant when seen in the light of the grace of ordination."

15 "The Guidance Counselor and the Spiritual Director: The Distinct Role of Each," in *NCEAB*, August, 1964, p. 112. See also Very Rev. James R. Gillis, O.P., "The Background and Preparation

Needed for the Office of the Spiritual Director," in *NCEAB*, August, 1962.

16 "The Priest and Spiritual Direction," *Cross and Crown*, September, 1965, p. 313 ff.

17 Fr. Adrian van Kamm's chapter, "Religious Counselling of Seminarians," in *Seminary Education in a Time of Change* is a very fruitful source of information about spiritual directing. Van Kamm is an advocate of a more flexible definition of the role, and he is opposed to any overly formalized manualistic and monologic concepts.

18 *Manual for the Apostolic Teams* (mimeographed, 1964). Italics mine.

19 See also in *Apostolic Renewal in the Seminary* (The Christophers, N.Y., 1964), the chapter "Spiritual Growth and Apostolic Formation in the Seminary," by Fr. Edmund Veillesse. Another exciting seminary is at Pontigny, in northern France, established for working-priests. Clerical garb is not worn. In a Spartan routine the seminarians study forty hours per week, do manual labor for ten. There is also a thorough preparation in the ideologies of the modern world.

20 "An Anglican in a Lutheran Atmosphere," in *Lutheran World*, Vol. XII, No. 3, 1965, p. 244.

21 A masterly article, highly to be commended to Protestant theological educators, is "The Quest for an Authentic Piety" by Dr. Edward Farley of Pittsburgh Theological Seminary, published in *Crossroads*, a magazine of the Board of Christian Education of the United Presbyterian Church U.S.A. (January-March, 1966). It is a superb description of the various forms of Protestant piety, their shortcomings and historical origins. Professor Farley claims that Protestantism must face bankruptcy unless it recovers an authentic piety, discarding pseudo-pieties.

22 See also his "A Catholic Foreword," this volume, pp. 9 ff.

23 "Yale Divinity School Reflections," in the seminary student newsletter, March, 1966.

24 For a fine elaboration of this point, see "Some Issues and Questions about Prayer" by John B. Coburn in *Theological Education*, Summer, 1966.

3

The Orbiting Worlds
of Clergy and Laity

A Shared Restlessness

Catholic seminaries clearly provide insight into the future shape of the Roman Catholic Church by the way in which its seminarians are joining in—sometimes leading—the crackling debate now going on regarding the proper relationship between clergy and laity.

In the thirteenth century Pope Boniface VIII thundered that the whole history of the Church showed that the laymen were natural enemies of the clergy. In 1965 one of the most articulate spokesmen for American Catholic laity, Michael Novak, reciprocated by maintaining that "The Church is much too valuable to entrust to the clergy."[1]

Mr. Novak is no anti-clerical, nor is there a major movement of anti-clericalism yet developing within American circles. There is, however, a remarkable display of a respect-anxiety ambivalence in the attitude of Catholic laity

toward their priests and their priests' seminaries. It is necessary that the Protestant reader remember particularly the
historical reasons for the respect, since the Protestant is
usually quick to pounce polemically on Catholic anxieties.

The love and respect which the Catholic feels for his
priest is of a markedly different type from the affectionate
but more casual regard which a practicing Protestant has
for his minister. The Catholic Church has always been hierarchical and sacerdotal, founded on an objective system of
salvation in which priests play an absolutely essential role.
Furthermore, Catholicism is a sacramental cultus at heart
which depends on the efficacious (*ex opere operato*) acts of
validly ordained priests (*ubi episcopus, ibi ecclesia*). The
Catholic clergy is self-reproducing, that is, there is no *necessary* consent or participation of the laity in the identification, and ordination of priests—not even in a priest's assignment to a given parish. Protestants may disagree with
the sacerdotal ecclesiology of the Church of Rome, but it is
a pat truism to remind Protestants that the Catholics do
not. Protestants must swallow the historical fact that a
sacerdotal view of the Church has been the prevailing one
since at least the third century in both the Roman and the
Orthodox communions. (Before Christ, the Jewish cultus
was also strongly sacerdotal.) The Protestant propensity for
jumping from the pentecostal account in the second chapter
of the Acts of the Apostles to a revival meeting in Madison
Square Garden certainly must test the irenicism of Catholic
historians. In any event, it is a grave error for the Protestant
to use the word "priest" as a synonym for a conspiratorial
perversion of Christianity. All whispering about purple
prelacy and priestly hocus pocus vilifies the vast majority
of the Catholic clergy and, far worse, makes it impossible
to appreciate the proper role which the priest has in the
mind and heart of the Catholic layman.

The American Catholic has an enormous regard for the priest, and for reasons which are as much social as ecclesiastical. The immigrant Catholic Church in the alien and largely Protestant and secular America of the eighteenth and nineteenth centuries owed its very life to its dedicated priestly leadership which—however defensive and obscurantistic it may have been at times—was tenaciously faithful in building the walls of its own Jerusalem. The parish priests and the bishops worked together to keep their families Catholic, to build parochial-school systems, to soften the sense of social inferiority, and to transplant seminaries to these shores. In this long and awkward pilgrimage to a full place in the American sun, the Catholic clergy won an allegiance which is not about to disappear.

The outspoken and often harsh but largely constructive manifestos now being issued by an influential minority of the Catholic laity need to be heard against that historical backdrop. Contemporary Catholic lay voices are, to be sure, in part a protest against too much priestly purview in American Catholic history. These voices are even more to be understood, however, as organically related to the opportunities afforded by *aggiornamento,* by the stimulus of American democratic society, and by the rise of members of the laity who now are often better educated than their priests.

The lay-clerical tensions within contemporary American Catholicism manifest themselves most strikingly in the debates over the education of the clergy, the parochial-school issues, birth control, and with regard to the complex question of Church authority and obedience. It is the first and last of those issues which concern the themes of this book. Members of the Catholic clergy are looking and listening, even *ad nauseam,* as some protests become tiringly repetitious; but among members of the American Catholic clergy there seems to be widespread agreement that the voices which they are hearing are no lay version of the old modernist controversy.[2] Any attempt to repress these laymen in the mood of a *nihil-obstat* censor, any defensive silencing, or any threats of excommunication would be catastrophic and would most certainly result in a heartbreaking alienation of many of the most promising members of the Catholic community. Let us now look at several of the specific lay criticisms.

The consensus among the outspoken laymen may be categorized as follows:

1. *A plea that the Church welcome and profit from the healthy and healthful secularities of the world around it.* The Church should not regard itself as a closed society, living off its own history, but must open itself to all the valid contributions of that vast society (also part of creation) which lives outside the Church. Putting behind it all forms of triumphalism and ghettoism, the Catholic Church should enter into serious dialogue with a predominantly non-Catholic, non-Christian world. Forty years ago one of three persons on earth was at least nominally Christian. Forty years hence, under prevailing trends, only one of six will be Christian.

With odds like this, if for no better reason, only those living in a dream world of yesteryear will not make every effort to be in close, sympathetic, communicable touch with the overwhelmingly non-Christian world around the Church. There is no room anymore for inward-looking smugness.

A part of this same plea by laity is an insistent objection to what elsewhere in this book is discussed as "total institutionalization"—Catholic *apartheid:* proliferating societies, clubs, and all other forms of "Mother System." One Catholic writer has suggested that if John Fitzgerald Kennedy had gone to Immaculate Conception High School and to St.

Aloysius College rather than to Choate and to Harvard, he would have crowned his career by being elected President of the Holy Name Society.

2. *Reform ecclesiology so as to give a proper role to the laity.*

"Why should the laity have all the gaiety? We clergy is Irish, too." That old quip is now being sung by the laity with different words: "Why should the priest be all the yeast? We laity is leaven, too."

Gary MacEoin, the prominent Catholic lay writer, underlines the desired stance of the Church in such an overwhelmingly non-Christian world by insisting that the clergy must first take seriously the Church's own laity:

I believe that what is developing in the United States is something essentially different from anti-clericalism. It is a consciousness on the part of the layman of a role and function within the Church which express themselves in the hectic dialogue [of clergy and laity] . . . If this attitude requires a name, it is that of contra-clerical. Every layman with any sense of his obligations as a Catholic is contra-clerical.[3]

That plea for a candid dialogue between clergy and laity is the precondition of clerical influence in the world. For if members of the clergy do not take the laity seriously, do not listen, do not communicate, then it is most unlikely that anyone else is going to turn an ear or open an eye.

In this connection it needs to be noted again that, good as is the Vatican II decree, *The Apostolate of the Laity,* it was written by the clergy—not by the clergy *and* laity. It is filled with such phrases as ". . . no undertaking should claim the word 'Catholic' for its title without the permission of legitimate ecclesiastical authority" (paragraph 24). Theoretically, yes; but does this mean that the Roman Catholic Church is so tightly organized, like a printed TV grid, that electricity must flow only through predesignated clerical channels? It would be just as much to the point to have reversed such an admonition by saying "the Church should at all times and in all places seek to operate on a basis of lay-clerical collegiality." There are many good and propitious phrases about the laity in that decree, but, when things are written by priests (as by ministers) alone, they smell too often of court favors awarded to *hoi polloi*.[4]

In asserting his fullest citizenship in the Church, the Catholic layman is not after glory or status; he seeks a working re-definition of the Church which gives more evidence of the whole people of God. "We need a new esteem for the priesthood of the layman, acquired through baptism,"[5] writes one Catholic priest, while a layman writes:

Probably the most basic additive needed is the concept of mutuality. This concept must end the centuries-old tradition of thinking in terms of lay and clerical separation, as if it were the consequence of the distinction of identities. In the broadest sense, we are all equal members of the Mystical Body of Christ; our equality simply takes different form.[6]

This lay resurgence, which ought to delight all clergy, stands in direct historical succession to the warnings of Cardinal Newman who had protested against that unconscious clericalism which assumes that the priesthood is a better or higher form of Christian vocation. This outlook is also illustrated by Fr. Yves Congar's reference to the way in which medieval language talked of the clergy-laity relationship:

Thus, for example, the clergy were the day, and the laity the night. The clergy were the heavens, the laity the earth. The clergy were like the gods or angels, the laity like beasts of burden. Texts were quoted from Scripture, such as Job 1:14: "The oxen were ploughing, and the asses feeding beside them;" or Numbers 22:22 "Balaam was riding on his ass" . . . and in either case, as we can by now guess, the laity was not doing any ploughing and wasn't Balaam.[7]

Again, this lay movement is not anticlericalism. It is, however, as Fr. Joseph Fichter says, "symptomatic of lay concern for potential improvement rather than of incipient anticlericalism."[8] An essential element in the lay movement is its hope that the priestly role and function can be better differentiated so as to give to the priest his valid sphere of influence by winnowing out those functions which more properly belong to the laity. Such also is the direct lesson of Cardinal Suenens' book, *The Nun in the World:* when members of the laity are given the responsibility they deserve and for which they are trained, then members of the clergy can be freed for their distinctive tasks.

The Catholic lay movement is thankfully aided in its aims by Vatican II's "thinking on the Church." *De Ecclesia,* as well as much of the writing of contemporary Catholic theologians, describes the Church much less juridically and with more emphasis on the mystery of the Church, the historical mission of the people of God, its liturgical functions, its biblical images. The new Catholic ways of speaking of the Church renounce many of the Scholastic and legal images.

This involves a loss of clarity and precision, but an immense gain in depth and richness as well as power of evocation . . . the recovery of the dynamic, cosmic, and eschatological dimensions in the biblical view of the Church has transformed the discussion of the place and function of the laity . . . starting point is rather the Christological formulation of Bishop de Smedt of Belgium: the people of God as a whole have been called and consecrated through the baptism of faith to participate in the one priesthood of the New Testament, that of Christ. The mystery of the Church is the presence of Christ worshipping through his baptized people, Christ teaching through his believing people, Christ exercising his lordship over creation through the labors in charity of his people in the world. The life of the laity is thus the life of Christ in the Church continuing his messianic work among and in his people.[9]

That is what the new Catholic layman believes, and he is grateful to the theologians who, in increasing numbers, are saying it. It is a far, far cry from the days when the layman was treated as what Fr. Karl Rahner labeled "an object in a clerical sanatorium for the cure of souls."[10]

Professor Albert C. Outler, Protestant Observer at Vatican II, in a widely publicized address to the Catholic laity of Dallas, Texas, on the subject, "The Laity in Vatican II's Constitution on the Church," had this to say:

Just as the hierarchy relate the whole People of God to the sacramental order, so the laity relate the whole People of God to the secular order. Neither is rival to the other, neither is superior or inferior . . . the call to Christian holiness is to all the people of God—the *cleros* in their sacral callings and the *laos* in their secular calling—each to seek the gifts of supernatural charity in those places and in that work wherein their distinctive witness to Christ is manifested.[11]

Certainly the fourth chapter of *De Ecclesia* is a powerful and satisfying statement which makes clear that the laity is the church in the world and participates in the salvific mission of the Church. This document gives ample basis for sharing of churchly authority between clergy and laity. It carries to commendable conclusions much of the seminal thinking of such theologians as Congar and Rahner.[11] Congar's article in the *National Catholic Reporter* is well worth quoting again:

History shows that the apostolate of the laity is only taken seriously when a real world exists to confront the Church and the Church is aware of it. Then the tension is felt between the Church and the world . . . the world that must be sacramentalized . . . but before the Church can go forth to be the sacrament of the world, she must find interior rapprochement. This means, of course, that Balaam must dismount forever.[12]

Congar's main point is superbly taken: *if the world is not taken seriously, neither is the laity.* The trouble, of course, is that it is easier to tell Balaam why he should dismount than it is to get him out of the saddle. The rule of architecture is reversed, as progressive clergy and laity now must try to get clerical function to follow ecclesiological form.[13]

Specifically and practically, the Catholic layman is asking for a system of workable communication, vertical communication, up and down the hierarchical structure.[14] This means that the clergy must rid themselves of any vestiges of medieval notions of "instant obedience" and display what the English Catholic layman Donald Nicholl has termed the two indispensable ingredients for effective clergy-lay rapport: the willingness to listen and the use of an understandable religious vocabulary. Nicholl's very good article[15] contains a dismal warning which is not peculiarly English: if communication does not occur, so that authority may be rationally presented and obedience made a mutual affair, then the layman becomes an *émigré à l'intérieur.* He writes:

After all, most of our energies are pre-empted by our professional activities, and if it looks as though any energies we devote to ecclesiastical matters will yield little fruit, then it seems reasonable to invest them elsewhere.

It is my impression that the number of these *émigrés à l'intérieur* is really enormous; I derive this impression from having noticed the Catholics who were my contemporaries at Oxford and from watching Catholics pass through to graduation in the Universities of Edinburgh and Keele. By the date of their graduation, or soon afterwards, almost all of them have come to accept that their particular talents are only marginally acceptable within the Church, and so the Church becomes rather marginal in their lives.

This is so striking a phenomenon that I am inclined to say that, if even a quarter of the talent lying untapped within the Catholic community had been available to the Communist Party, Britain would now be a Communist country. Conversely, if the Catholic Church in this country does not wish to lose more ground, it will have to learn how to make maximum use of this latent talent, for the simple reason that the tasks facing it in the second half of the century will make demands of a magnitude far in excess of the talent available from within the ranks of the clergy. Moreover, the laity will not be drawn into those tasks if they are not allowed to share in the decision-making process; this is a fact based not on any recalcitrance from the side of the laity, but simply because in the rest of their lives, in their professions, professional associations, trade unions and voluntary societies they are accustomed to play their part in the decision-making process. And it seems to them unnatural, monstrous, that it should be otherwise within the Church.

Bluntly, it amounts to the layman saying to the clergy, "Move over, more playing room on the field and a turn at bat, if you please." The layman wishes to claim more fully his Christian inheritance in the liturgy, in parish life, in education, and in the councils of the Church. The layman, understanding better his role in the Church, does not want to be merely an obeying subject in an authoritative church. The Catholic layman is no longer content unquestioningly to dance to clerical pipers. Words which delight the ear of this new "Liberal Catholic Establishment" are such as these from the pen of Mgsr. A. Pailler, Auxiliary Bishop of Rouen:

Authority in the Church at every level, whilst fully preserving its genuine character as a sacred authority, will always aim to elicit a religious and not a purely human type of obedience. And this implies that the religious reasons for any given directions should be completely explained. . . .

It cannot be denied that the Church's ideal should be that of a community in which the mediatory function of hierarchical authority would remain essential, but in which, at the same time and by the same token, the guidance of the hierarchy would be counterbalanced by the greatest possible degree of spiritual liberty, and this because the community, as a body, is quickened by the Holy Spirit. This means that spiritual liberty is not the opposite pole, but the correlative of the hierarchical idea. It means that no obedience should be asked for which it does not involve, at least to a small extent, a response dictated by love on the part of the believer under the rule of the hierarchy. It means that the ideal state of the Church is not to be found in a plethora of canonical prescriptions, but in a minimum of these. To quote the witty remark of a well-known theologian: "where the Spirit of God has faded away, Canon Law proliferates."[16]

As the Catholic layman looks at his Church, his seminaries, and his clergy under the rubric of authority and obedience is quite clearly influenced, as he cannot help but be, by two other surging moods of society. The first is the revolutionary protests against all inherited forms of authority—family, class, Church, Nation. This protest is rampant everywhere, from long-haired beatniks to younger politicians. It is a sign of our time which may be deplored or accepted, but which cannot be avoided. Such validity as it has is anchored in its protests against injustice and hypocrisy and conventionality. The *status quo ante* of church and society is ruthlessly questioned or ignored.

The second mood or tendency is a much older one: the autonomy of the democratic man. This is the person accustomed to pluralistic society, to the free combat of opinion, to the "rights of man." It can easily be carried to extremes of Promethean idolatry, but in most societies it is healthy and necessary if personhood is to be honored. It creates a layman who does not *automatically* bow before churchly authority.

Three factors, then, have revolutionized the contemporary Catholic layman's understanding of authority and obedience: a more biblical ecclesiology; the anti-authoritarian syndrome in modern society; the tradition of the rights of man. One should add the influence of lay Protestantism. But without further attempt at analysis, let it simply be asserted that neither the Catholic nor the Protestant churches can coast along under clerical-magisterial concepts of authority and obedience.

Given a keen lay awareness of the Church as the whole people of God, conjoined with a desire to bring the world and Church to a fuller encounter, one can easily understand the Catholic layman's rising interest in the seminaries of his Church. It so happens that clerical criticism of the seminaries has paralleled this lay stirring.[17] This has made for a propitious and radical re-evaluation of Catholic theological education. The 1960–65 period undoubtedly has been the most tempestuous and exciting time in the history of American Catholicism as far as seminaries are concerned. It may be that not since Trent has there been such an outpouring anywhere of lay concerns about theological education. In these last few years it is a rare issue of a Catholic periodical or an unusual volume by a Catholic layman which does not contain sharp and specific references to the key role of seminaries.

Parenthetically, while the nature of Protestantism has always involved laymen much more directly in the affairs of church life and, to a lesser degree, in the counsels of theological education, there probably has never been a period of such *intense* lay concern for theological education within Protestantism as there currently is among Catholic laymen.

What are the major themes to be found when Catholic laymen write and speak about Catholic seminaries?

There is the brooding over the geographical, cultural, and psychological isolation of seminaries. The Christian layman—or at least that minority which thinks about it—usually wonders about the mysterious ways in which clergymen are trained and educated. But that is no more than the normal amount of curiosity which surrounds any professionally educated group. At the moment, the vocal Catholic laity are disturbed even more by the unjustifiable *degree* of seminary separation from the lay and the secular world.

In *The Trouble With Catholics,* Frank Getlein writes:

Apartness is a very real apartheid: the avowed policy of seminary recruiting officers is to obtain their recruits at as early an age as possible, preferably before beginning high school, and certainly before college. It is quite true that seminary studies are both extensive and intensive, yet the urgency of the plea for early commitment reveals the sometimes explicit desire on the part of the ecclesiastical authorities that the candidates be safely in the seminary harbor before they are "contaminated" by the world. Contamination, in the apparent view of many seminary directors, is also a danger from the families of candidates for Holy Orders. Hence, early in training, the seminarian develops a sense of distance between himself and his parents, brothers, and sisters. He has entered a new world, that of the Church; that world, the Church, has nothing to do with the other world, the world outside, where, among its most distinctive features, people get married.[18]

It is true that many seminaries are straining to close the gap between the world of the Church and the "other world";

but it is no less true that this is still a minority response to the aggravating fact that increasing numbers of Catholic laity feel that the seminary life and outlook is, indeed, formed in a cocoon. These lay people are desperately eager that their priests-in-formation share the larger world of secular and non-Catholic dynamics. As mentioned previously, the healthy secularities of the natural world must be phenomena in which the seminarian is educated, not dimensions of life from which his education is divorced. The layman finds the ersatz-world of so many seminary communities one which makes for unintelligibility in language and thought forms, so that there is diminishing coinage of the faith in circulation. He is also afraid that seminary isolation perpetuates the defensive and militant manner of "doing theology."

The English Protestant theologian, Daniel Jenkins, succinctly makes the same point as these Catholic laymen:

. . . the theologian badly needs what H. R. Niebuhr has called "the gift of the Catholic vision." He must have a synoptic view of Christian truth which enables him to see how his special interests are related to the rest and which enables him, as T. F. Torrance puts it, "to think through every doctrine into every other doctrine." This vision is one of the greatest gifts which theological education should provide, and those concerned with theological education must always carefully consider how they can best put their charges in the way of it. That provincialism and sectarianism should be associated in many people's minds with theology is a sad commentary on the failure of theological education to do its job. What the theologian needs to see in these days more than ever is that he will fail to avoid these dangers if he has a purely seminarist approach to his task. Theology is often most true to itself when it holds active conversation with other disciplines. The theologian of all men must realize that he cannot protect the integrity of the faith by bury-

ing the talent of God's truth in the ground. He must be prepared to put it out to usury in the commerce of the world,
especially in the greatly enlarged world of today. This means
running risks—but again, the theologian of all men should
know that it is only as we lose our lives that we shall find
them.[19]

The laity are asking, "When you finish seminary, are you
in touch with the main thought forms and problems of the
world, as well as with the content of the Christian Gospel?
Are you able to speak the language that we speak, to share
our troubles, to understand our dilemmas, to enjoy our
joys? Are you buried in the thirteenth or the fifteenth centuries? Are you still living in nineteenth-century Ireland or
eighteenth-century France? Do you regard the world as
essentially soiled and naughty? Is your spirit fed with a false
self-righteousness nourished on closeted virtues? Do you
expect us to react to you with the same instinctive genu-
flection that you show to your seminary superiors?"[20]

These are barbed questions, often unfair, increasingly
repetitive. They do record, however, the layman's concern
for his Church, not the lessening of his loyalty. Such questions bespeak the layman's hunger to share the ministry of
the Church alongside a clergy which has been educated in
such a fashion as *to be able to share.* On the whole, these
criticisms must be understood as a demand that the secular
clergy be educated in less of a monastic, medieval, and
fortress ethos.

The lay critique of seminaries most assuredly concerns
itself also with the present styles of spiritual formation. The
Catholic layman, more so than the Protestant, is proud of
and insists upon the essentially spiritual nature of the priesthood; the Catholic layman no less than the Holy See is
going to insist on the primacy of this in theological educa-

tion. The difference of opinion concerns the methodology and the language, even the sense of taste (rejection of tawdry and the cheap) in spiritual formation. Does seminary spiritual formation lend itself to a fake other-worldliness which then becomes distrustful of the real world? Does it concentrate too much on overly precise cultic practices?[21] Is priestly formation far too dependent upon ancient cultural presuppositions (medieval and scholastic)?

Furthermore, the laity wish to have an appropriate role in the life and teaching of seminaries. Catholic seminaries are still priestly fiefdoms, fully and absolutely. Catholic laymen seldom venture into the affairs of these seminaries. Members of seminary faculties are almost all ordained. The Boards of Control of the seminaries have no corporate autonomy; they are, in effect, advisory committees to the Bishop, and they are appointed by him. This raises a nice point. All professional graduate schools—medicine, law, or theology—will, of course, be dominated by the respective professions. It may be well and inevitable that a medical school is operated and run by physicians, but the Church is more open to the lay world, to lay teaching, and to lay guidance. Why should not competent laymen, particularly educators, social scientists, philosophers, do more full- and part-time teaching? Why should they not actually exercise jurisdiction as well as write checks? Why should not competent non-Catholics in certain fields be part of the interior landscaping of theological education? How can seminarians be brought into close and realistic contact with the Church-in-the-world during the seminary years?

The seminary is different only in degree, not in kind, from most of the structures of the Catholic Church insofar as lay participation is involved. Vatican II had no laity with a vote and precious few on any of the preparatory commissions.[22] Up and down the hierarchical structure,

Catholic laymen are conspicuous for their absence in key ecclesiastical affairs. To the Protestant eye, it is as if two large circles of Church life, one lay and one clerical, intersected only at a very small area of sacramental and parish life: the bulk of the clergy circle operating within a closed and official ecclesiastical world of its own; the bulk of the lay circle enclosing its own Church sub-culture. A figure of speech from the writing of Paul of Aquileja makes clear the necessity for members of the laity to play their proper role:

If one of the estates of Christendom is missing it is like a city, fortified on one side only and the other side exposed, thus giving access to the enemy; and it is like a ship: be it made ever so well, if there is a leak in one single plank it will sink to the bottom of the sea.

Secular Institutes and Seminary-Lay Apostolate

François Mauriac, noted Catholic layman and writer, states in his *Pierre d'Achopement* something which has great attraction to the Protestant mentality: that if he had to relive his life exactly as it had occurred, he would have taken as much care to hide his Christian faith as he had taken to display it. By this he meant that he would, as it were, have buried it in the soil of his life, that he would have incarnated it in his daily pattern of living. The task for the "prophet," he claimed, is to enter into communion with the natural community of which he is a member, to root himself unobtrusively there so that he grows to a spiritual maturity redolent of the soil from which he has sprung.

This is dangerous and profound advice for Christian laity. It is dangerous when the layman is not deeply rooted in a worshipping community (Mauriac is not talking romantic nonsense of the "more secular than thou" type of Christian-ity). It is profound advice because there is a way of living one's faith without constantly advertising it or referring to it only in ecclesiastical terminology.

Within Roman Catholic life in the United States today there are forms of lay witness well worth careful study by Protestants. There are types of discipline commendably in keeping with the spirit of Mauriac's words. If the Protestant imagination and the sturdy tradition of Protestant lay life is put alongside these experiments, there could be a variety of chain reactions—not imitation (for the same clothes won't fit), but new adaptations of Protestant lay witness based on Catholic experience.

Deserving of particular notice are the Secular Institutes (together with Third Orders Secular) and the Seminarian-Lay Apostolate Conference.

Secular Institutes. These are societies of men and women liv-ing in the world who dedicate themselves by vow or promise to observe the evangelical counsels and to carry on apostolic works suitable to their talents and opportunities in the areas of every-day life. Members oblige themselves by vow to observe perfect chastity, and by vow or promise to be obedient to superiors of the institute, and to practice poverty to the extent that it can be practiced in their position in the world. They do not wear a distinctive religious habit, nor are they bound to live in com-munity like the members of religious orders. They remain in the world, pursue their own professions and earn their own livelihood, and perform their apostolic tasks in the environ-ments in which they live and work. . . .[23]

"Secular Institutes," writes one of their leaders, "satisfy the desire of those who wish to belong entirely to God, while remaining in the world with their fellow men, with-out distinguishing themselves from them so that they may share their life, their work, their sufferings, and help them to return to Christ."[24] A typical member of such an Institute is Dr. X, a woman physician, who each year takes vows of chastity (renewed year by year) and who lives on the minimum income necessary to her professional and social obligations. In most cases membership in an Institute is kept *secret* from her family and friends in order that she may not be regarded as some sort of pseudo-nun. This woman pledges herself also to a daily discipline of Mass and private devotions. She is a lay missionary. When seven such persons are so pledged to this type of apostolate, they constitute themselves an Institute with a priest superior. Another example, this time a man, is John Y, a public-school teacher, who each day maintains a schedule of spiritual discipline, seeking total dedication to God, and attempting to sanctify his job or profession by making an apostolate of it. Quoting from Fr. Abbott's booklet:

Ludolf Baas, president of Catholic Action in the Netherlands, has charged that secular institutes at present are "simply religious congregations in disguise." They are not. On Feb. 2, 1947, Pope Pius XII added a new chapter to the law of the Church. He approved a movement that had been attracting priests, laymen and laywomen. From that day, associations of people professing poverty, chastity and obedience in the world—not, therefore, in the manner of religious orders—had a special position in the Church. On March 12 of the following year the Pontiff confirmed his decree.

Members of secular institutes live the life of the vows or promises without the protections of religious habit, cloistered room and daily spiritual exercises in common. More significantly, however, as Pope Pius XII pointed out when he gave his official approval to the movement, "the apostolate of secular institutes is to be faithfully practiced not only *in* the world, but as if it were *of* the world, and therefore with avowed aims, practices, forms, and in places and circumstances corresponding to this secular condition." The worst thing that could happen to the secular institutes, Cardinal Cushing has said, would be for them to approximate too closely the character and functioning of religious congregations. The Cardinal added: "There is no need for secular institutes if they are to concern themselves merely with the problems that religious institutes are already meeting."[25]

Some Catholics, like some Protestants, still suffer from the delusion that a life of "total Christian discipleship" is possible only to priests, ministers, nuns, and monks.

If an outside critic may say so, however, one views with anxiety—even given the Catholic view of juridical states of perfection—aspects of the secular institutes which threaten their evangelistic impact. Would they not be of broader appeal to more laymen if their status in the Church were divorced from all the language of "comparative perfection"? For example, Fr. Haley in his description of these lay institutes employs such phrases as "moral minimum of virtues," "canonical states of perfection," "superior to Catholic Action," "superior to marriage," "an elite," etc. This is a typically Catholic way of speaking about vocations; when applied to lay institutes, however, this vocabulary often gives exactly the opposite impression and image desired by the lay members.

Third Orders Secular. These are

bodies of faithful living in the world who strive for Christian perfection in association with and according to the spirit of various religious orders. Members of these orders, called tertiaries, do not live in religious communities, but maintain their customary way of life in the world. Priests, as well as lay people, may be tertiaries. They have distinctive habits . . . they promise to live according to their rule (Franciscans, etc.) . . . in general they do not bind themselves by vow or under pain of sin.[26]

There are at least ten such orders in the United States. One tertiary writes of his way of life:

From personal experience, it should be evident to every tertiary that the Third Order is a fraternity of those trying to be holy and not a clique of those already saints. It is a school of perfection, not the alumni of the perfect. Like every other human organization, the Third Order of St. Francis has its dedicated, its pedestrian, and its discontented. There are saintly, mediocre, and sinful tertiaries.[27]

This brief attention to the Secular Institutes and to the Third Orders Secular provides an appropriate opportunity for mentioning their relevance for Protestant ecclesiology. The main lesson would seem to be that Christian discipleship permits of a much wider variety of organizational forms than is customary for Protestants. Despite all the talk about new forms of the Church, not enough attention has been given to the suggestiveness of these and other forms of Roman Catholic witness.

Protestant denominational forms, particularly those deriving from the Calvinistic and Wesleyan traditions, more and more look alike, are alike. Even in lands where some form of Protestantism has been or is an established Church, the variety of ecclesiological styles and liturgical practices is disappointingly limited. Emphatically, this is *not* an argument for more denominations. God forbid! But Roman Catholicism does rightly raise the question as to why Protestants cannot achieve more organic unity *and* more diversity. In the United States, at least, the present main-line Protestant churches reveal an extremely bland and homogenized pattern of church life. The ecclesiological spectrum has too few colors.

Protestant secular institutes would give opportunity for imaginative flexibility in apostolic tasks. Too many forms of church and parish life are frozen in postures, or burdened with outmoded historical functions which make it difficult to adapt to twentieth-century situations. Such institutes deliberately keep themselves free to respond to need wherever the Christian wisdom of the institute seems to dictate. The institutes also provide much more stability and continuity for lay dedication than does the ever-changing parish population or even the cell-group. As Miss Virginia Leary, a Catholic leader in the Institute movement, writes, "The problem of instability and immaturity in leadership and inadequate training of leaders constantly plagues some U.S. lay movements." Furthermore, the institutes are much less likely to develop the *status-quo* mind which constantly threatens the professional clergy. Inevitably this means also that these institutes are the source of responsible criticism and needed change in otherwise lethargic churches.

Roman Catholic lay institutes and religious communities are a viable challenge to Protestants to use their imaginations in devising new types (or modifications of old) of religious organizations. Protestant "ecclesiological vacuums" surely exist with regard to lay institutes (married or celibate), with regard to the enlistment of unmarried women, of men who prefer the celibate life, and, above all, with regard to a much greater liturgical diversity and richness. Men and women in all Christian communions have a wide-ranging variety in which they can respond enthusiastically to their Christian calling. The parish congregation for a long time to come will be the usual church home for most laymen. But local parishes of any given denomination should be encouraged to develop a wider variety of worship styles. Further, the diversity of personality types demands that Protestantism thoughtfully develop new forms for discipleship. Protestants can look with gratitude to Rome for keeping this obvious bit of common sense before them.

Let us be more specific. What might a Protestant version

of a secular institute look like? It would be non-cloistered, with no distinctive garb. There would be a pattern of daily devotional discipline, probably under an agreement (not a public vow) or covenant concerning financial practices and standard of living. (Poverty is too slippery a concept; economic identification and restraint is what is involved.)[28] These communities would not be designed as exercises in piety for the eye of a naughty world, but as Christian task forces, highly mobile, prayer-centered Christian groupings addressing themselves to the toughest and most pressing frontiers of twentieth-century urban living—frontiers which the most high-minded ordinary (and necessary) local parish cannot reach: dope, prostitution, delinquency, anonymity, illiteracy, mass industry, special occupational groups, sexual deviates and the like.

Such an institute would be based for the most part on participating family groups, living nearby, gathering regularly for prayer, study, and discussion. Home-mission financial support for certain of its needs would come from national denominational boards, but financial self-sufficiency ought to be an objective. The laity presumably would work part- or full-time in secular employment. Some of the institutes might be designed for single men or women. At all costs, they should avoid becoming entrepreneurial peace-corps groups of the avant-garde. They would need specialists; a few clergy, for example, a competent theologian, a sociologist. It could appeal to the laity of professional competence in any field who wish a heroic and pioneering type of Christian living. The possibilities are endless.

The Seminarian-Lay Apostolate Conference

Another heartening example of current Catholic efforts to balance off clericalism in the Church is the recently formed *Seminarian-Lay Apostolate Conference* (SLAC).[29]

Beginning in 1962 in the Chicago diocese, under the direction of Father John Pawlikowski, O.S.M., there has been a series of annual conferences which bring together three to four hundred seminarians, seminary teachers, and laymen. SLAC corresponds exactly to one of the recommendations made in *Apostolic Renewal in the Seminary*.

Seminarians should also be encouraged, through conversations, publications and correspondence, to develop a two-way communication not only with those laymen with whom they have common interests, but also with those who are indifferent or even hostile to the faith. Besides gaining new insights from laymen, seminarians could stimulate them to take constructive steps . . . in problems of common concern . . . which in the divine plan may have beneficial effects on mankind.

SLAC, in the words of Fr. Pawlikowski, was born of the effort "to discover the factors which contribute to the present lack of understanding, of meaningful and sincere dialogue, between clergy and laity." He lists these as:

First, *inbreeding.* Instructed for six or eight years by faculties overwhelmingly, perhaps exclusively clerical in composition, the seminarian of necessity developed a clerical mentality, one that made him aware of his personal problems as a priest, but seldom gave him any feeling for the difficulties the laity must face. The area of marriage would be a case in point.

Second, *clericalism:* the identification of the Church with the clergy. The seminarian realized that he was "in," a member of a select circle, and the attitude of family and friends unfortunately reinforced the tendency to consider himself unduly special. A second cause of clericalism is the almost sacred stature given to the *status quo* in many seminaries. Here often was a prime criterion for judging whether a student was fit for ordination. And it would not seem to violate any rule of logic to trace the effects of this continual emphasis on anti-boat-rocking.

Third, *lack of maturity:* Seminarians' interests are often self-centered, and the lack of opportunity to exercise responsibility quite naturally resulted in a collateral stifling of leadership development. The lack of trust, characteristic of many rectors, also carried over after ordination. . . . It may be said that clerical possessiveness with regard to the direction of the parish and the Church at large may hide a feeling of inadequacy in leadership ability among priests, one that would quickly manifest itself if leadership were to be shared with responsible laymen.

Fourth, *Organization-man mentality:* because he was so often forced to live under an intricate and highly organized system of rules, the future priest likely acquired the twofold system attitude: "How-to-beat-it" and "How-to-climb-it." This attitude would, in turn, carry over into his approach to parish work where often what he did and what he said was done and said with an eye to future promotion.

It makes little sense to deluge a seminarian with minute details about each and every lay organization, the majority of which he will never encounter in his apostolate. But if the seminarian can leave his formative period convinced that he and the layman *together* form Christ's Church, then he very likely will be able to work with any type of layman.

Everything about SLAC testifies to its realism, its honesty about the Church, and its desire to break through acquired patterns of clerical thinking.

Notes

[1] *A New Generation* (New York: Herder and Herder, 1965), p. 22.

[2] Modernism was the term used by the Church to describe Catholic heresies of the 1900 era. For a listing of these heresies, see the decree of Pius X, 1907, *Lamentabili.*

[3] *New Challenges to American Catholics* (New York: P.J. Kenedy and Sons, 1965), p. 52.

4 The Catholic Code of Canon Law reflects clericalism insofar as that, of its 617 canons dealing with persons, 574 have to do with clergy, only 43 with laity. This is unconscious clerical narcissicism.

5 George H. Tavard, *The Church Tomorrow* (New York: Herder & Herder, 1965), p. 67.

6 Edward Keating, *The Scandal of Silence* (New York: Random House, 1965), p. 94.

7 *National Catholic Reporter,* August 18, 1965, p. 6.

8 Joseph H. Fichter, *Priest and People* (New York: Sheed and Ward, 1965), p. 199.

9 *Dialogue on the Way,* George A. Lindbeck (ed.), (Minneapolis: Augsburg Publishing House, 1965), p. 60.

10 Cardinal Dopfner, *The Questioning Church* (Westminster: Newman Press), p. 18.

11 *Information Service,* June 19, 1965, p. 2. National Council of Churches, N.Y.C.

12 Yves Congar, O.P., *Laity, Church and World* (Baltimore: Helicon, 1960). This work represents probably the best statement by a priest theologian on the place of the laity. See also Karl Rahner, S.J., *Theology for Renewal* (New York: Sheed and Ward, 1964), and Jean Guitton, *The Church and the Latiy* (New York: Alba House, 1965).

13 *National Catholic Reporter,* August 18, p. 6. It has even been advocated that the Pope might be elected for a term (ten years) rather than for life and that bishops be elected by both lay and clerical votes.

14 See "Elections in the Church," Fr. Joseph O'Donoghue, *Commonweal,* May 21, 1965, p. 281.

15 As Fichter notes, "The pivotal functions of the priest, and the conception that the laity has of them, are largely determined by the internal organization of the parochial system. The authority structure is relatively 'flat.' Responsibility and decision-making rest directly in the hands of the priest, while the laity remain in an ancillary position. This implies that the 'new emergence' of the laity in the American Catholic Church will alter both the image of the priest and the organizational structure of the Church." *(Priest and People,* p. 196).

16 "The Layman and Ecclesiastical Authority," in *The Clergy Review,* July, 1964, p. 393 ff.

17 *Problems of Authority,* John Todd (ed.), (Baltimore: Helicon, 1962), chap. 2.

18 It is no coincidence that the critiques of theological education by Putz and Lee, by Poole, and by the Christopher colloquia came out

at the height of the "new breed" lay critiques of Church and seminary.
[19] *The Trouble with Catholics* (Baltimore: Helicon Publishing Co.,
1964), p. 147.

[20] *The Scope of Theology*, Daniel Jenkins (ed.) (Cleveland: World
Publishing Co., 1965), chap. 6.

[21] "The real crime of seminaries," wrote Adrian Cunningham in the
Spring, 1965, number of *Slant*, "is that they are designed to produce
good seminarians rather than good priests."

[22] See Michael Novak, *op. cit.*, p. 67 ff.

[23] The role of laity at Vatican II was an instructive symbol of the
old plight and new status of laity. The Council began with only
two laymen as "invited experts" (lay *periti*) meeting with some of
the Commissions. No laity had any vote in the Aula at any session
of the Council. But by adjournment in December, 1965, there were
close to forty lay auditors, including seven lay women and eight nuns.
It may be that they were there only as a gesture, but it is probably
more significant than that; in the United States, at least, there was
a noticeable spurt in lay activity in circles formerly dominated by
clergy.

[24] Definition given in *The National Catholic Almanac* (Garden City:
Doubleday and Co., 1965), p. 518.

[25] Some suggested instructive literature about secular institutes:
Walter M. Abbott, S.J., *Vocations for Catholics* (New York: America
Press, 1962); Stephen Hartdegen, O.F.M., *Like Burning Lamps* (Patter-
son: St. Anthony's Guild Press, 1962); Patrick M.J. Clancy, O.P., *Secu-
lar Institutes in the United States* (Huntington, Indiana: Our Sunday
Visitor Press): *"Aggiornamento* in Vocations," article by Virginia Leary
in *America*, April 17, 1965; "Secular Institutes," article by Fr. Joseph
Haley in the *NCEAB*, August, 1960.

[26] Abbott, *op. cit.*, p. 5.

[27] *The National Catholic Almanac* (Garden City: Doubleday and
Co., 1965), p. 520.

[28] Daniel O'Rourke, O.F.M., *How to Live in a Layman's Order*,
(Chicago: Franciscan Herald Press, 1964), p. 59.

[29] There are monastic communities today, for example, which have
every convenience known to modern man (including Italian marble),
plenty of good food, laundered habits, expense accounts, and the rest.
It is not poverty so much as a "drip-dry hair shirt."

[30] Information about SLAC, as well as its newsletter, may be secured
from the Stonebridge Priory, Lake Bluff, Illinois.

4

Pipings in Academe

Professionalization

An analysis of Catholic seminaries as *academic* institutions, whatever else they may be, is a marked characteristic of contemporary seminary criticism. It is also one of the areas in which a consensus seems to be emerging: at least an agreement that there must be a severe academic reappraisal of the seminaries and a much more affirmative attitude toward the university world. This chapter is devoted to various positive and constructive suggestions with regard to academic changes in Roman Catholic theological education.

The category of "professionalization" is one of the most central and rewarding ways of analyzing Catholic seminaries. The issues which are here raised also furnish excellent insights into the larger problems of the whole Catholic Church. Proper professionalization, conscientiously worked out, permits any number of specific and important reforms to be carried out. Without a comprehensive notion of professional theological education, Catholic seminary reforms tend to be superficial patchwork, comparable to rearranging furniture in an old room.

Roman Catholic theological education has existed too long in a well nigh self-sufficient educational world of its own. This world has inhibited the development of Catholic seminaries to such an extent that they now must begin to run simply in order to catch up with other forms of professional education which have achieved a long lead by steady walking over the years.

If Roman Catholic theological education in the United States becomes truly professional, it will soon be in a good position to lead the entire Catholic world.

Professionalization should operate at all levels of theological education simultaneously and continuously:

1. *Seminary self-study:* Periodically, without constantly pulling up one's roots to look at them, studies must be carried on under seminary initiative and with the cooperation of knowledgeable experts. Competent outside advice, Catholic and non-Catholic, is invariably a good move. Which questions to ask, how to get and to interpret statistics, how to implement findings—these call for experienced minds. But the most important matter is that a seminary genuinely desire a full and free scrutiny.

2. *Pan-seminary study:* The evaluation of individual seminaries will be much more beneficial when done in a context of regional seminaries, diocesan, inter-diocesan, provincial, and national studies. Obviously, there is a very sensitive interdependence between the many Catholic seminaries, and major advances are to be achieved only in concert and with a synoptic regard for the welfare of the whole Church.

3. *Accreditation:* Regional academic accreditation is such an obvious virtue that the speedy adoption of the 4–4–4 system in order to achieve such accreditation would seem beyond argument.[1] Negatively, any seminary unable to

achieve regional accreditation should be asking itself the most basic questions about its future.

4. *The American Association of Theological Schools:* Catholic participation in the A.A.T.S., the dominant professional organization for Protestant theological education, is an opportunity not to be missed.[2] It would be easy, of course, to set up a Catholic equivalent; but this would be a major blunder, almost a tragedy. It would perpetuate parochialism and would not permit the Catholic seminaries to take advantage of the present strengths of the A.A.T.S. Membership in the A.A.T.S. has no theological party lines. It provides the types of services, judgments, and stimuli which Roman Catholic theological education badly needs, and from which Protestant seminaries have so markedly benefited. There would quickly and fairly be established an *unus inter pares* sharing of office and leadership roles between the Protestant and the Catholic membership. Furthermore, there is no reason why certain specific Catholic concerns could not operate as subdivisions of the A.A.T.S. In presenting the possibility of such membership to the hierarchy, every effort must be made to avoid any confusion which would make membership in the A.A.T.S. smack of syncreticism or "Protestantizing," because this is strictly an educational and professional matter. The Protestant seminaries in the A.A.T.S. very much need the Catholic presence and experience.

When one studies the history of Protestant theological education in America, it will be seen quite unmistakably that there is a definite, really quite extraordinary, correlation between the strength of Protestant seminaries and the increasingly beneficial influence of the A.A.T.S.

5. *National Staff:* There is immediate need for a small national staff of even two or three highly qualified Catholics (one might be a lay educator) who have as their full-time

job that of knowing and leading Roman Catholic education in the United States. When everyone is responsible, no one is responsible. There is a leadership vacuum, not by intention, but because those now concerned for theological education are not able to give full time to national dimensions.

Given a small staff, where should it be located: National Catholic Education Association, National Catholic Welfare Conference, or elsewhere? Fortunately, this is a matter for decision by Catholics, not for a Protestant observer's guess work. But the main point is that two or three competent persons (or even one) need to be giving full-time professionally "savvy-type" leadership—thinking, criticizing, suggesting, dreaming about Roman Catholic theological education. It cannot be done from Rome; it cannot be done on a part-time basis.

At this very moment in Catholic history when there is a staggering amount of profitable discussion, writing, and self-criticism abroad, plus the whole atmosphere of Vatican II, it is a great pity that there is no such professional staff.[3]

6. *National Study:* It follows from the above points that *now* is the time for a Catholic version of the Niebuhr-Williams-Gustafson and the Bridston-Culver type of study of Protestant theological education—a study authorized by the episcopacy.

7. *Professional Organizations:* Professionalization is enhanced by appropriate participation in various educational organizations. To what extent are Catholic seminary rectors, administrators and teachers involved in the vocationally specialized communities of American higher education? Are they active in such groups as associations of deans, of guidance people, of learned societies, American Council of Education? There is a professional society for almost every discipline and speciality.

8. *Faculty Education:* The post-graduate education of

seminary faculty is a key issue in professionalization. The remarkable Catholic concern for spiritual formation makes it unlikely that the Catholic faculty will err in the direction of becoming graduate schools of religion. However, there certainly seems to be a clear need for the development of a larger cadre of Catholic seminary faculty which has doctoral degrees from a wider range of outstanding graduate schools:

a) More doctoral study at the very best graduate schools, particularly the secular schools.

b) A balanced reappraisal of the tendency to have so many men do graduate study at the Roman Athenaea, at Louvain, and at one or two other Catholic graduate centers.

c) The need for regularized sabbatical study leaves.

d) Enough secretarial help so that Catholic scholars can be freed for study, counseling, and writing.

9. *Faculty Control:* By definition, any first-rate university is operated on policies controlled by the faculty, especially the senior faculty. This is especially true of graduate schools. Basic academic policy, appointment, curriculum matters, etc., must be under faculty purview. It is the business of the rector and the trustees to make these things possible. Something comparable to a Committee on Committees is usually the key to this type of faculty supervision. A wise faculty will deliberately give to the administration as many chores as will free the faculty for its main task; but the faculty must never surrender its basic autonomy and authority.

It may be argued that a seminary is *sui generis* and, therefore, an exception to such faculty control. I think not, however. At the very minimum the principle of academic collegiality should be operative. Bishop and rector *and* faculty, but with the faculty as *primus inter pares.*

10. *Faculty Competition:* It is intriguing to ponder the

fact that most Catholic seminary faculties do not operate under the competitive pressures of tenure, promotions, faculty incentives, publishing obligations, and the whole professional pecking-order which, whatever its drawbacks, makes for a "taut ship." More such pressures and standards are needed.

11. *Episcopal Power and Professional Education:* As a final variation on a major theme, one must ask how episcopal jurisdiction and leadership in the United States can be harnessed to the professional improvement of Catholic seminaries.

It is precisely here where the monarchical episcopate, plus Catholic notions of obedience, may undercut professional upgrading. Even in many Protestant church colleges and seminaries, where there is nothing comparable to Roman Catholic episcopal tradition, it is the curse of education that the wrong people often dominate the institutions. *Ex officio* church control, however enlightened or personable the officials may be, "is no way to run a railroad."

The Vatican document on priestly training gives ample opportunity and encouragement for national episcopacies to exercise their muscle and wit with regard to their own seminaries. Will this be done in the United States—and how? Suppose, for example, that an episcopal sub-commission of the National Catholic Welfare Conference, charged with the welfare of seminaries, were to address itself vigorously to this task by (1) setting up a small survey committee to make a thorough study of seminary education and (2) coming up with a list of priorities. What then? Would the bishops, as a group, be willing to subordinate their own diocesan seminary plans to a national agenda? How much national planning is possible? How do the bishops cooperate with religious seminaries, and vice versa, in national planning? Which bishops individually have the *courage* to risk some experiments? These are the types of questions which this observer finds himself asking. Is it not clear that the national episcopacy is going to play the crucial role in major, long-range seminary changes? Is it not equally true to say that seminary progress at high professional levels must proceed, in this day and age, not by autocephalic hit-and-miss-experiments, but by sustained cooperative programs based on serious study?[4]

The University Challenge

One of the most widespread criticisms of seminary life by both Catholic laity and clergy is the isolation of seminaries from major university and cultural centers. The burden of this complaint may be appropriately prefaced by a few remarks from a speech of President William H. Conley of Sacred Heart University, Bridgeport, Connecticut:

The outcome of a program of liberal education is a civilized intellect. The civilized intellect is one which has been developed in all its capacities through knowledge. It is one which knows things as they are, and can judge, reason, discriminate, and discern. It can analyze and synthesize.

It has intellectual taste. It can unify and recognize the hierarchy of knowledge. In its highest form of development it can create. The knowledge through which this development takes place must include the totality of knowledge. Contact with each branch contributes uniquely to development. General knowledge which is necessary for any educated person includes the humanities, the natural sciences, the behavioral sciences, philosophy, theology.[5]

It would be a mistake, and a grave one, to read these paragraphs as the typical clichés of a commencement address.

It is a quite precise index to the concern of an increasing number of highly honed, liberally educated, broad-gauged Catholic laymen and priests who are insisting that their seminarians be given a more comprehensive educational background.

There may be no more striking paradox in American education than that the Catholic Church, whose medieval universities were the source and protector of Western learning and whose theology faculties once queened it over all, now finds its American centers of theological education stubbornly separated from the mainstreams of education and culture. This cannot be overstated. It has a history going back at least to Trent:

The humanism of the early sessions of Trent yielded to a revitalized Scholasticism in the later phases of the Council. Thus the priest-seminaries, which the Fathers decreed in 1563, developed more under the scholastic influence than the humanistic. Guided more by traditional than progressive considerations, the architects of these new schools sought inspiration in the distant past, as far back perhaps as the monastic schools of the Carolingian Renaissance. In view of the formative elements of this new clerical education, its subsequent development is normal. Thus the urban faculties of theology were gradually deserted, for in the Post Tridentine ideal the priest was to be educated in a private seminary rather than at a public university. His priestly training was more moral than intellectual.[6]

Theological education, to an uncomfortable degree within Protestantism and to a shocking degree within Catholicism, is the only major professional field largely separated from an organic and living relationship to the graduate faculties of great universities. Most Catholic seminaries are not even related to major Catholic universities.

The greatest cluster of seminaries related to a Catholic

university is found at The Catholic University of America, Washington, D.C. Some twenty-seven seminaries, with an affiliate relationship to The Catholic University, have buildings there. Students from affiliated seminaries are granted the Bachelor of Theology degree by The Catholic University at the end of the fourth year. Seminarians in the Catholic University's own major program at the School of Theology are granted the Licentiate in Sacred Theology.

The typical Catholic seminary is either well out in the countryside or set off by a park-like island within a city. Physically, the seminary is a well-kept, rather austere, and military-style building. A hundred or so seminarians will spend six or seven years there. More and more of them are wondering about the academic and cultural life which they are missing and to which they should be contributing. At one seminary visited by this writer, the students were circulating a petition entitled *"De Movendo Collegio."*

It is admittedly easy to be doctrinaire about the advantages of a seminary education in a university complex. One priest, after an evening of discussing this issue, was moved to write: "Intellectual formation is not a matter of a large campus or richly provided college buildings . . . in any seminary of any size today the superiors are appointing men who teach out of religious dedication, men who are intellectually alive to today's scene . . ." The same voice is heard, this time from an Irish mouth:

Let's leave scholarship to the universities and equip our future priests with a theology that is biblical, pastoral, and liturgical in bent. A bourgeois conception of the educated man is not verifiable in the pages of the Gospel. Of course we must have learned theologians and research scholars . . . a seminary close to a cathedral has an inestimable advantage . . . If our seminaries could say that priests leave their halls and chapels as masters of the Bible, the missal, the breviary, and the sacramental ritual, all would be well. . . .[7]

This type of deep attachment to the traditional seminary, though it may be more nostalgic than wise, is widespread. Most educators, however, assume that in any professional or graduate field genuine intellectual and creative advances are inextricably related to the great universities. That theological educators in any number should doubt such an assumption is wearily regarded by the secular educators as another sign of theology's cocoon world.

Catholic arguments in favor of isolating seminaries are not simply the result of a quarrel with the surrounding culture or a defensive ghettoism, powerful influences though these have been. From Rome itself, both Pope and the Sacred Congregation of Universities and Seminaries, through bishops and local ordinaries up and down the line there has been a strong conviction that, if the seminaries are to accomplish the spiritual formation of the celibate priest, they must have a definite geographical and psychological distance from distractions. This is a *sui generis* argument which does not lend a ready ear to analogy with other professions. Spiritual formation is a heroic enterprise, so precious that many other lesser goals must be forsworn in order to achieve it. Spiritual formation is, they say, an esoteric type of life which demands a controlled environment. There is a need for much quiet, for congenial surroundings, for a community which is able to possess its own soul. Just as the world needs men and women (priest, monk, or nun) who exemplify to a singular degree the pattern of Christ, so the educational and cultural world can well use a few educational communities of similar function. Although this argument does not downgrade or even subordinate the proper goals of university communities, either Catholic or secular, it does contend that the seminary is not primarily to be put in the same category as the graduate professional school of law or medicine.

Protagonists of the separated seminary are agreed that spiritual formation is to be construed in the classical forms of a disciplined community horarium. They are also agreed that celibacy itself favors a definite removal from society in order both to permit celibacy to achieve its maximum ends and to avoid drop-outs which come as a result of too much intermingling with the secular attractions of a hetero-sexual and glittering society.

There are weighty practical reasons for continuing separa-tion. Bishops must work within limited budgets. Moving (or merging) a seminary is very expensive. Bishops and everyone else concerned also have a heavy investment of affectionate and nostalgic capital in the present system. They came up through the system at the seminary, deep ties were formed, and the "old-school clerical collar" tightens a notch when moving or abandonment is suggested. There are matters of benefactors, trusts, wills, and the whole apparatus of the *status quo ante* with which to contend. Nor should anyone forget—and this is a deliberate under-statement—that bishops, dioceses, and religious communi-ties are prone to an imperialism of status seeking, one of the hallmarks of which is the proud possession of a seminary.

There are additional reasons making for separation. A very difficult one to analyze may be termed the fear of heresy. What will happen to the closely knit fabric of the Faith and the Church if it is, in the person of its sem-inarians, exposed too much to the ruthless criticism or discouraging indifference shown by wide-open intellectual communities? Give this argument its due. It is not ideo-logical tyranny to insist that, if Christian priests are to be formed and strengthened to endure and to lead in this world, there must be a prolonged time when the full impact of the Christian Faith and life can be felt and expressed in a community situation with maximum in-group impact. Advocates of the present system maintain that separation and isolation do not mean that the faculty and the students are naive about the realities of the world; rather, they urge, it would be naive to believe that the spiritual and intellectual formation of the priest can be achieved in the usual graduate-school milieu. No one claims that being part of a university complex *guarantees* anything, any more than it does for the individual student who refuses to take advantage of such surroundings. It is rather a matter of comparative possibilities. And what are they?

The case for integration with the larger academic community is a powerful one which has time and tide running for it. There is a high pressure built up within the Catholic faculty community, particularly among the younger men, to be part of the centers of American cultural and intellectual life.[8] There is no defensiveness about lack of competitive ability.[9] The better Catholic scholars and students are like pitchers who have been kept under wraps too long. They want to play in the big leagues. There is an eagerness to learn, to contribute, and an understandable pride to show the academic world that Catholics do have live and able minds.[10] This is a proper pride, for there can be no doubt but that, under the present system, far too many extremely competent and personable men and women in seminary and religious communities are not being given the chance to make the contribution to mankind which a university setting would afford.

This same eagerness is born of the conviction that Catholic theological education would itself benefit immensely from the interplay of a wider stage setting. Muscles get flabby if they are not employed against the best competitors.

Theology can easily become unreal, aimed at issues and opponents no longer alive. If the Catholic Church is all that it claims to be, and if all truth be of God, then how can the seminary fail to be in close touch with the intellectual nerve centers of our world? And what sort of spiritual formation is it which will adequately prepare the priest for the world in which he must minister? One carried on behind a moat, carefully ritualized and protected, or one which is forced to find its strength and its style from the very angularities of the world about it?

There is also the telling argument related to the supply of men for the priesthood. Analogies from the Protestant recruiting experience as well as from other professions should be pondered very carefully by Catholics, namely, that the best men are attracted by the best schools. If one wishes to strengthen the drawing power of a graduate professional education, it must be upgraded, made highly competitive, situated in an exciting milieu, given the best faculty and library, and so on. No person of competence wants to feel that the precious years of graduate education are being spent in a mediocre situation, apart from a yeasty community.

Professional accreditation is a substantial reason for encouraging the movement of Catholic seminaries into university centers. The vast majority of Catholic seminaries need much finer library facilities, a better student-teacher ratio, sabbatical programs, and all the other criteria which the university must meet. Any university, in short, would be forced to insist that a seminary community joining its ranks, coming under its umbrella, must bring its professional standards into line. The corollary of this is a life-giving sharing of facilities and the much wider variety of courses open to seminarians. This means, too, that many more lay faculty will be available.

Theology itself deserves and demands a university setting. One could conceive, let us say, of a narrowly defined field of marine biology having as its chief scholarly headquarters an isolated laboratory on the coast of Greenland. Christian theology can never be so conceived and remain Christian. It must be in touch with all the disciplines which have to do with human nature and human welfare, even though it cannot possibly absorb all that the non-theological disciplines have to offer. The day-by-day presence of an alert community of students and faculties, many of whom certainly do not live existentially by the assumptions of a seminary community, means that theology is always forced to talk a language which the world can understand, to search out superstition in its midst, to develop the open ear leading to an open mind. In religion, which lives always on the border of mystery, few things are as healthy as the constant reminder that where mystery is, obscurantism and ignorance are never far away. Clerical communities, as do all professional in-groups, develop a jargon and cultus which insulates them. There is a justifiable technical language and conceptual framework, of course, for advanced theological education, but it should be kept to a minimum. The presence of other equally literate persons who say, "I don't know what you are talking about," helps to do this. Even more, there are key areas of Catholic theological education which sorely need the sandpaper treatment of inter-disciplinary dialogue. The whole Thomistic vocabulary, natural-law categories, juridical approaches to ethics, the tendency to authoritarian pronunciamentos—these and such as these, one knows, would be thoroughly reworked in the open forum of a great university.

Catholic theological education will profit immensely from the redemptive secularities of an open culture. Standing grim guard against such openness is a long Catholic tradition of celibacy and the monastic virtues *vis à vis* the world, the flesh, and the devil. "Secular" thus becomes an epithet, and spiritual formation is seen as, negatively, a retreat from the mainstream of life. More and more Catholics are saying that this ought not to be so. For example, the present seminary schedules offer precious little time for cultivation of the theatre, music, the fine arts. The heady and constant offerings in lectureships, visiting scholars—all the apparatus of higher education should be open to seminarians without the false clothing of pietistic program notes. A close examination of the word "secular" always reveals that it has a contribution to make to our understanding of life and that it is also a part of God's creation.

As American Catholicism scatters from its old ghetto, the educational world is increasingly aware that Catholic theological educators—the very best among them—have a unique contribution to make to American thought and culture. Not only the gifts of individual Catholic scholars are to be sought after, but also the example of Catholic worshipping communities of scholars—which is what a seminary is. Higher education needs this Catholic "presence," and seminaries too isolated from the highways of culture will not be able to make their proper contributions. Universities which lack theological communities suffer from a peculiar malnutrition. The Protestant seminaries at many universities need to be supplemented by Catholic ones. *Above all, Catholic seminaries must be encouraged to move 'to the secular private university worlds and not simply to huddle alongside a Catholic university.* To migrate to a Catholic college or university campus, while it is an improvement over isolation, is only the "big-brother" mentality, a toe-in-the-water instead of the high dive. Nor are private-campus locations the only possibilities. There are many state-campus situations which can be opened up and where the administration would encourage any arrangement which would meet the academic and State-Church protocol. It is of the *highest priority* that a major Catholic seminary be firmly fixed in the matrix of one or more of the twenty or so great secular universities. (Reference to the "British Case Study" in this chapter is very much to the point.)

Since the Vatican II *Decree on Priestly Training* is permissive enough, national hierarchies will now be able to adjust their respective seminary systems to local educational landscapes instead of pretending they are on the Palatine Hill. This means that the better seminaries will be able to fit into the requirements of university patterns and that seminary officials enter diligently into the local task without undue glancing at Rome.

In a following chapter, "Fitly Joined Together: An Ecumenical Reflection," there is presented a profile of what a Roman Catholic House of Studies or Seminary might look like in close juxtaposition to a fine secular university.

Catholic theological education is at the present far, far too unbalanced in the direction of isolation.[11] Not all seminaries should be at universities, but more should. The obvious surfeit of seminaries might well be rectified, then, in three different ways:

1. Merge and move many present seminaries into clusters or theological consortiums.

2. Shift a substantial number of seminaries into a vital and geographically close relation with a few of the better Catholic universities.

3. Make every effort to establish at least three or four of the very best seminaries alongside an equal number of the great secular universities.[2]

Fortunately, the first two proposals above are more than theory, and much movement can be expected within the near future. Take, for example, the clustering going on around St. Louis University or at St. Meinrad's. Number three above is on the drawing boards, but is still wishful thinking. A good beginning has been made at the Graduate Theological Union at Berkeley. The University of Chicago is also amenable to Catholic seminary neighbors. This trend, too, will mount; but it will be much slower.

A good and an encouraging place to end this section is the following quotation:

> Not long ago, at the request of two dioceses and two religious communities, the National Catholic Educational Association sent a letter to all Catholic colleges, asking if they would accept seminarians on their campuses for education at the college and theological level. Of the 285 Catholic colleges in the United States, 65 answered that they would be happy to take them for college studies; 8 of these replied that they would also offer four years of theological studies. It was encouraging to note that a number of the college officials polled were not only willing, but very eager, to have a nucleus of these dedicated young men on their campuses. It would add something valuable, they felt, to the educational and religious tone of their institutions.
>
> The nub of the NCEA's proposal was to bring the seminarians to "centers of learning" where they would meet a more competitive educational situation. There they would encounter all the intellectual problems their future ministry would plunge them into; they would learn to understand better the emotional difficulties their young contemporaries are experiencing. After four—or eight—years in such a stimulating atmosphere, these students would reach their ordination more mature, intellectually and psychologically.[13]

A British Case Study

Catholic life in Great Britain affords a dramatic illustration of what happens when the laity and the clergy receive substantially different educations. American Catholic educators would do well to study the English scene. It certainly should bring them to a pause.

It was not until 1871 that Oxford and Cambridge, theretofore Anglican fiefdoms, were opened both to Catholics and to free-church Protestants. The English Catholic hierarchy, understandably defensive after so many centuries of battle with the English establishment, refused to follow the advice of Cardinal Newman who pleaded that Catholics, both clergy and lay, be educated at the great universities. Cardinal Manning opposed Newman by making every effort to keep the scions of the ancient Catholic families away from Oxbridge. In retrospect, that decision, plus the isolation of the Catholic seminaries, was a disaster. It resulted in the building into the Catholic community of England of two essentially different stances toward life and education. By and large the Catholic laity ignored Manning and did send their sons to Oxbridge, while on the other hand the Catholic seminaries did not closely affiliate with Oxbridge and have remained until this day in splendid isolation, socially, educationally, and geographically. The Protestants meanwhile quickly moved their seminaries into the midst of the educational complexes at Oxford (Mansfield, Regents Park, Manchester) and at Cambridge (Wesley House, Chestnut, and Westminster).

American Catholics should note that the English lay group did *not* pull out of the mainstream of British education. "Thank God," remarked one prominent Catholic layman to this writer, "The Catholic Church in England didn't start a national Catholic university. We didn't make the mistake of American Catholics."

In England today there is thus no Catholic University, nor has either Oxford or Cambridge an undergraduate Catholic college.[14] None of the Catholic major seminaries is affiliated with an English university. None of the universities has a Catholic theological faculty. Catholic institutional participation in the life of the universities is minimal.

The two major theological seminaries in England are St. Edmunds, Ware (not to be confused with St. Edmunds Hall at Cambridge) and Ushaw. It is at these seminaries and in Rome that most of the English priests are trained from minor seminary through ordination.[15]

Over the years, therefore, a cultural and educational gap, growing geometrically, has developed between priests and laity. A difference always exists between clergy and laity; but in England the lack of common participation in a basic educational experience (the sharing of the best in the secular and humanistic culture) has resulted in conversations between clergy and laity being carried on at shouting distance.

This polarization of clergy and the better educated laity accounts for the caustic comment of an outstanding Catholic layman: "During the last hundred years or so, a number of Catholic theologians have exerted a considerable influence on English intellectual life. They were Cardinal Newman, William Ward, Lord Acton, Von Hügel, Abbot Chapman, and Ronald Knox. All of these men received their significant intellectual formation outside the Church's training establishments. The seminaries have never produced a theologian of the same calibre, or near it."[16]

The relations today between clergy and laity are not unlike what they were a hundred years ago when Newman and his lay friends were editing *The Rambler Magazine* and causing chancery officials to claim that Newman was "the most dangerous man in England"—a charge which seems to have been caused by Newman's faith in the contributions which a well educated laity can make to the life of the Church. It was Newman who wrote:

So far as I can see, there are ecclesiastics all over Europe, whose policy it is to keep the laity at arms-length, and hence the laity have been disgusted and become infidel, and only two parties exist, both ultras in opposing directions . . . You will be doing the greatest possible benefit to the Catholic cause all over the world, if you succeed in making the University a middle station at which clergy and laity can meet, so as to learn to understand and to yield to each other, and from this, as from a common ground, they may act in union upon an age which is running headlong into infidelity.[17]

The closed circuit world of the clergy, and the wide-open world of the laity (to caricature the extremes) has created within the English Catholic Church an uneasy, edgy hierarchy, critical priests writing pseudonymous letters to editors, and the perfectly normal Christian newsletter, *Search,* edited by laymen, being mailed to seminarians in brown, unmarked wrapping paper.

Without becoming too simplistic about the matter, all this is largely the result of misunderstandings caused by lack of enough significant common experience between priests and laity. This is not to claim that sweet harmony would prevail had most of the priests shared the educational experience and world of their lay peers up to the first year of major theology (age 18 or 19); nor is it to claim that professional theological education should not have its own specialization. It is, rather, to point out that the clerical leadership of a church has a much better chance of being understood, of being effective, and of getting a better educational preparation for their priesthood if the Church would put its seminaries in the main centers of the better secular educational traffic. The minor seminary does nothing to alleviate matters, either.

It is beguiling to conjecture, on comparing the English with the American situation, if Oxford, Cambridge, and the better provincial universities may not produce a Catholic lay constituency of much more rugged independence and discriminating taste than in the United States where a far larger percentage of the laity are educated in Catholic colleges. It may fairly be expected. If so, will it not provide a classic test case as to the type of laity produced by two different types of educational systems?[18]

The English situation has a sure tendency to make the recruiting of seminarians more and more difficult. Vocations figures in England bear this out to a discouraging degree.

There is now at hand a series of recommendations drawn up by a committee of Catholic scholars which, if implemented, should do nothing less than completely revolutionize theological education for Catholics in England. Page for page, it is a most succinct and helpful document. The recommendations are listed here because they have such cognate relationship to similar issues in the United States and because they so clearly reflect lay criticism of seminaries:

1. Do not isolate philosophy from theology.
2. Do not separate scriptural study and liturgical study.
3. Avoid overcrowding of lectures.
4. Avoid superficial outlines and manuals.
5. Reject any study which is irrelevant to modern man.
6. Keep in touch with the apostolic needs of the church and make certain that seminarians are educated accordingly.
7. Conceive of theological education in the most ecumenical terms possible.
8. Give more room to individual needs, adapt curriculum to individual seminarians where desirable and feasible—give more leeway to the talented.
9. Introduce more of the modern studies in social sciences and psychology and anthropology.
10. Let national episcopacies have more freedom to deter-

mine the shape and destiny of their own theological systems, without so many guidelines from the Sacred Congregation of Seminaries and Universities.[19]

Like so many other countries (Holland and France, for example) England will now be forced to make haste in seminary reform. The United States still can afford a wasteful amount of duplication. In this comfortable culture there is still not the sense of urgency, still not a ruthless facing of the fact that all churches are disestablished in a hostile or indifferent world. The churches and seminaries of the United States may be the last to adjust their structures and proud empires to the shapes required by an ecumenical era. The fat of a vanishing Christendom still clings to American bones.

Notes

[1] See Appendix on "Catholic Seminaries: Logistics and Manpower."

[2] At the 1966 Biennial Meeting of the American Association of Theological Schools, five Catholic major seminaries were admitted to membership. This step will merit watching in terms of results.

[3] I have often wished that this modest study of Catholic seminaries could have been done in tandem harness with such a staff person. Also, there is need, on the Protestant side, for a Catholic to study Protestant seminaries.

[4] I suspect that a sociological analysis of the strengths and weaknesses of the hierarchical pattern would indicate that the more administrative-educational autonomy seminaries can achieve, the better it will be.

[5] "A Layman Views Seminary Education," *NCEAB*, August, 1963.

[6] Robert McNally, S.J., *The Unreformed Church* (New York: Sheed and Ward, 1956), p. 99. It can be maintained that on many counts it would have been better to have kept most of the Catholic seminary life within the university pattern rather than so much under the control of chanceries.

[7] *Herder Correspondence,* July, 1965, quoting Fr. Patrick J. Brophy of St. Patrick's College, Ireland.

[8] See "Should The Theological Seminary be Located on a University Campus?" by Rt. Rev. Mgsr. Gerard A. Green, *NCEAB* August, 1965. p. 66.

[9] The problem is, rather (as one priest put it), to know what competition is like.

[10] One dilemma of theological education for the Protestant results from the pressures of professional scholarship—not only publish or perish but publish or "parish." A survey taken by The Fund for Theological Education, Inc., revealed that the number of Protestant faculty members with more than a year of parish experience is declining rapidly. The usual young Ph.D. in religion now goes directly into either college or seminary teaching. The demands upon him by his own scholarly conscience, plus the competitive pressures for employment and promotion, make it a grave risk for him to serve in a parish even for a year. The reasonable expectation is that a similar dilemma will mount within the Catholic camp.

[11] Within Protestantism the situation is not so isolated, but it is serious enough. See "A Model for Theological Education," in *Theological Education,* Winter, 1965, by Walter D. Wagoner.

[12] One unsung American Catholic prophet was the Paulist Father, J. Elliot Ross, who in 1918 suggested that the Paulists establish a seminary that would be affiliated with the University of Texas.

[13] Fr. Hilary Ottensmeyer, O.S.B., "Blueprint for Seminaries," in *America,* Dec. 18, 1965, p. 780.

[14] There are Catholic private resident halls at Oxford (Campion) and Cambridge (St. Edmunds Hall)

[15] One quip has it that there are two requirements for being consecrated a bishop in England: one is baptism and the other is an education at the English College (Rome), and of these the former can be dispensed.

[16] *Search* (newsletter), Dec. 1963.

[17] Quoted by Guitton, *op. cit.*

[18] Fr. Andrew Greeley, prominent Catholic sociologist at the University of Chicago, would not agree. See his "Catholic Education," in *America,* April 17, 1965, p. 526.

[19] At this writing, this document was not available for final public circulation.

5

Celibacy and the Church Militant

A cloud no larger than a fig leaf is forming on the horizon of Catholic theological education and church life, fanned by the mounting breezes of discussion and argument concerning the appropriateness of celibacy for all members of the secular clergy. The implications of celibacy for the priestly life, for seminary years, and for the shape of the Church are so enormous that they can no longer be treated *sotto voce*.[1] The subject must be taken out of the realm of the prurient and gossipy in order that the genuine virtues and handicaps of celibacy may be better understood and, crucially, in order that celibacy's influence on the missionary effectiveness of the Church may be more fairly evaluated. The primary task of the Church—to embody Christ and to witness to his gospel—ought to be the great criterion. Does enforced celibacy inhibit that task?

No one is debating the vow of chastity for those in religious orders and communities. At least in these pages, no such issue is being raised. However, what is being questioned is whether the Church is justified in its juridical ruling that all its secular clergy be celibate. May there not—ought there not—be an option exercised by the seminarian as he contemplates ordination and by the priest following his ordination? A noticeable feeling is abroad in the Catholic community that the time has come for a free, frank and open debate on two questions: 1) "Resolved that married life be optional for secular clergy"; 2) "How does celibacy influence the effectiveness and nature of seminary education and thereby the apostolic witness of the Church?"

Celibacy is not an essential part of Catholic dogma. Some forty popes were married. The rise of a celibate clergy paralleled the slow growth of monasticism, and celibacy only gradually became the normative pattern. An open difference of opinion still exists among historians of the Church as to relation between monasticism and celibacy. Celibacy existed from St. Paul's time, apart from monasticism; whether as an evangelical counsel of perfection or as a monastic vow and ascetical discipline, it was well grounded in the first centuries of the Christian Church. Gregory VII in 1073, in his *Dictatis Papae,* outlined the role of priests *as monks in the world.* After about the fourth century, celibacy was largely monastic and, indeed, the role of secular clergy in the twentieth century has been confused by the celibate-monastic tradition.

Since the Council of Trent, the overwhelming juridical tradition of the Church has bolstered celibacy for secular clergy. Celibacy, be it repeated, is not a dogmatic assertion; it is not a matter of faith and morals from which there can be no departing; it may be discussed by Catholics as an open issue, but the resistance to such discussion is very powerful.[2] Like Thomism, which also is not of the *esse* of the Faith, celibacy is so interwoven in the fabric of the normal pattern of clerical life that most Catholics cannot conceive of the cloth remaining whole without it. It is not that these Catholics are insensitive or illiberal; it is simply that the celibate life has been so much a part of the picture for so long, with so many personal sacrifices having been made in its name, that it is exceedingly painful to bring the matter out for re-examination.

The position of Pope John XXIII on the question of celibacy was not as simple as official declarations, especially as they appeared in print, made it appear. No doubt he did feel that the Church should maintain celibacy. This kindly pontiff was touched by the burden of celibacy which, to judge from the complaints of some priests, represented a real martyrdom. A most poignant illustration of this is found in the famous interview between Etienne Gilson and Pope John in December, 1960.

The Pope's face grew sombre, and then he went on: "Shall I tell you what is my greatest pain, not as a man, but as Pope? The thought of these young priests who bear so courageously the burden of celibacy is a continual grief to me." Then he said, with a sort of violence, almost a cry: "It is a martyrdom for some of them, yes, a sort of martyrdom. I often seem to hear a sort of lamentation—oh, I am not speaking of here, it comes from much farther away—as if voices were being raised asking the Church to relieve them of this burden. Can I do it? In itself, it is not impossible. Ecclesiastical celibacy is not a dogma. It is not imposed by Scripture. It would even be easy. We take a pen, sign a decree, and tomorrow all the priests who wish to can get married. But we cannot do it. Celibacy is a sacrifice which the Church has taken upon itself freely, generously and heroically. I said so recently to the cardinals. Can we agree that the Church will soon no longer be spoken of as One, Holy and *Chaste?* We cannot. No, we cannot do that."[3]

Celibacy, freely entered into by mature persons, and joyfully lived out in a eucharistic community is an exemplary and desirable contribution to the Christian witness in this world. This is not said as a *noblesse oblige* preface to an all-out attack on celibacy. Quite the contrary, for Protestants, in particular, have much to learn from the Catholic experience with celibacy. It may add bright rather than gloomy colors to the ecclesiastical spectrum. At its best, celibacy forms men (and women) of quite remarkable and engaging personality, free to serve the Church where need exists, and making of their lives a striking parable of the covenant between Christ and his Church.

Cardinal Suhard of Paris sings the praises of celibacy:

The priest is, above all, a witness through his voluntary chastity. . . . It is not purely asceticism assumed in the best interests of the apostolate. It is the pledge of a future kingdom where God will be all in all, the anticipation of a spiritualized humanity. . . . It detaches the priest from the flesh and its entanglements, but also from human love, a love which is valid and sanctified since Christ made it a sacrament. But it is a very demanding bond. The husband belongs to his wife and children. He can give to others only a part of his time, of his thoughts, of his heart. Voluntary virginity, on the contrary, as St. Paul remarks in his praise of it, while it detaches the apostle from a limited circle, binds him to all, without distinction and without reserve.[4]

Fr. Bernard Haring, C.S.S.R., whose books are among the most widely read and genuinely respected in Catholic seminaries, and whose voice must be accounted to be eloquently on the side of *aggiornamento,* summarizes the glories of the celibate priesthood with these points:

1. It is a divine witness to the superabundant grace of the Holy Spirit in creating totally spiritual men and women. The vow of chastity supposes a greater maturity than matrimony.
2. Celibacy is a spiritual unction, a cult practice within the eucharistic sacrifice, which brings with it, to an exceptional degree, the gifts of joy and adoration and grateful service.
3. It permits love of God and neighbor to be first in one's life.
4. It encourages the spirit of poverty and humility in a way not possible for married men.
5. Virginity is a more adequate witness than marriage to the covenant between Christ and the Church. It is a credible sign of that supernatural reality. The celibate priest may represent Christ in his sacrificing and redeeming love for all men without exception.
6. Celibacy is an eschatological symbol. It is a sign of the fulness of time, of life not under law, but under the fulness of grace. It is a witness of Christian hope, foreshadowing the final kingdom of the freedom of the sons of God.[5]

Haring's plea for celibacy is duplicated in hundreds of manuals of devotion, in scores of books written for the edification of seminarians. The overwhelming number of published Catholic writings agree with Pope John XXIII. "What a grace it is for the Church to have priests faithful to such high virtue! With St. Pius X we consider it the purest glory of the Catholic priesthood."

The psychological dynamics of celibacy, insofar as they shape seminary life and the ordained life, are exceedingly powerful and just as controversial.[6]

One well-known American Catholic writer, for example,

makes much of the danger of the repressions, distorted personality identities, and occasional homosexual problems brought on by celibacy. With some justification he elaborates on the effect that celibacy has had even on "the image of Christ himself as that image is presented for veneration in Catholic churches, homes, and publications, has become saccharine, sweet, feminine, emasculate—to paraphrase a hundred critical appraisals."[7]

Whatever the validity of such arguments, it needs to be said most emphatically that psychological-sexual proof-texting, *pro* or *con,* with regard to celibacy is quicksand for the amateur psychiatrist. There abounds far too much easy and strident dismissal of celibacy by those who regard it, *ipso facto,* as a mental aberration, an affliction of sacerdotal eunuchs. It must be remembered that marriage, too, brings many problems with it, and that there is no guarantee that an immature celibate will become mature simply by marrying. Nor is homosexuality unknown among married clergy of other churches and, for that matter, some of the most cloyed-feminine images of Jesus Christ can be found in the stained glass windows and Sunday School books of Protestant churches.

There are, of course, terribly crippling aspects to celibacy, but celibacy is by no means an inevitable personal disaster endured for the sake of Church discipline. A Catholic psychiatrist, Dr. Conrad W. Baars, in an address to an Institute of Spiritual Theology goes to great lengths to reassure his hearers that celibacy is no obstacle to a full and mature human life. He maintains, in fact, that the celibate life may make it possible for some persons to attain maturity at an earlier period:

The only two conditions for a celibate to reach emotional maturity are the same emotional capabilities as the married person *and a seminary atmosphere which does not force him to repress and distort his emotional life.*

Like his married counterpart, the celibate will not attain this happiness without difficulties and inner struggles, particularly in the 30's and 40's when man's drives and desires are normally the strongest. That they have these difficulties and conflicts in common proves that their happiness has nothing to do with their ability to learn the love of restraint.

Further credence is given to the absolute importance of this love (*amor amicitiae*) when one realizes that the celibate who remains deeply aware of the noble reason for his choice of life will attain the maturity of the love of restraint and its attendant joy earlier than the married man whose path of life is easier and less dangerous in some respects, but who therefore requires more time to reach full maturity . . . priests have neither more or less sexual difficulties than married men.[8]

While this writer feels that in a majority of cases the personal damage caused to the celibate outweighs its personal satisfactions, it is by no means a psychologically open and shut case.[9] Apart from the personal-psychotherapeutic dimensions of celibacy, there are other implications of relevance for theological education and the Church.

Celibacy, in a very mixed cause-and-effect relation, has all kinds of ramifications for the daily style and methodology of seminary life. Overly solicitous and protective rules abound which are designed to protect the celibate from the temptations of the world without necessarily allowing the seminarians the initiative to develop the personal strength to live unprotected lives in the world after ordination. Celibacy certainly contributes to the hot-house atmosphere of many seminaries. The absence of women (as wives, teachers) from seminaries obviously makes it more difficult for the future priest to move with ease in heterosexual society. This absence of women, when combined with the tradition that virginity

is a higher virtue than marriage, can produce almost unconscious suspicion of sex itself:

> . . . to a certain Catholic mentality, is there not something in-
> congruous in the thought of a priest (if marriage should be al-
> lowed) rising from his marriage bed to celebrate the Mass? It
> has struck many people as very strange, for example, that in
> the Roman liturgy there is no term to describe the Mass and
> Office of a widow except that of the negative designation "nei-
> ther a virgin nor a martyr." An even less defensible attitude is
> displayed in one of the antiphons for the Office of a Virgin,
> the Latin of which may be rather freely but accurately trans-
> lated, "This is she who has never lain on a bed of sin." At the
> very least, one might observe that there are countless mothers,
> Catholic and otherwise, who have never lain on a bed of sin
> either![10]

The cloistered, all-male seminary community gives very
little chance for such attitudes toward natural sexual relations to be aired. The co-educational Protestant seminaries,
many of whose students are married, certainly enjoy a more
conducive atmosphere in this regard. Even without a married clergy, however, the Catholic seminaries could do more
to fumigate Manicheism. A feminine presence of a few
women teachers, for example, more coming and going of
families, allowing seminarians to get out more, to take classes
in nearby co-educational universities—this sort of thing
would help immeasurably to shed the "celibate mystique"
which so insulates profitable conversation and mission.

In his *Priestly Celibacy and Maturity,* Fr. David O'Neill
has an extremely interesting point to make about the relation between celibacy and theological education. For one
thing, he is eager that celibacy not be embraced in any *pro
forma* fashion simply in order to be ordained, but that it
be a decision postponed until the seminarian is mature

enough to realize its full meaning and implication. He suggests that celibacy might be separated from the vows of the subdiaconate. He emphasizes that celibacy as a "total dedication of love" is a step of such consequence that no man should take it without being genuinely prepared for it. O'Neill ventures the estimate that about ten percent of the priests in the United States leave the practice of the priesthood, and he thinks celibacy to be a prime cause of this attrition—an attrition directly related to men who enter the priesthood without first comprehending the impact of celibacy. That is, so many young men are eager to become priests that they might accept celibacy unthinkingly. O'Neill maintains that there are many who "would not have chosen a celibate life if there were any other way of becoming a priest."

Another of Fr. O'Neill's intriguing observations is related to what he terms "biased intake," namely, that seminaries tend to attract not only those of a certain type of ability and aptitude, but "also those with characteristic personality development. There may be many mature and well-integrated young men who do not desire to be married, but we inevitably have among the non-marrying group all those who hesitate to marry because of their lack of personal growth, their high basic anxiety, and their inadequacy in any close interpersonal relationship."[11] This indicates clearly, as O'Neill elaborates his argument, that celibacy narrows the type and range of men who attend seminary and it eventually makes more difficult the relationship between clergy and laity:

In fact, the whole emphasis of seminary training, as it is now conceived, seems to be rather in the direction of immaturity than of mature responsibility. It seems often as if the Church does not particularly want strong and vigorous characters in its junior clergy, and makes little attempt to develop strong, mature, and responsible men within the walls of the diocesan seminary.

During the seminary years, celibacy serves also as a major sociological and psychological device for achieving total institutionalization and the total priest; it is a means whereby the "separateness" of the priest is confirmed and understood; it builds a moat around the priest; it is a status-conditioning instrument, a rite of passage into the priest-hood. Fr. John Donovan in *The Catholic Priest: A Study in the Sociology of the Professions*[12] has this to say about celi-bacy from the sociological perspective.

In the Western Church the unmarried state of the clergy has the dual function of contributing to their recognition by the laity as a superior and of insulating the priestly office from the personal spheres of influence which might threaten the uni-versalistic treatment expected of him in his specific area of competence and authority.

Celibacy also —and this cannot be stressed too much— has shattering implications for vocations, for the supply of priests. Here we return to the central point: the manner in which celibacy for secular clergy is badly wounding the primary mission of the church. There is very little justifica-tion for anyone maintaining that celibacy has an insignifi-cant relation to vocations. The interrelationship will, of course, vary from culture to culture. In some places like Oceania, sub-Saharan Africa, and many spots in Latin America, celibacy so controverts the conception of mascu-linity that it is very difficult to win vocations. But even in the West and in the United States, where a celibate secular clergy has the authority of long tradition, one must ask how many priests would have remained in the work of the priesthood had marriage been permitted them, how many more young men would seriously consider becoming priests, and how many ex-priests would enthusiastically return were marriage allowed. No attempt is here made to cite *conclusive* evidence about the answers to these questions. For what it is worth, all that the present writer may say is this: after talking with hundreds of priests and seminarians, both here and abroad, and after a good deal of reading and work in the field of vocations, a clear and distinct impression exists that the insistence on celibacy is very seriously hampering the witness and the work of the Catholic Church because it discourages priestly vocations. The Christian world too much needs a powerful and persuasive Roman Catholic Church for so subordinate a matter as celibacy of its secular clergy to stand in the way of that Church's witness.

One quite typical, oft repeated, testimony is of the following sort. It proves nothing, but indicates much:

I have conducted a simple opinion survey while teaching in a Catholic high school over the past six years. I asked the junior and senior class boys how many would want to be priests if it were possible for them to be married. I am still amazed by the positive response I regularly receive from a full one-third of the boys. Our young men have not lost all idealism, are not devoid of a sense of sacrifice or rotten with materialism; God is giving His grace of vocation to the priesthood in ever increasing abundance to fill the needs of His Church. We are either too blind or we are simply refusing to recognize that grace.[13]

It would be naive to claim that optional marriage would result in a massive increase in vocations. Things are more complicated. But it is the worst sort of blind traditionalism which will not accept the fact that optional marriage will help substantially the number of vocations and thereby, since married clergy often achieve a more natural entrance into the evangelical and apostolic frontiers, greatly strengthen the advance of the Church.

There is an appealing candor in the quotation from Professor Leslie Dewart, St. Michael's College, Toronto:[14]

History has ever more clearly shown what may well have been unavoidably obscure at one time: there is, at bottom, a contradiction between professional celibacy and secular priesthood. Religious celibacy may well have seemed like a mere approximation to the religious life. But an approximation to religion that begins with celibacy is rather like the camel's approximation to the tent. One of the two, celibacy or secularity, had to be imperfectly and superficially realized; it had to be more apparent than real. And since celibacy cannot be had by halves and is, moreover, easily detected and, as it were, mechanically controllable, what has in fact suffered—all the more to the extent that celibate chastity has prevailed among the clergy after the fairly widespread irregularities of the late medieval clergy—is the worldliness, the secularity of the priesthood. As we know, the Church as a whole has become increasingly divorced intellectually from the reality of the world since the end of the Middle Ages, and most radically so since the beginning of the 19th century. It is not difficult to suppose that one of the principal causes at work in this process has been the gradual loss of the secularity of the priesthood.

Finally, the whole reassuring witness of Protestantism, Anglicanism, and Orthodoxy should carry weight with Rome.[15] These other churches are no less effective; they manage to survive; they are not corrupted by having a married clergy.

Naturally, Rome has a staggering economic investment in celibacy. The whole structure of Catholic schools, hospitals, charities is heavily staffed by celibates whose sacrificial service provides an incalculable financial saving for the Church. This is nothing to be debonair about. It would be a catastrophe in many places were some of these services to be seriously weakened. All that can be said—again—is that other churches and institutions make the grade without depending on celibate labor. A start can be made by the Roman Catholics as well. And if cheap labor is one reason, in a minority of instances, for being able to keep alive enterprises which are marginal or mediocre, then the economic pressures of a married clergy would contribute to a much needed shake-down cruise.

Celibacy need not and should not be made the whipping boy for circumstances which are infinitely complex; neither should it be a monomania. But it is a very, very important and pervasive factor in theological education and in almost every aspect of the Church. What is badly called for is a healthy, open, plenary debate. Get the whole subject out from behind the reredos. Bring in the sociologists, educators, psychiatrists, laity, and clergy—Catholic and non-Catholic. Set up conferences and symposia. Talk about it until it settles down to its natural proportions. Then, as the years go by (and it may be very few years), the Church surely will have the wisdom to do what is called for in this ticklish and troubled matter.

Finally, the close friendship which this writer has been privileged to enjoy with priests confirms two opinions: first, a profound admiration for what grace of character so many of the men have been able to acquire (either because of or in spite of celibacy); second, a poignant sense of personal tragedy in the lives of some of them which comes from an unnaturally truncated life. Celibacy has called forth heroic sacrifice, both painful and joyful. Before such sacrifice a married Protestant clergyman feels both respect and exasperation. Why can it not be a secular priesthood both married and unmarried?

With understandable strength of feeling it may be protested that celibacy is in a very intimate and special way a "family matter" for Catholics. This feeling must be respected. The only trouble is that all Christians are members of one family, and our denominational and churchly clan gatherings are so interrelated for weal and woe that we all wince when any one falls short of the mark, and we all rejoice when a fellow Christian Church adds muscle and mind to the family of Christ. Indeed, it is in this very family spirit that all Christians must be concerned for the proper role of celibacy within the Roman Catholic communion. In the same spirit, Protestants can make much more of an effort to evaluate the effectiveness of celibacy in certain circumstances and should reconsider if, under those limited circumstances, it might not have a greater place within Protestant church life.

Notes

¹ There is still far too much writing about celibacy by priests and others who use pseudonyms. One Catholic reader of such epistles to the editor finally wrote, "Let's have no more of this Mickius Mousiensis. Sign your real name." The whole subject suffers both from the pornographic approach of nineteenth-century "monks and nuns" stories and from the musty Manicheism of those who believe that the whole business is taboo for public discussion.

² Attempts to secure plenary discussion of celibacy at Vatican II got nowhere. Paragraph 16 of the decree on *Priestly Life and the Ministry* contains a vigorous endorsement of celibacy. Pope Paul requested that the issue not be debated in the Aula, despite requests from some bishops, notably a few from South America. The action of the Pope in closing the discussions on celibacy caused strong reactions immediately: One was a private meeting under Monsignor Ancel, Coadjutor-Bishop of Lyon, which was held to discuss the problems of celibacy (married priests will increase vocations, will not decrease the dignity of those who remain celibate, and will decrease the numbers of priests

not faithful to their vows of chastity). The other reaction was the petition sent to Vatican II by 81 Catholic laymen, including sixteen psychiatrists, urging a reconsideration of celibacy. Similarly, in January, 1966, a group of Catholic priests in southern Italy urged Pope Paul VI to abolish celibacy as a Church discipline.

3 Etienne Gilson, "Souvenir du Père," in *La France Catholique,* no. 862, 7: vi: 1963.

4 *Le Prêtre Dans La Cité,* 1959, p. 34 ff.

5 *National Catholic Reporter,* July 7, 1965.

6 Dealing with celibacy and indicative of the yeasty discussion now going on are the following three worthwhile books: David P. O'Neill, *Priestly Celibacy and Maturity* (New York: Sheed and Ward, 1965); Ida F. Gorres, *Is Celibacy Outdated?* (Westminster: The Newman Press, 1965); Pierre Hermand, *The Priest: Married or Celibate* (Baltimore: Helicon Press, 1965).

7 Frank Getlein, *The Trouble with Catholics,* (Baltimore: Helicon Press, 1964), p. 146.

8 *National Catholic Reporter,* July 14, 1965. Italics mine.

9 There can be no doubt that in many cases the psychically crippling effects of celibacy are agonizing: loneliness, drink, façades of authoritarianism. What the church loses in this type of misplaced anxiety and energy is impossible of measurement—even when put alongside what it gains by the devotion and service of mature celibates.

10 *National Catholic Reporter,* February 16, 1966, p. 6, Edwin Smith (pseudonym). That pseudonym again!

11 See O'Neill, *op. cit.,* particularly pages 55–68.

12 Unpublished Ph.D. dissertation, Harvard University, 1951, p. 134.

13 *National Catholic Reporter,* July 14, 1965. Letter from a priest-teacher in a parochial high school.

14 "The Celibacy Problem," *Commonweal,* April 22, 1966, p. 149.

15 Is there not an anomaly in the Catholic case for secular-clergy celibacy when Rome in no way protests married clergy in Roman Catholic churches of the Eastern rite?

6

Total Catholic and
Partial Christian

Ignatius Loyola vs. Henry Ward Beecher

The current torrent of talk about a crisis in authority
and obedience within Catholicism can easily be misinter-
preted by the Protestant. The Protestant is apt to regard
this as another sign of rebellion against the essential nature
of the Roman Catholic Church, a rebellion extending down
into the ranks of its seminarians. Rebellion there is, but it is
rebellion against the wrong interpretation of obedience
and the wrong exercise of authority.[1] Basically, this is a
protest against neither authority nor obedience. Few opportunities appeal more to ancient Protestant instincts than
the chance to shout that Roman Catholicism should reform
its version of Christianity by ceasing to be so rigidly authoritarian. This is a polemical blind alley. Within the ranks of
the Church itself there are enough voices as anyone could
wish expressing disturbance over abuses of Church authority.

"The duty of loyalty is no excuse for failing in intelligence," writes one Catholic. Protestants who seek to learn from their Catholic brothers in Christ need to look at quite the opposite side of the issue by asking this question: "Is there not a basic and valid Christian witness in the Catholic understanding of authority and obedience—a witness, which however manhandled by Catholics from time to time, still has a profound truth embedded within it?" As we shall see, this witness is central to Catholic seminary education, and it is to be found there as a paradigm for the whole Church.

A succinct presentation of the Catholic understanding of obedience within the church can be made by paraphrasing the words of one Catholic priest:[2] obedience implies that a man ought to give an *audience,* a dutiful hearing, to the voice of his Creator speaking through his conscience. All authority comes from God. Human authorities may claim obedience only to the extent that such a claim does not violate the will of God. Catholics believe that this will is discernible in the Church of God through its lawful authorities and that Catholics are called upon to subordinate otherwise legitimate personal desires and opinions to the general good of the Christian community. This is "reasonable obedience."

Catholic respect for Church authority does not mean that Church leaders, lay or clerical, do not make mistakes; certainly it does not mean that a Church superior should compel anyone to act against his conscience. In doubtful matters and in most affairs, however, the authority of a Church superior enjoys a presumption of validity.

A trenchant argument for Christian obedience, Catholic style, is found in the following words:

Obedience does not mean surrendering one's power of decision into the hands of a superior. It means deciding freely and, after mature reflection, to follow this particular leader because one sees in him the embodiment of an authority which one recognizes as necessary, as the depository of a promise, even if the leader himself is not always competent or infallible. In the Church, the Catholic obeys his bishop or the Pope because he believes that they are the historical successors of the Apostles and thus have received from God himself the command to feed his lambs and his sheep. In obeying, the Christian is conforming to the logic of his faith. Obedience, for him, means acting according to his conscience, and hence remaining free. . . .

However, it makes no sense for a Catholic who has faith to separate himself from the Church. The Catholic cannot fail to realize that, by breaking the bonds of ecclesial unity, he is committing an evil action, that he is giving in to pride, and that he is actually preferring himself to God. Henri Marrou put it very well: "No cause, however just, can justify rebellion and schism; unity is so transcendent a good that a Catholic cannot entertain the idea that he, a mere twig, should cut himself off from the rest of the Lord's vine."[3]

Naturally, this delicate balancing of individual conscience and institutional authority can and often has been corrupted by clergy who take advantage of the Church's intrinsic authority to flaunt their power and wave the sword of the spirit in an irresponsible fashion. But what is going on today within the Roman Catholic Church is a major redressing of any such clerical propensities. A lay-clerical collegiality is fast emerging. With it comes the agreement that authority and obedience work best when there is true dialogue, when clergy speak out of friendship and respect, avoid excessive and trivial commands, when maturity is sought rather than docility.[4]

Any Protestant whose empathy cannot stretch far enough to grasp the Catholic understanding of ecclesiastical obedience misses one of the most meaningful dimensions of

Catholicism, and he misses a great learning experience. The Protestant would do well to forget his mutterings about obscurantistic prelates and church politics. He ought rather *sentire cum ecclesia,* as Yves Congar labels it.

The Catholic abuse of Christian obedience is centripetal: to hug too closely to the institutional center, neglecting the critical autonomy and dignity of the individual. The perfect illustration of this abuse is the attempt, in some seminaries, to create total priests.[5] The Protestant abuse of Christian obedience is centrifugal: to go spinning out in personal orbit, losing touch with the institutional center. The perfect illustration of this abuse is the chaotic communityless, raggedly individualistic styles of education at some Protestant seminaries. Protestantism's healthy regard for scriptural authority seems somehow or other to have resulted in an illogical downgrading of the Church's authority. Centrifugal Protestants, therefore, are too much concerned for individual salvation and too little for community-oriented obedience.

Protestant appreciation of Catholic obedience will cause the Protestant to modify and discard the outmoded language with which he so often talks about the Catholic Church: "Bishop" is not a epithet; it describes a man invested with lawful church authority. "Rome" is not a title for a conspiratorial headquarters; it is the seat of authority and obedience for five hundred million Christians. "Priest" is not the designation for a thin-lipped martinet; it refers to one who is essentially a man and who, in an act of obedience, has given up wife and family and dedicated his talents to the Lord of the Church. "Catholic layman" is not to be defined as a dumb Pavlovian stooge, blindly obeying the dictates of an arcane hierarchy. He is a layman who believes deeply that the Catholic Church is the Church which Christ founded and in which his divine will operates.

Protestantism has as many stupidities and errors on record, in the name of individual conscience, as has Rome in the name of institutional obedience. A sympathetic study of Roman Catholic convictions about obedience and authority will go far to cleanse Protestantism of many of its most egregious errors.

The obedient Catholic reminds the American Protestant that entrepreneurial individualism is not the prime virtue for the Christian disciple. Loving obedience to Christ in the Church is at the heart of the matter. The Catholic reminds the Protestant that the well-being of the Church, i.e., its evangelistic effectiveness, its theology, its worship, its service, has a prior claim over the individual Christian's desires. The Catholic bishop should represent for the Protestant seminarian a living witness to the fact that the future minister is called to serve where the Church most can use his talents, and that the ministry is not primarily a "job" which one secures by virtue of his talents. The Catholic priest should help the Protestant minister to remember that higher salaries, hungry pastoral-supply committees, and rubbed oak chancels do not necessarily represent the certain will of God. The Catholic layman should be a testimony to the Protestant layman that the local congregation belongs to God, not to the bank, or to a circle of friends, or to a particular social class.

Protestant notions of Christian obedience are still predominantly individualistic and pietistic. What is the will of Christ for *me?* What shall *I* do to be saved? or—one step up—what is *my* congregation supposed to be doing? The Catholic vision of obedience is more inclusive. Through its structures of authority, however stultified, the Church of Rome is forced to think in universal terms. Protestants are often semi-docetists, that is, they often forget that God's Church is an entire body, not simply an eye or an arm.

If extremes are to be caricatured, one might contrast Ignatius Loyola with Henry Ward Beecher. Insofar as Loyola symbolizes a militant unquestioning obedience (which, incidentally, is far from typical of the American Jesuits), then he must be held at arm's length; insofar as Beecher symbolizes free enterprise, *laissez-faire* discipleship, then he must be discarded as normative. If all goes well with *aggiornamento*, the Catholic extreme may be rectified faster than the Protestant. There is a very impressive group of Catholic educators and writers, particularly in seminary circles, who are wasting no time in reminding their Church authorities that obedience and authority are not normatively to be defined in medieval or military metaphors. Obedience is not blind, servanthood is not slavery, authority is built on understanding, laity are not puppets, seminarians are not push-buttons.

Fr. Charles Davis, perhaps England's outstanding contemporary Catholic theologian, addresses himself to the correct understanding of Christian obedience with admirable insight:

Fundamental to Christian obedience is that it is obedience within a community, and it is the communal nature of the Christian faith and life that makes obedience such an essential virtue for every Christian. Faith is deeply personal, but we do not have it as individuals but only by sharing in the faith of a community. Our life in Christ, too, is life with others. Obedience for the Christian is a willingness to believe and think his faith in union with the community . . . it implies that he submits his personal ideas and desires to the test of reception by the community and does not refuse to learn from others within the community . . . only by recognizing the fundamental obligation of living and thinking with the whole Church can we act with Christian freedom toward fallible holders of local authority without falling into the license of individual caprice.[6]

The American Catholic community and seminaries still stagger under a heavy load of canon-law obedience. Whatever its merits, canon law is always corrupted by martinets and by those who cannot sift law through the sieve of charity. It is thus encouraging to notice that many members of its clergy are seeking to demonstrate that clerical authority, although rooted in divine authority, does not imply the imposition of arbitrary personal fiat. Legalism and heavy-footed canon-law attitudes (let-no-layman-bark) are twins who today walk gingerly in parishes and seminaries. The future is really with the viewpoint expressed by the Jesuit biblical scholar, Fr. John L. McKenzie:

The base of the power of authority is the love which those in authority exhibit; for the mission of the Church is the work of the love of Jesus Christ for men. Authority is a commission to lead in love and in the service of love; this, and not a grant of dominative or jurisdictional power in the secular sense, is what enables authority to exercise its leadership and to demand the assent of the other members of the Church. This conception of authority, far from diminishing its scope, increases it; for all men know that love can demand and obtain a response far in excess of the response which can be demanded by mere dominative and jurisdictional power.[7]

In that context, *aggiornamento* is, as another Catholic writer puts it, an attempt to make certain that outmoded concepts of authority and obedience do not "continue to hold up those baroque dikes of order and constraint erected to keep the flood tide of modernity from the faithful."[8]

Such sentiments with regard to obedience reveal, in American Catholicism, the influence not only of a more biblical view of the Church, but of the more general American political and pragmatic tradition. American Catholics find it impossible to thrive in American society under any Church tradition which exalts medieval language and notions about obedience and authority.

Moving along now into seminary circles, one finds that the students are pledged to obedience, that they wish to give their lives for the greater glory of God's Church; by no means, however, are they inclined to equate a seminary with a military school or a medieval court. For one thing, the sense of humor is outraged by some older Catholic practices: "To see one who is at once a prince of the church (a bit of medieval imagery which so many younger Catholics cannot abide) and a successor of the apostles disguised as an aged dowager prinked out in lace is irresistibly comic."[9]

The present generation of seminarians is busy, night and day, questioning so-called authorities, whether they be popes or seminary theologians. In this they are part of their peer-culture, which has few heroes. Like his Protestant seminary counterparts, the Catholic seminarian is not about to prostrate himself before St. Thomas or any other thinker who does not seem to be particularly relevant (even propositional "truth" can be irrelevant). Of course, as Fr. Andrew Greeley has remarked, the "new breed" of seminarians is alternatively desiring to storm the barricades and then sit down to undergo an identity crisis.

Obedience and seminary discipline are closely related, but they are not the same. Catholic seminarians are obedient enough to the "Catholic vision" and to the intrinsic authority of the Holy See and its delegated agencies. Nevertheless, the peculiar forms of abrasive discipline often exercised try the souls of priest, teacher, and seminarian alike. The following quotation from a personal letter to the writer by a very well educated priest is indicative:

Rectors and teachers complain that the students resist obedience. Now I find this judgment to be superficial. What we are witnessing is, instead, the exposure of a long-suffered but uncorrected weakness in seminary faculties. It is well known that the Army has an attraction for insecure people who crave nothing more than complete control over a small group of their fellows. Seminaries have their share of such insecure men as teachers. They fancy that the Church for which they are preparing priests is one wherein all orders and initiative come down from above, and the chief duty of the cleric is to respond. In this set-up, the ideal virtues of the seminarian are roughly those of a cabbage. The end-product is a priest who must have explicit instructions before acting, and who will, in turn, bully the laity into passive submission to his own whims. This is a procedure which has been attributed to the kings of the heathen, but was not recommended to disciples of the Lord. I trace it back not so much to any wholesome conviction that priests are agents of a vast apostolate to which they must accommodate themselves, as to a pettiness of character in the teachers. They overpaternalize the students because they are not themselves adult enough to deal with adults—only with children. They insist on verbal repetition of their lectures and notes, because any synthetic creativity in the students would be a threat to their own incompetence. They speak constantly of obedience to Christ and to the Church, but so often resemble nothing more than small children dressing up in their parents' clothing, as they themselves play at receiving the homage due to Christ and the Church. I totally repudiate the notion, still current, that the seminary experience is like pouring concrete: the cement is poured as liquid into the forms, which can be removed only after it has had time to harden. This suggests a long regime of imposed conformity on the presumption that habits long imposed will become habits freely maintained after ordination.

Too often obedience in seminary life implies that the docile, quiet, non-questioning student with the fat notebook, the good memory, and no critical apparatus is the one who finds graduation, ordination, and parish assignment to pose few obstacles. This is one obvious result of confusing obedience with the wrong kind of discipline and expectation. Although this confusion is no exclusively Catholic problem, it is much more accentuated in Catholic than in Protestant seminaries. The Catholic seminary tradition has abused obedience in the name of prudence. The Protestant tradition has worshipped individualism in the name of freedom.

Today within Catholic seminary communities there is more restlessness than has ever been the case within Protestant American seminaries. Vatican II, as the major reason among many, has raised the threshold of expectation so high that no seminary can be expected to adjust easily, wisely, and fast enough.

The Victorian age of seminary and religious training has ended. The present problem will not be solved by a retreat into the past. Many of the repressive aspects of religious formation programs are out of fashion now. The space age finds a new breed questioning the unquestionable and thinking about the unthinkable. This is a heady wine for a generation bred in prosperity and enflamed by banners that demand "Freedom Now." Veteran religious and priests, as well as laymen, whose faith has been tried by prejudice, depression, and wars, are genuinely upset at the pace of and passion for change in the Church in which they grew up. Young liturgical geniuses have ridiculed their habits of piety, as well as their religious dress, and questioned their apostolic techniques. If that isn't enough, they have given them Protestant hymns to sing, along with an abrupt change in their manner of saying and hearing Mass. The members of the older generation believe that they have received little consideration as to their feelings and little credit for their contribution to the Church.[10]

Catholic seminarians and many priests especially fret, during this period of readjustment, about the respect due a superior who in the name of tradition and office seems himself to violate Christian ethics. Protestants are too quick to whisper darkly about, not the keys, but the chains of Peter. It would be more charitable to admire those Catholics who criticize and witness under duress,[11] but who do not leave the Church or go off to play God, Jr., in the name of prophecy. Catholics abhor schism; they will protest, resign posts, submit to censure; but they shudder at the thought of breaking the unity of the Body.

The martyrdom or personal hardship suffered by conscientious Catholics needs two qualifications. The conscience of the protesting Catholic is no more apt to be right than the conscience of the superior is apt to be wrong. Each case must be judged on its merits. Also, Catholic authorities have no right to abuse the communal loyalty and ecclesial obedience of Catholics simply in order to perpetuate things as they have been.

This observer, for one, suspects that much of the agitation behind "new breed" or related syndromes of Catholic restlessness about authority and obedience is not a protest against the dogmatic and magisterial rights of the Church so much as an existential discomfort about the whole influence, impact, meaning, relevance of the Church's present style and strategy. Could it not be that the most sensitive spirits in the Church are demanding an obedience of themselves and others which cuts far deeper, demands radically new forms for the Church's apostolate, asks that obedience go beyond saying a prompt yes to chanceries, or hat-doffing toward Rome, or kneeling before a rector. There may be here a Catholic version of Kierkegaard's protest against "mere" professional Christianity. Do the "formal" authority structures and respectable acts of obedience go far enough? Indeed—and this is a very painful question to raise—do even the formal structures of religious orders, vows, etc., permit the more radical forms of Christian obedience which Christ calls for in our time?

Lord Acton, as one well ahead of his time, once observed that "three centuries have so changed the world that the maxims with which the Church arrested her decline now arrest her progress." This is never seen more clearly than in the *sturm und drang* accompanying contemporary Catholic redefinitions of authority and obedience. Acton's warning should not be lost on Protestants who have much to learn from Catholics in this area and who must not permit aberrant Protestant styles of obedience—also formed centuries ago—to straitjacket more faithful responses to that obedience which Christ seeks both in the individual and in the whole Church.

The Total Priest

Karl Rahner's splendid definition of the Church as "the visible presence of Grace upon the earth" is a reflection of the pervasive Catholic instinct to root the Church deep in the supporting culture. This habit has created a Catholic sub-culture in every land where that Church has had an active history. Sometimes this has hardened defensively into a ghetto, as it did in the United States for so many years and for so many reasons. Today, however, it is a cliché and simplistic to describe that sub-culture as a ghetto.[12] The pockets of ghettoism and the associated mentality are fast breaking up. What is not breaking up, however—and this has direct implications for seminaries—is what may be called "Mother System."

Roman Catholic seminary leaders should consider seriously whether it may not be more healthful to cut the umbilical cord not to Mother Church, but to Mother System. A sub-cultural system is justifiable as long as one breathes other atmospheres and is not hermetically sealed within a packaged universe. One Protestant seminary dean remarked at a faculty luncheon: "I am sick and tired of these first-year seminarians showing up, umbilical cord in hand, looking for some place to plug it in." These maternal-culture co-coons exist in all strong communities, political and religious. By the Catholic system is meant that vast network of Catholic this and Catholic that: hospitals, schools, orphanages, parochial papers, colleges, the Roman presence, sodalities, Serra, Knights of Columbus, Holy Name Society, and such like. Within this network of structures and attitudes the Catholic seminarian is too neatly enfolded in Laodicean self-sufficiency. Whatever the ecclesiological advantages which Mother Church sees in this system, it is not without sharp limitation for any seminarian formed too exclusively within it. The System confines the seminarians to worlds of their own, inhibiting their ability to adjust to a wider world—the future parish of the secular priest; it is overly protective regarding scholarly processes; it looks out on the world through narrow windows, confusing obedience with docility.

When overly dominant, Mother System is not the sanest way by which to prepare priests for a world which is boiling with change, resounding with pluralistic battle cries, and threatened by both secular and religious idolatries. More tragically, it atrophies the appreciation of the virtues of the secular world. Priests and ministers must be educated in a way which encourages them to be broad-gauged human beings, able to stay on their feet in a dizzy scene.

The priest should have the opportunity of becoming a "worldly Christian" (shunning angelism and Manicheism) so that he can both love and judge his fellow humans while standing naturally alongside them in their own world. In that way, the priest's notions of sin, for example, are not apt to be artificial and juridical; he will base his compassion on the existential situation; he will bring prophetic criticism into focus on the real heresies in all their worldly camouflage.

All efforts to move seminary education out from under the *full* eclipse cast by the shadow of Mother System will motivate seminarians to be better students and pastors, animated by a lively sense of being in that place so sought after by all students: "the real world." By and large, it does seem that too much of Catholic seminary life is pre-Copernican, that is to say, it operates in a two-level universe, of which the main one for the student is the "churchly world." Is this congruent with the incarnation? In short, does the System tend to produce *total priests* rather than worldly Christians who are priests of the Church?

Having asked that question, we can move on to a more detailed analysis of this total priest, *né* seminarian. The sociologist, Erving Goffman, provides an exceedingly useful analytical method in his concept of "total institutionalization."

A total institution may be defined as a place of residence and work where a large number of like-situated individuals, cut off from the wider society for an appreciable period of time, together lead an enclosed, formally administered round of life.[13]

Given this definition as preface, Goffman proceeds to an engaging description of groups in our society which possess such characteristics: prisons, mental institutions, military schools, ship crews, etc. Goffman makes quite a few references to Catholic seminaries, monasteries, and sisterhoods. If one keeps in mind that descriptive sociology is not to be confused with normative language and value judgments, much of what Goffman has to say is quite suggestive and profitable in analyzing seminary life. Those characteristics of total institutionalization which Goffman sets forth are: 1) barriers to social intercourse with the outside world;

2) a definite demarcation between the supervisory staff and the managed group; 3) a tightly regulated daily life; 4) a coherent plan designed to fulfill the official aims of the organization.

Goffman is careful to point out that total institutions range from the vicious (concentration camps) to the altruistic and benign (cloistered religious communities). With regard to religious communities he mentions how names are changed, dress is the same, belongings are uniform, old identities changed, deference patterns established. All of this is at odds with the outside world where there is more adult self-determination, autonomy, freedom of action, and a minimum of ritualistic formality.

Monastic communities and nunneries are clearly classic cases of total institutions. Catholic seminaries exhibit a wide range of this type of institutionalization, but most of them have such characteristics to a marked degree.

It is most important to remember that religious "total institutions" differ from a prison or mental hospital at the crucial point of *voluntary* entrance. Furthermore, all organizations, even families, share some of these characteristics to some degree.

Goffman's analysis does stir up reflection on the suitability and effectiveness of such seminaries for the training of secular clergy. How far should such regimentation, loss of identity, automatic deference, ritualized living, and the like be allowed to go without socially and culturally castrating a man? In some cases, it is as if the seminarian must, the moment he is ordained, enter a societal decompression chamber and learn to breathe a new atmosphere or else get the bends.

To what extent, one must also ask, is such a stylized regimen congruent with the full human dignity of the individual? This is not a question about the way in which total institutionalization cripples effectiveness of the priest so much as a question about how the Christian understands the meaning of "being human." The Christian regards it as idolatrous for the State, the army, or a political party (communism, for example) to demand total loyalty. Is the Church an exception to this logic? Can the concept of Christian obedience, which has been so sensitively developed within the Catholic Church, be stretched to the extreme of such regimentation? Is the Church still intent, as Fr. John D. Donovan has so skillfully documented, on claiming the whole life of the individual priest, putting him through a process of institutionalized depersonalization? Is "Keep the rule and the rule will keep you" the first law of survival for the priest? Is it correct to say, "In a sense which no secular profession could envision, the official and the personal spheres of his life were being integrated into a total status that, upon ordination, would be his for life"?[14] Use marriage as an analogy. Is it a healthy marriage which demands that the basic autonomy, dignity, and freedom of either partner be sacrificed?

These are fair questions, even if the answers are not always crisp and clear. When one looks at many Catholic seminaries, questions of that sort come to mind, and the clear implication is that a penetrating debate is in the offing.

One would immediately and rightly raise equally serious questions at the other extreme: Can there be effective or Christian discipleship without structural and organizational discipline? This is an arrow to aim at Protestantism. There is, indeed, a quiver full of such arrows to shoot in the direction of Protestant seminaries; this, however, is another archery tournament, and not the chief concern of this critique.

It would seem dubious to maintain that the Catholic commitment to the dogmatic authority of the Church necessitates such institutionalization. The two phenomena are related, but not logically concomitant. Because one freely obeys, in good conscience and with reason, the dogmatic authority of the Church does not imply that the Church is justified in violating the proper humanity of the seminarian.

Just where and when the line is to be drawn within the life of seminaries is a very delicate and debatable matter. The answers will vary from faculty to faculty whenever there is a plenary discussion of these issues. A faculty will first have to arrive at an understanding of the function and role of a good and effective priest, and, secondly, at an understanding of Christian humanity—a humanity which the priest shares equally with all other men. It may then proceed to analyze the curriculum, the rules, the manners, the ethos which is necessary to cultivate such maturity. The faculty must try to disabuse itself of *a priori* commitments to any present or past seminary patterns and, insofar as possible, try to design, *de novo,* an ideal or archetypal seminary. It will then be in a position at least to argue with history and circumstance and to make whatever changes are possible. The changes will be, without doubt, in the direction of more freedom, more flexibility, less juridical pettiness, a more realistic dovetailing of the "outside" and the "inside" worlds.

Since so much of what has been implied here would seem to be (and is) an adverse criticism of monastic models for diocesan seminaries, it is only fair to say that monasticism, as such, is outside this critique. It would be extremely useful, just to make sure that the rich and sustaining monastic tradition is not summarily dismissed, if Catholic theological educators would carefully and ruthlessly examine monasticism in order to isolate those elements in it which are valid for the secular seminary. It would seem unlikely that monasticism is all of one piece, with no transferrable parts. It would be cavalier irresponsibility to be so put off by the misplaced forms of monasticism in secular seminaries as to be blind to its appropriate merits.

Notes

[1] Such, fairly accurately, is the theme of Fr. John L. McKenzie, S.J., in his *Authority in the Church* (New York: Sheed and Ward, 1966).

[2] Fr. Joseph Gallagher, *The Catholic Review*, Baltimore, January 15, 1965.

[3] Henri Fesquet, *Catholicism: Religion of Tomorrow?* (New York: Holt, Rinehart & Winston, 1964), p. 71.

[4] See Conrad W. Baars, M.D., "Psychological Aspects of Obedience," *Cross and Crown*, March, 1965, and June, 1965.

[5] See concluding section of this chapter.

[6] *America*, November 7, 1964, p. 558.

[7] *Authority in the Church* (New York: Sheed and Ward, 1966), p. 61.

[8] John Ratte, "The Specter of Modernism," *Commonweal*, July 23, 1965, p. 532.

[9] J.M. Cameron, "The Transformation of the Church," *New York Review of Books*, July 1, 1965.

[10] Eugene Kennedy, M.M., "*Aggiornamento*, Anxiety and the Seminary," *The Critic*, June–July, 1965, p. 33.

[11] Painful examples of this are to be found in the 1965 founding of The Institute for Freedom in the Church, in the priestly protests against the racial attitudes of Cardinal McIntyre, and in the uproar occasioned by priests clashing with ecclesiastical authorities over the issue of political protest.

[12] There does remain, however, much of what one Catholic terms not a defensive closed ghetto, but an "open apostolic ghetto" which still sees the world as something apart from the Church, as something which Catholics "go out and confront." See Luiz A. De Souza, "Christians and Social Institutions," *Catholic Mind*, January, 1966, p. 23.

[13] Erving Goffman, *Asylums* (Garden City: Anchor Books, Doubleday and Company, 1961). See especially the first chapter.

[14] "The Catholic Priest: A Study in the Sociology of the Professions," doctoral dissertation, Harvard University, 1951, p. 239.

7

Whence Cometh Melchizedek?

Vocational Furor

Anyone who studies Roman Catholicism is immediately impressed by the amount and the intensity of attention given to vocations.[1] There is nothing in all of Protestantism which can match the Catholic campaign for vocations. It is a campaign which is built on the serious interest of clergy and laity alike. Father Joseph Fichter believes the laity may be, if anything, more concerned about the problem than the clergy.

From the Pontifical Office of Vocations[2] to the smallest parish and parochial school, there extends a network of scouts, advisors, magazines, newspapers, conferences, books, vocational clubs, and other strategic vocational apparatus which makes the New York Yankee farm system look like the Little League. Catholics may feel that their vocational efforts are inadequate, but in comparison with any other

Church it is far ahead in the sheer quantity of concern and energy expended. One finds himself asking if the search for vocations doesn't occasionally reach frantic, obsessive proportions. If one were to ask, "In proportion to the size of the vocational campaign, how are the results?", then the answer would have to be carefully worded, and probably on the sober side.

On the whole, however, Catholic vocational efforts form an impressive object lesson for other Christian churches. For one thing, the other churches need to appreciate the reasons behind the intense Catholic drive for vocations. While a competent and professionalized clergy is important to Protestantism, the Roman Catholic Church customarily defines itself in terms which make the sacerdotal office of the *esse* of the Church. The engines of the Church, to use a harsh figure, are manned by priests; the soteriology is posited on priestly actions; the hierarchy is completely priestly. Without a priest a local congregation of Catholics would be rudderless and almost inoperable.[3] The Church must have an ample supply of priests. So must Protestantism, but the lay structures of Protestantism permit much more non-clerical stability, and a ministerial shortage is not felt as acutely or as immediately.

Futhermore, the Catholic fright over the prospect of a shortage of priests is severely multiplied by the leadership needs of the Catholic Mother System—that sub-cultural cluster of schools, hospitals, clubs, leagues, philanthropies, and other agencies of good work to which the world owes so much. This system is very heavily staffed by religious and seculars. Their personal services bring a remarkable degree of dedication and an equally significant measure of financial savings. Cardinal Suenens and others are arguing persuasively that too many religious, too many vocations, are placed in positions where specially trained and educated lay people can do just as well or better. Catholic critics are increasingly upset by the plethora of Catholic organizations. Yet, despite all such criticism, it will be many a year before there is a noticeable decrease in the vocations necessary to the System. The situation now, with burgeoning populations and demands, is one in which an arithmetical drop in the number of vocations has functional results which hit the System with geometric intensity.

One bittersweet lesson in the shortage of vocations may be that the Catholic Church and all churches must learn to educate and then to place clergy where their distinctive functions are needed. It simply is not necessary for so many clergy to be occupied in a daily work that does not need ordained persons: administrative posts in schools, church offices, etc. Church leaders, both Protestant and Catholic, need much more rigorously to ask, "Does this particular position require a person who has been educated for a sacramental and pastoral ministry?"

An additional object lesson is the seriousness with which the Catholic Church attempts to challenge young men and women with the vocational possibility. Protestants would do well to match the intention and the scope of such recruitment activities, even if some of the means need to be changed to fit the Protestant view of the ministry. While most Protestant churches (largely with the exception of the predominantly Negro churches) have national and regional programs and staff in the area of ministerial recruitment, the scope of these efforts is much smaller proportionately than the Catholic effort.

All Christian churches have the responsibility of presenting the claims of the ordained ministry to as many appropriate persons as possible. Far too few Christian students have ever been asked the legitimate questions, "Have you thought seriously about the ministry or about the seminary as a place to consider ordination?"

One way by which the Catholic Church presses the vocational challenge is through the program of Serra International. Protestants should take a close look at this organization. It is "a voluntary association of outstanding Catholic laymen who dedicate themselves to a two-fold objective; fostering and sustaining vocations to the priesthood and furthering Catholicism through enduring friendships among Catholic men." Founded in 1934, Serra now has a United States membership of about ten thousand men, each of whom must be active: no dead weight is allowed in the membership. Attendance is compulsory. Serra sponsors movies, essay contests, vocation rally days, and some eighty other activities aimed at stimulating an interest in the priesthood. The entire Serra program is carried on in closest cooperation with diocesan offices.

The prospect of having thousands of competent laymen systematically recruiting for the ministry of the Protestant churches is an extraordinary example and challenge.

Furthermore, most Catholic dioceses have Directors of Vocations whose task it is to bring effective vocational stimuli to students and to families. Tons of vocational literature are published; sermons are preached on the subject; bishops talk vocations at Confirmations; priests visit homes; essay contests are held; posters are distributed. The Pope speaks regularly on the need for vocations. Vocational institutes for priests are held wherein they discuss the latest vocational strategies. There is a World Day of Prayer for Vocations. Films are produced and televised. "Some place in the United States there is a Maryknoll film being shown on television every day of the year." Even plenary indulgences are given under certain circumstances for apostolic work on behalf of vocations. The Pontifical Office for Religious Vocations edits a magazine on vocations for international distribution as well as a monthly newsletter for priests.

The net influence of this tremendous effort is difficult to

estimate, but it certainly breaks the sound barrier. Most Catholic youths can say that they have heard in one way or another the cry of the Pope, *"Te io chiamo"* (I call you). Like modern advertising, some of these vocational efforts may be done because the sponsor is afraid not to do it, and certainly some of the activities are jejune and maudlin. The very intensity of the program causes extravagant claims to be made for the "product," that is, the priesthood is often over-sold, and to such a degree that the status of the lay Christian is wittingly or unwittingly subordinated. On the whole, however, the Protestant observer can only cheer the effort and wish that his own tradition were doing as much.

It would be a mistake to think that the Catholic vocational recruitment campaign is all instrumental, but non-theological. Actually, the Catholic Church conceives of ordination as a long process involving personal fitness and conviction, education and preparation, the examination and call of the Church. It differs from classical or Reformation Protestantism only insofar as such Protestants insist on the examination and a call involving a lay-congregation as well as clerical approval. The Catholic Church will do all it properly can by human instrumentality to stimulate thinking about vocations. It always understands the sacrament of Holy Orders as including the interior call of God and the exterior call of the Church.

What is the extent of the vocational-supply problem? The answer is extremely difficult to find, even in a Church which has such a hierarchical organization. There is mounting apprehension about the supply of vocations, and one proceeds on the assumption that there is a correlation between the cries of dismay and the actual situation. The true figures are maddeningly elusive, but not because the Church is hiding anything. The Church has so many separate agencies from which to cull the data that the most responsible officers of the Church are not certain of the figures and disagree among themselves. Nowhere, not even at the Pontifical Office of Vocations, is there yet a reliable tabulation of the number of secular and religious, of seminary drop-outs, of comparative progress or decline over the years. Furthermore, after data is accumulated, there remains the interpretation. Does the Church ever have enough vocations? How many clergy are manning positions which should be filled by laity? Are there too many parishes? What is the relation of numbers of clergy to quality of clergy? These questions need to be kept in mind in evaluating the current hue and cry about the supply of vocations.

The cry of woe is loud. Cardinal Shehan, of Baltimore, speaking at a 1965 convention of Serra International, termed the shortage of priests "desperate." Merely a superficial reading of Catholic periodicals reveals a constant flow of articles on the alarming statistics of vocations. For example, in 1963 the Chicago diocese had 624 men entering major theology; in 1965 it had 450—a 27 per cent decrease. One New York seminary has had a 30 per cent decrease over the past four years. The Catholic population in the United States has increased almost 100 per cent in the last 20 years, whereas the number of priests has increased only about 50 per cent. There has been a 68 per cent drop in the rate of increase of new priests since 1955.

Nor is the worry confined to the United States. In France, Italy, Portugal, England and Holland, for example, the situation is worse. Vocations to the religious life are dropping even faster than vocations to the secular priesthood. Clergy supply is amazingly dependent on the United States and Canada, with close to half of all the vocations in the world now coming from the United States.[4] In any case, the Western world is supplying two thirds of the entire

Catholic priesthood and three fourths of all missionary priests. One of the most impressive and realistic reports on vocations is found in a 1965 special survey conducted by the White Fathers and published at their motherhouse in Rome. This published report, *Sedos,* maintains that 10,000 priests must be ordained each year simply to care for the current needs of the Church, but that only 5,000 men are being ordained yearly in all countries combined. In 1965 the United States furnished 1,700 priests.[5]

In the United States, where the population has increased some forty per cent within ten years, all circumstantial evidence indicates a steady decline in the proportionate number of Catholic priests, even though there has been a slight increase in absolute numbers. In 1966 there were 59,193 priests in the United States serving 46,246,175 baptized Catholics—or one priest for every 781 members of the Catholic laity. Since about 36,000 of these priests are secular clergy and since thousands of both secular and religious are engaged in teaching and non-parochial types of ministries, it is easy to see that the supply of parish priests is stretched far too thin.

Comparison or contrast between the Catholic and Protestant ministerial-supply pictures is hopeless. There are so many differences and variables that it is fruitless to compare oranges and apples. To be sure, there are profitable exchanges of wisdom and experience which will help each tradition to evaluate common factors behind increase or decrease in enrollment; but the comparative "numbers game" should be avoided.[7]

Because there is a general loss of faith, because culture offers beguiling lay careers, and because the professional ministry is less esteemed or in disrepute, the number and quality of both Catholic and Protestant newly ordained will suffer. Neither tradition at the moment has cause for despair or for self-congratulation; both have every reason to be worried about quality more than about numbers; each could do much more than it is currently doing to utilize ordained ministers more effectively.

An analysis of all the reasons and excuses being offered by both Catholic and Protestant vocation directors shows the same items on both lists: disenchantment with the Church as an institution; lack of information about the ministry and seminary; conviction that Christian lay vocations get to the power centers of society; hesitation about the professional standards of the clerical education; confusion over the nature of God's call to ordination; the glitter of the monetary marketplace; the countervailing values of family life. One or another analyst will arrange these items in varying orders of priority, yet it is true that most of these reasons appear on the vocational fever charts of both Protestants and Catholics.

Another and more general way of stating the common problem is to assert that the supply of competent clergy is a very complex matter related to the general health of the Christian Church in our time. No one solution by itself is available. Gimmicky devices, high-powered salesmanship, bits and pieces of special programs—even when well designed and devoid of false motives—will not carry the day. It may be, as has so often happened in history since Calvary, that the Church must be born of worldly failure. Dedicated work on many fronts simultaneously is imperative, always remembering that, however important members of the clergy are or may consider themselves to be, God works with them and without them. *Sedos* is absolutely right in maintaining :"To present the need of vocations as an emergency case is a bad point of departure for the apostolate of vocations. Who likes to board a sinking ship? Moreover, it is not a case of saving a ship from wreckage; Christ is the very ship and rock." Too much shouting and hand-wringing only causes potential seminarians to be the more suspicious.

The Protestant observer of the Catholic vocational dilemma cannot but notice several aspects which differ sharply from the Protestant dilemma. It is quite clear that the Catholic priest, or his image (that most pejorative sociological term!), stands well with the Catholic laity. Fichter remarks:

In comparing the pastoral image as seen by the clergy and by the laity, the most significant finding is that the laity thinks more highly of the priests than the priests think of themselves. One may suggest also, however, that the judgment of the laity reflects the genuinely high status that the clergymen occupy in American society. Catholic lay people are by and large satisfied with their parish priest. They make use of his services, express high esteem for him, and are fairly cooperative when the need is manifest.[9]

Compared with Protestant problems of recruiting for the ordained ministeries, the Roman Catholic problems are both easier and more difficult. Protestant conceptions of the ministry now circulating among college and high-school students are undergoing a fast and confusing change: in terms of office, function, and relevance the ordained ministry is unclear and not well differentiated from that of the layman. As a profession, the ministry lacks sharp definition. Many students believe that the minister suffers from functional unemployment and that the parish minister doesn't make much of an impact. Theologically and ecclesiologically, the Protestant minister has nothing like the crucial role of the Catholic priest. Catholics may feel that the image or role of the priest is fuzzier than it formerly was, but, contrasted with Protestantism, the priestly function and status is much clearer in terms of "job definition," has a much more precise and critical role in ecclesiology and soteriology, and thus is easier to focus upon and to define in vocational recruitment campaigns.

What makes matters more difficult for the Catholic than for the Protestant is the celibate life, the greater degree of "separateness" in the priestly life, and the high standards of personal sanctity required for ordination. There are many other factors, but these are among the most "uniquely Catholic" obstacles to recruitment. The problems of celibacy are discussed elsewhere in this book. "Separateness" is closely related to celibacy, but it includes other aspects of the priesthood as well: clerical groups; the isolated impact of seminary life; clerical dress; the priestly authority structures.[10]

The requirements of personal sanctity are, of course, a compliment to the Church's understanding of the priesthood. The vigorous manner in which spiritual formation and moral standards are espoused in seminary years certainly causes—no matter how compassionate and understanding the faculty—many men either to stay away from seminary or to drop out after entrance. More than any Christian likes to admit, it is the spiritual and moral demands of the faith, even more than the theological assent or the intellectual rationale, which cause men and women to stumble and lose heart. In a very perceptive article, Fr. Richard Klaver, O.S.C., presses home the thesis that the failure to develop personal sanctity and spiritual growth during the seminary years is one major cause of a decline in candidates for ordination:

A priestly vocation will take care of itself, if the young man allows himself to be sanctified according to God's intent. This henceforth must be his prime objective . . . it is our sincere conviction that the seminarian who lives his vocation and allows himself to be formed interiorly will keep his vocation, while the one who neglects this means of personal sanctification will either weaken it or lose it entirely . . . the first duty of a seminarian consists in striving after the perfection of holiness. The acceptance of this obligation will guarantee his vocation while the reverse will inevitably result in vocational disaster. We can readily see that the young aspirant does not yield to this urgent demand of holiness easily, and seldom immediately. But, unless he does, at least gradually, he is on his way out, even though it may be several years before the issue reaches its climax.[11]

Fr. Klaver discusses spiritual discipline as a reason for seminary drop-outs, but the same reason serves also to explain why some men will not enter seminary. And it is a valid reason. One may lament that the Church is hoist with the petard of its own standards; yet one may hardly expect the Church to lower those standards. What is so astounding in this day and age is not that fewer men are going to Catholic seminaries, or that more are dropping out, but that so many do arrive at Holy Orders. If contemporary Protestantism, with its diffuse conception of ordination and its ambiguous standards of spiritual formation, were to add the sacrifices of celibacy, sanctity, and separateness, it undoubtedly would have staggering problems in ministerial recruitment.

Although some adversely critical things are said here concerning the present details and style of Catholic theological and spiritual formation, the Catholic Church knows very well—and it is a lesson which it taught Protestantism after Trent—that a well educated and formed priesthood is, like marriage, not a matter which is to be accomplished inadvisedly or lightly, but soberly and in the fear of God. This means that priests (monks and nuns as well) are not "produced on some fast-moving assembly line." One cannot sprinkle vocational holy water over well-intentioned laymen and have instant clergy. The long, arduous preparation for ordination is not a standard which Rome is about to drop, even thought it presents grievous vocational problems.

Where Have the Students Gone?

In September, 1966, at least two thirds of all U.S. Catholics in colleges and universities were not in Catholic schools. By 1980 there will be close to four times as many Catholics on secular campuses as under the ivy of Mother Church. In this type of distribution Catholics are not much different from Protestants.[12]

There is a telling difference, however, and it is one to which Catholics must pay attention. This is most definitely a place where they have much to learn from Protestants: namely, the necessity of being where the *better* students are —where *most* of the students are.

The Catholic apostolate to Catholic students at secular colleges has been carried on largely through Newman Club organization and strategy. The Newman Club is a student-center house with a priest-chaplain. Like most of the Protestant denominational foundations, it functions on "religious fraternity row." Now fifty years old, the Newman Club movement has had to fight an uphill and testy battle to win the confidence of hierarchical leadership. One bishop of the pre-1960 period said of Catholics on secular campuses in his diocese: "I look after them as I do Catholic prisoners in our jails. It's the same thing: taking care of people who shouldn't be there."[13] The bishop was simply revealing the deep trap into which the Catholic Church has fallen: the either/or mentality about parochial or secular schools. At the Third Plenary Council of Baltimore in 1884, the trap was dug: "Every Catholic child in a Catholic school." The limitations of such a goal, whatever the merits of parochial schools and colleges, has, until quite recently, effectively insulated the Catholic Church from its proper influence on the secular campuses of the United States and thereby minimized the flow of vocations from such campuses.

The force of numbers, the sudden realization as to where the Catholic students have gone, is now causing a major reappraisal of strategy. This is paralleled by a welcome re-thinking of the nature, role, and contribution of the secular campus. This re-thinking is similar to that going on in some seminaries which wish to have a closer relation to the university world. Here are two quotations indicative of this new Catholic attitude. Each quotation represents a radical departure from what has been heretofore the normative Catholic party-line.

Specifically, of course, the Church must begin to accept secular universities for what they are, a central if not dominative fact of American life. They are not important merely because the vast majority of America's college-educated citizens, and this includes Catholics, are educated in these institutions. It is rather that within these institutions our society has what Charles Davis, in a phrase borrowed from John Wain, calls its "creative center." There is such a center in every culture. In Father Davis' definition: "It consists of those artists and thinkers who do not shirk reality but are prepared to face it. And reality is for them a present thing: they are not content with past descriptions or received ideas. They grapple with reality itself in its disturbing greatness and unexpected newness, in its unresolved problems and unexplored mystery. And they react to it creatively. They allow questions to arise that give them no rest, making life unendurable for them."[14]

And:

Shouldn't we think in terms of the Catholic students' *right* and even necessity to attend secular schools? Father Schillebeeckx gives grounds for this kind of thinking when he writes: "In the plan of salvation, the concrete world by definition is an implicit Christianity; it is an objective non-sacral but saintly and sanctified expression of mankind's communion with the living God; whereas the Church, *qua* institution, is the direct and sacral expression of that identical communion."[15]

The Catholic investment in its own educational enterprise is so massive that there is a natural (and, to many Catholics, a maddening) reluctance to assign new funds and manpower to secular campuses.[16] It has been easier for Protestants to adjust to the educational facts of life, especially since many of the great secular schools (Yale, Vanderbilt, Oberlin, and the like) were originally Protestant fiefdoms. Protestantism in the United States never has been as suspicious of secular education as the Catholic Church. Now the Catholics must come running up with reinforcements and seek to capture lost ground.

The Newman Club and similar student movements see the situation clearly and they are slowly winning new support within Church circles. But the Newman Club strategy, in and of itself, is inadequate when it is defensive or if it is regarded as an excuse for Catholics talking only with Catholics (or with Protestants). The key dialogue is with the agnostics and skeptics who compose such a large proportion of the collegiate population.

Furthermore, there are well over a thousand major secular campuses where there are no Catholic ministries to students at all. By no means should all existing Newman Clubs and programs be classified as soundly established. Catholic college campuses average one priest to each thirty-five Catholic students; secular campuses claim a ratio of one priest for each thirty-one hundred Catholic students. Church tail wags vocational dog!

A sore point must here be touched, if only to encourage lively rejoinders: many educators—Christian, non-Christian, and non-religious—are willing to argue long and hard that the better students, per square mortar board, are on the secular campuses.[17] This is particularly true at the rapidly growing number of selective colleges and universities. This assertion can be made only if one recognizes the many individual exceptions; in the educational marketplace today in the United States, however, the weight of opinion would be on the side of maintaining, let us say, that, per one thousand undergraduates, the greater quality would not be in the church-related colleges and universities, either Protestant or Catholic.

Argue the case as one may, no Catholic concerned with vocations dare neglect the secular campuses. Nor can anyone avoid the plain fact which vocational-guidance persons keep reiterating: the vocational and career decisions of American youth are progressively postponed to later years, and such decisions are powerfully shaped by the persons with whom they identify during the college years.

If anywhere there is a priest or Catholic layman who stigmatizes or makes uncomfortable a Catholic student for not attending a Catholic college, then there is a person who misunderstands God's grace in Creation, who sadly misreads the education scene, who misjudges the psychodynamics of career decision, and who undercuts the Church's drive for vocations. There are good reasons for some Catholics attending Catholic colleges. There are equally good, at least as good, reasons why many more do not. Educational chauvinism is something no church can afford today. Conversely, secular educators with any statesmanlike sensitivity for national health and public virtue should do everything possible to cooperate with the churches as they seek to minister to their students.

Minor Seminaries: The Broken Escalator

The role of minor seminaries in Catholic theological education is currently being debated with such heat and contentiousness that a Protestant commentator is tempted to sidestep the whole argument. Yet minor seminaries are a central and normative feature of preparation for the priesthood. There is no avoiding the debate.

A minor seminary is a boarding school (there are a few which are day schools) for high-school-age boys who wish to consider ordination and for those who definitely are planning to attend major theology and seek ordination. It is a form of priestly preparation inherited from the European tradition. Protestantism has nothing at all comparable to it, unless it be the few preparatory high schools of the Missouri Synod Lutheran Church. There are about 216 minor seminaries in the United States with an enrollment of 33,200.[18] Most priests now living in the United States began their education as minor seminarians.

It is still the prevailing vocational system to encourage potential priests to attend these schools.[19] The typical minor seminary is isolated in a place of quiet remoteness. The curriculum includes the basic high-school liberal-arts subjects, plus courses in religion—all set in the daily round of communal and private devotions. The boys generally wear a distinctive clerical-type dress: either black suits or soutanes. The faculty is clerical, carefully selected as men suitable to work with youth and giving an attractive image of the priesthood. The daily life, as in any high school, includes athletics and the usual extra-curricular activities.

Parents may visit at stipulated times, and the boys are permitted vacations with their families.

The rationale of the minor seminary is well expressed in the literature of St. Joseph's College, operated by the Vincentians at Princeton, New Jersey:

... the parents should realize that age has nothing to do with vocation. God calls a boy to His priesthood in His own good time and at His own good pleasure. It may be at 12, or at 13, or at 16, or at 22. This is the clear teaching of the Church, for she has established hundreds of minor or junior seminaries throughout the world to provide for the earliest vocations ... the minor seminary, therefore, is the place where a boy and his parents can be sure about his vocation.[20]

The clear intention of the seminary is to encourage the boys to continue on to ordination. The spiritual requirements for ordination are made perfectly plain to the students. These schools dove-tail the educational requirements for major theology into the curriculum, giving enough Latin and religious instruction to facilitate passage into the advanced levels of theology.

There is scarcely a diocese in the United States without one or more minor seminaries. The Jesuits, Dominicans, Paulists, and others take candidates only after high school, while Franciscans, Precious Blood Fathers, Oblates of Mary Immaculate, Maryknoll, and Divine Word missionaries are among those religious orders which actively seek eighth- and ninth-grade candidates.

The Catholic priesthood has depended so heavily on minor seminaries as the major source of candidates that any weakening of these seminaries poses extremely serious consequences. Two factors in minor seminary training are under radical re-examination: the first is the lamentable attrition rate: only about sixteen per cent of those who enter at the ninth-grade level continue on to major theology; the second is the whole educational and pedagogical assumption involved in isolating boys for specialized vocational training at such an early age and in such closeted circumstances.

A consideration of the attrition rate, in the words of one priest, "reminds you somewhat of methods of continental warfare through World War I, when troops advanced in close formation upon the enemy, dying by the thousands but finally winning through by sheer weight of numbers."[21] It is a very slim argument which can maintain that the money and energy devoted to such seminaries is a valid vocational effort or justifiable Christian stewardship. One may have the highest personal regard for the men who teach in minor seminaries, and one may understand the historical origins of the system; but who can refrain from asking questions and lifting an eyebrow that such a system, with so low a yield, is worth the candle. God may, indeed, call boys to the priesthood at various ages, but whether the minor-seminary system is a necessary part of such providential action is very much open to debate.[22]

There is one key question to be asked, and it concerns the assumptions of vocational guidance which underlie minor seminaries. The normal young person goes through marked periods of vocational ambivalence as he tests out his various abilities against various possibilities. While the Church certainly should make every effort to present claims of a clerical vocation to as many of its young men as it possibly can, neither the Church (any church) or any other institution or profession should be permitted to do vocational arm-twisting at too early an age and over too long a period. Each young man should have a greater sense of freedom, should put his toe in many ponds, and should not in any sense "play priest." Human individuality has an autonomy and an integrity which should not be violated. The Church and society both profit when its citizenry get as much intelligent vocational guidance as possible, without too premature a forcing into a mold.

No one is proposing the complete abolition of the minor seminaries. However, they do need to be put in a much more subordinate role, with more reliance placed on the regular Catholic parochial schools and the public-school system as a feeding ground for vocations. It is hard to believe that the minor-seminary system will be able to cope with the vocational needs in the United States. There is no reason for the Catholic Church to be so negative and fearful about the vocational potentiality in ordinary school systems of our country. Further, the intense pressure to get boys into minor seminaries displaces the attention which the Catholic Church ought to be giving to vocational work at secular colleges and universities.

In the end, the minor seminary strategy is probably back-firing in two ways: it presents too stereotyped and too narrow a picture of the route to the major seminary; its drop-outs (those who do not continue to major seminary) may not be the best advocates of the priesthood.[23] The minor seminary is being re-evaluated on many counts. Its influence on vocations needs the most careful scrutiny. One conclusion is obvious: if the resources now devoted to minor-seminary life were more adequately scattered over a broader high-school and collegiate level, the results for vocations would be far more rewarding.

Two Proposals to Catholic Vocations Directors

One. In 1954 the Rockefeller Brothers Fund initiated a tremendously significant program for the recruiting of high-quality Protestant seminarians.[24] Its success has been so marked, and its assumptions so tested, that Catholics would do well to give it close attention. Its basic features can be modified to fit the Catholic vocational situation.

The Rockefeller Brothers Theological Fellowships are "trial-year" seminary awards, given on the basis of a stiff, nationwide competition to outstanding Protestant college graduates who, without such an award, probably would not have attended seminary. The fellowship covers the costs of the one complete school year. No Fellow is under any obligation to continue. The grant is, indeed, made to provide these men a more comprehensive view of the Church and its ordained ministries in order that the decision either to continue or not to do so may be a wise one. The assumption of the program is that there are a great many young men of academic competence and personal promise who, while seriously interested in theological matters, have either such a stock of misinformation about the church and the ministry or who have never really been challenged to think about it, that the normal recruitment channels and vocational appeals fail to touch them. The opportunity to spend a year in solid theological study, plus relevant field-work, parish situations, is one which has immense appeal. About sixty-five per cent of the Rockefeller Fellows continue beyond the first year of seminary.

There is nothing in the Catholic understanding of the call to Holy Orders which is at odds with this type of program. The Catholic Church, as with the classical Protestant reformed tradition, sees the act of ordination as involving both a personal conviction, an educational preparation and testing, and a call and confirmation by the Church.

Catholic vocational literature and campaigns have much to teach Protestants. But one of the weak points of the prevailing Catholic vocational strategy is that it does not take into account enough of the deep-seated vocational ambivalence which affects more and more young men as the educational system prolongs adolescence. On the whole, it is true that more Catholic young men than Protestant are "formed in the faith." The Catholic catechetical system, the parochial-school system, the powerful sense of in-group loyalty, has effectively promoted a steady supply of men for the priesthood. There is every reason to believe that this system is fast weakening, and there is even more reason to suspect that a very substantial number of the most qualified young Catholic group is never really touched by the usual vocational appeals. The minor-seminary system, plus the fact that the great majority of Catholic seminarians enter the major theologate without completing the B.A. degree, is a further barrier to recruiting. The worrisome number of seminary drop-outs ought to make the Catholic seminary fraternity even more eager to experiment with the trial-year type program. And what has already been said about the vast throngs of Catholic young men in non-Catholic colleges and universities should double this willingness.

The Catholic Church itself or a Catholic philanthropist would perform a noteworthy service by underwriting a Catholic version of the trial-year program. It can be done in two ways: either by granting a fellowship for a year's study at a regular major seminary, with suitable tailor-made counseling and course adjustments; or by establishing a special one-year program in connection with a university-related house of studies. The Rockefeller experience indicates that the latter will be more attractive to the potential Fellow. The usual sequence of courses must be waived, and the Fellows must be permitted a choice and balance of courses which will speak to their immediate personal and theological questions and still give a fair overview of the realities of Church and ministry. The details can be worked out by Catholic educators, if they see the plausibility of such a fellowship program. Its great merit is that, while it will not add quantitatively in significant numbers, it will attract a leaven of blue-ribbon human beings. There are also many laudable side-effects: 1) the paper work and interviewing in a national competition gives much depth insight into vocational dynamics, particularly the question, "Why are not more and better men thinking of the priest-hood?"; 2) Fellows attract other men who are impressed that outstanding members of their peer groups should give it a try; 3) those who do not continue in seminary will give significant lay service to the Church.

The implications of a Rockefeller type of trial-year pro-gram for Catholic seminary education would go far beyond the Fellows. One implication is that the major theology years be freed from too close a connection with minor and collegiate seminaries, that it be made more feasible for a Catholic graduate of a Catholic or secular college to enter major theology without backtracking. Another implication is that there is a wealth of Catholic students who have, during their college years, not planned on the priesthood and who have majored in economics, or history, or science, etc. This diversity of educational background is healthy in the clergy. Every effort should be made to encourage voca-tions among good men wherever they may be and whatever they may have studied in college.

Two. Catholic vocational endeavors would be much more effective if they were somehow more coordinated. Here again we find an illustration of an area where the Catholic Church is much more competitive than the Protestant churches. Vocational marksmen from hundreds of different armies—diocesan and religious—are shooting at the same Catholic targets. John Smith, a high-school senior, and John Jones, a college sophomore, both being promising Catholics, may be besieged by visits, literature, and various combinations of the hard and soft sell from a score of Orders as well as by the systematic urgings from their parish priests. Only a church with more men to choose from than it knows what to do with can afford the intramural competition now going on. It is bad enough within Protestantism. It is worse within the Catholic Church. The moral of this suggestion is not to eliminate the religious orders and communities (though the number of orders which can justify their existence is a story in itself), but to work out a more systematic method of cooperation.

The Protestant experience teaches two lessons with increasing clarity. First, there must be maximum regional and national cooperation between the churches as they endeavor to seek seminarians on college campuses. The campus administrators, chaplains, *et al.,* simply do not wish to be inundated with competing "salesmen." Secondly, more and more students can only be interested in the ministry of the Church of Christ, not *initially* in this or that seminary, this or that denomination. *Mutatis mutandis,* it probably is true that Catholic collegians will not be stopped in their tracks to think about the priesthood if the primary approach is to "consider the Paulists" or "think about being a Christian Brother," and the like. The *priesthood* of the Roman Catholic Church should be the priority. Priorities can be worked out only under a coordinated strategy. The first step here would seem to be the appointment, under the National Catholic Welfare Conference, of a National Director of Vocations.

Notes

1 "Vocations" is a peculiarly Catholic word. A person with a vocation is one called to be a priest, monk, or nun. Protestants do not use the word in this specific sense.

2 A word of appreciation is expressed here for the courtesies and cooperation offered the writer by the Rt. Rev. Godfrey Poage, C.P., Director of the Pontifical Office of Vocations. His books on vocational problems are well worth the reading.

3 The priest in the Catholic Church should be regarded as not the only normative Christian or as the sole generator of the Church, but as one of the chief sources of the Church's reproductive process.

4 See Godfrey Poage, C.P., and G.L. Lievin, C.Ss.R, *Today's Vocations Crisis* (Westminster: The Newman Press, 1962).

5 Even so, the priestless areas in the United States, when taken together, make up an area that is greater than France, Germany, and Great Britain combined. See Charles Schleck, C.S.C., "Vocations in Crisis," *NCEAB*, August, 1965, p. 569.

6 Figures taken from the 1966 *Official Catholic Directory* (New York: P. J. Kenedy & Sons).

7 The number of seminarians and ordinations in Protestant churches which expect a college and B.D. education as a prerequisite for ordination has been steady for the last ten years. However, this means that the supply is not keeping up with the proportionate increase in collegiate, national, and church population.

8 Report published at the motherhouse of the White Fathers in Rome.

9 *Priest and People,* p. 198.

10 The caricatured extreme of public image about "separateness" is found at the shrine in Lourdes where there are three public baths: one for women, one for men, a third for "priests and small boys."

11 "Why do Seminarians Leave the Seminary?", *NCEAB*, October, 1961.

12 Catholics in the United States form the largest body of college-educated Catholics in the history of the Church.

13 See the helpful article, "The End of the Newman Club" by Fr. Richard Butler, O.P., *Commonweal*, September 3, 1965, p. 627.

14 John J. Kirran, C.S.P., "The Newman Apostolate Is Not Enough," *Catholic World*, August, 1965, p. 300. The argument here is that the Church must go beyond Newman Club strategy to build a cadre of Catholic lay teachers who can win posts at the secular universities.

15 Rev. Joseph L. Quinn, *Catholic World*, December, 1965, p. 166.

16 Ernest Bartell, C.S.C., of the Department of Economics at Notre Dame, estimates that *65 percent of all of the income* of the American

Catholic Church goes to its parochial school system, grades 1–12. Add to that the cost of Catholic colleges, universities, and seminaries!

[17] The newsletter of the Pontifical Office for Religious Vocations, January, 1966, carried the following item: There are 2.9 million Catholic students in public grade schools in the United States and 1.1 million Catholic students in public high schools. This past year Msgr. Ralph Miller, Rector of the Diocesan Minor Seminary, Buffalo, New York, reported that only 3 out of 113 applications were from public schools. Many other dioceses and religious communities have reported the same thing. For this reason, Bishop John J. Wright of Pittsburgh told the National Convention of Diocesan Vocation Directors of America: "You must seek vocations where they are and as they are . . . This means more intensive efforts to find them in so-called secularized areas as public schools and secular universities, as well as among older people."

[18] For a fuller description of the minor seminary, see pp. 194 ff. of this volume.

[19] The average minor seminary has about 160 students, with a 1:10 faculty-student ratio.

[20] *Miraculous Medal Magazine,* Philadelphia, September, 1965, p. 21.

[21] Rev. Joseph Noland, "Why Seminarians Seek Elsewhere," *National Catholic Reporter,* December 22, 1965, p. 8.

[22] This debate is carried on, in no uncertain terms, in the volumes by Putz and Lee and by Stafford Poole. See also the following: Rev. J.F. McGrath, "Where Have the Young Men Gone?" *Clergy Review,* May, 1965; Msgr. James A. Hickey, "Vatican II and Its Proposals for Seminaries," published and privately circulated by St. Paul Seminary, Saginaw, Michigan, 1965; Cornelius Cuyler, S.S., "Minor Seminary Outcomes," Catonsville, Maryland, 1965.

[23] Under the leadership of Fr. Earl A. Eilts, Vocation Director, and of Dr. C. Kermit Phelps, clinical psychologist, the Kansas City, Missouri, diocese has carried out studies which give fairly good marks to minor seminaries on such issues as social adjustment. But even well-adjusted minor seminaries can scarcely justify the enormous investment of the Church.

[24] This program is administered by The Fund for Theological Education, Inc., 163 Nassau Street, Princeton, New Jersey.

8

The American Negro
Catholic Community:
Priest and People

In 1966 there were at least 20,000,000 Negroes in the United States. That is the equivalent of the entire population of Canada. In view of the size of this ethnic community, its crucial role in American democracy, and the challenge which it presents to the whole Christian community, any sober analysis of the future strength and integrity of the Roman Catholic Church in the United States must appraise the adequacy of the Catholic Negro priests (numbers, education, and placement after ordination), the supply of Negro seminarians, the dimensions of the Negro lay community, and the general response of the Catholic Church to the needs of Negroes in American society.

The Catholic Church in the United States was late in

addressing itself to the Negro community. In the nineteenth century the Church was so involved in fostering and protecting its massive waves of immigrants that it may be pleaded with some justification that it could not readily find the energy or the vision to seek for new members among the Negroes. The Catholic community at the time had more excuse, if anything, than the Protestant for neglecting the political and religious life of the Negroes:

> The Church of the colonial and pioneer periods was a small, persecuted body, made up, for the most part, of immigrants and families of lower-class means . . . The whole energy of this tiny, threatened body of scattered Catholics was spent in efforts to escape the public eye, so as not to excite the renewal of persecution . . . Such an unimportant and timid group could hardly have been expected to accuse the public conscience and to attack the deeply rooted social disease . . . Catholic higher education was in its infancy. As a result, the only intellectuals with enough aplomb to criticize social patterns and to champion new causes were converts such as Orestes Brownson and Father Isaac Hecker. If the American Catholic Church did not assume leadership in the nineteenth-century struggle for Abolition and Negro rights, it was because the Church itself had yet to produce confident and capable leaders.[1]

Immediately after the Civil War, the white Protestant churches displayed, at best, an attitude of benevolent paternalism toward Negro Protestants. It must be remembered, however, that much of the anti-slavery and abolition movement had strong Protestant origins, as did most of the post-Civil War support for higher education of Negroes in the South. Also, in the 1820's and 1830's hundreds of white Protestant missionaries had been working with Negroes. Even so, Negroes found that their religious life had to be developed in their own churches and not in the balconies of the white ones. By 1880, American Negroes were finding not only their major spiritual homes in their own Protestant churches, but also a keen sense of group identification, protection, and leadership—a fact which accounts for the massive leadership given even today, particularly in the civil rights movement, by the Protestant Negro pastors.

When the Third Plenary Council of the American Catholic Church met at Baltimore in 1884, it took cognizance of the estimated 125,000 Negro Catholics in the United States.[2] This Council decreed that the parishes of the United States henceforth take a special collection on the First Sunday of Lent for the work of the Church among Negroes. This income amounts now to almost $2,000,000 per year. The Third Plenary Council's concern for Negroes did eventuate slowly in a wider stirring of conscience and action, primarily among religious orders, most notably among the Holy Ghost Fathers, the Divine Word Missionaries, and the Josephite Fathers. These and a few of the sisterhoods began special apostolates to the Negroes.[3]

Particular tribute should be paid to the Divine Word Missionaries for their apostolate to the Negro community in the United States. This order has taken the most responsibility for encouraging Negro vocations. Both the Divine Word Missionaries and the Holy Ghost Fathers had missions in Africa. In 1906, when the pioneer German Divine Word Missionaries undertook their first Negro mission in the United States (in Mississippi), the prevailing ecclesiastical missions strategy was that congregations with African missions were best suited to understanding American Negroes. It was Congregation of the Divine Word which in 1923 founded the first seminary for Negro candidates. More than one third (62) of all Negro priests in the United States have been educated at Bay St. Louis. In 1934 the first four Negro priests educated at that seminary were ordained.[4] The seminary is now fully integrated.

Special cognizance must also be taken of the Commission

for the Catholic Missions among the Colored People and the Indians, headquarters in Washington, D.C. Organized in 1886 as a result of the Third Plenary Council, this Commission administers the funds collected through the annual contributions for this purpose, and some 800 priests, dedicated primarily to convert work among Negroes, are currently being supported. Usually this is carried on through local churches, school systems, and social facilities in predominantly Negro communities. The more than five hundred missions and parishes supervised by the Commission are located in 68 dioceses; as of 1965, the 52 schools connected with them had an enrollment of about 100,000 Negro pupils.

It is estimated that, as of 1966, there are about 780,000 Negro Catholics in the United States.[5] One out of every 56 Catholics is a Negro; one out of every 24 Negroes in this country is Catholic. Almost one fourth of all Negro Catholics are to be found in Louisiana. It is claimed that "of the various ethnic groups (Indians, Negroes, Orientals, *et al*) which compose the American population, it is the American Negro who is entering the Catholic Church at the fastest rate."[6] Negro accessions to Catholic Church membership are growing at a faster rate than the American Negro population as a whole.

What are the current figures regarding the number of Negro priests, seminarians, and religious in the United States? According to a very careful census[7] issued in November, 1965, there were 159 Negro priests in the total American priesthood of 59,000 (one out of every 3,100). By Negro constituency alone, this is one Negro priest for each 5,000 Negro lay Catholics.

The Negro vocations are divided as follows:

1. Secular diocesan priests: (two of these priests are military chaplains; four are overseas): 45.

2. Religious: these priests are found in 19 orders, of which the main ones are Divine Word (62), Benedictines (18), and Josephites (9). Ten of these 114 priests are serving overseas, and a dozen are teaching in seminaries: 114.

3. Major seminarians: about 70

4. Brothers: about 200.

5. Sisters: about 1,100.

It is startling to notice that 70 per cent of the Negro priests are in religious communities. Nationally, the distribution of all priests is about 60 per cent diocesan and 40 per cent religious, percentages which the distribution of Negro priests more than reverses. This reversal can be attributed to the fact that the Negro apostolate has been carried on largely by religious communities. Furthermore, in the words of Fr. Charles D. Burns, S.V.D., Rector of the seminary at Bay St. Louis:

Another consideration is the placement of the Negro priest after ordination. Some diocesan bishops would be at a loss (are at a loss) as to an assignment for their Negro priests. If little effort or advance has been made in the integration of diocesan parishes, the bishops of such dioceses are in for trouble. A mature Negro youth knows about this placement problem and is discouraged from entering such a diocesan set up. Religious life, moreover, offers a poor Negro aspirant a modicum of security in his youth and especially in old age. He cannot be guaranteed this security as a diocesan priest.

Even though most of the religious do part-time parish work, the number of Negro priests manning the diocesan parish is, when contrasted with the urban concentration of Negro Catholics, like dew on the Sahara. Negro diocesan priests are currently stationed in twenty-five dioceses, only six of which have two or more priests: Chicago, New York, Raleigh, Brooklyn, Lafayette, La., and Alexandria, La. This indicates a severe lack of Negro priests in the large cities.

There can be no doubt but that an increase in vocations from any minority and ethnic group depends directly on the number of priests with whom young men of such a group can identify. Furthermore any significant increase in Negro vocations must be correlated with the population centers of American Negroes.

The absence of a significant number of Negro priests in the urban centers means also that the Catholic Church cannot play, as much as it may wish to do so, its fair share in the current struggle to win fair play for Negroes. Furthermore, in addition to the extenuating circumstances of the nineteenth century, the Catholic Church has been kept somewhat under the wraps in the civil-rights struggle by 1) cautious canon-law chanceries,[10] 2) the lack of social-ethics courses and related field work training in seminaries, and 3) the above-indicated lack of an adequate supply of Negro priests.

At this point it is necessary (but not for merit-badge purposes) to compare and contrast the Protestant American Negro community with its Catholic counterpart in order to understand better the strengths and weaknesses of the Christian Church, both Catholic and Protestant, among American Negroes.

There are two reasons why statistics regarding American Negro Protestants are unreliable:

1) They are badly out of date. Of the six predominantly Negro denominations, only two cite membership figures gathered since 1960, and all of them are making educated guesses.[11] Not one of these denominations operates effective central departments on a national scale. Not one has a national "Department of the Ministry." Thus, there is no one who really knows very much either about the size of their membership or the numbers of their clergy.

2) Although six denominations claim 90 per cent of the Negro Protestant membership in the United States, no one has assessed the effect upon membership of the vast migration of Negroes from rural to urban areas over the past twenty years. There is evidence to suggest that many of those who have so migrated do not resume active church membership.

Taking into account the above uncertainties, a fair guess would be that there are probably no more than 11,875,000 Negro Protestants in the United States. This figure includes available estimates for the six leading Negro denominations (c. 10,500,000), plus about 725,000 who are members of the smaller Negro churches, plus those in the predominantly white denominations, including the Central Jurisdiction of the Methodist Church (650,000).

In contrast to the Negro Protestant clergy, the Catholic Church is fortunate in that all of its priests have a formal seminary education. This stands in sharp contrast to the double standard of Protestant denominations, and it reflects the seriousness with which the Catholic Church regards educational preparation.

The Negro Protestant denominations have suffered from the lack of educational standards to such an extent that probably no more than eight per cent (4,000) of the estimated 50,000 Negro pastors with charges have both a college and a graduate-seminary education. This crippling situation can be laid very substantially to decades of cultural deprivation under a white hegemony.[12]

The poor educational standards have been exploited by the extremist congregational autonomy of Negro Baptist churches in particular, wherein the local congregation is so normative that almost any man who feels that he is "called" can form his own congregation. One result of this has been that many Baptist Negro pastors in effect preside over hereditary fiefdoms. There is probably no other sector of American Protestantism in which pastors wield so much influence over congregations.

When such a role is abused and when such posts are filled by incompetent men, it only makes it the more difficult to persuade the well educated Negro college student to attend seminary. If the Negro Protestant does attend, he (like his Catholic opposite) is still faced with a parish placement problem of discouraging proportions.

The Negro Protestant experience underlines the Catholic leadership dilemma: Negro ministers obtain the best response from Negro communities (this is not a subtle argument, however, for maintaining segregated congregations), and if there are not enough Negro clergy leading and sharing the burdens of their people, it is far from adequate compensation to have white clergy, much as they may help.

Notes

1 V. Rev. Bernardin Patterson, O.S.B., in *Our Sunday Visitor,* July 26, 1964, p. 5.

2 There are no reliable statistics as to the number of American Negroes at that time. Estimates by reputable historians range from four to eight million!

3 Olmstead estimates that, in 1906, fewer than one percent of American Negro Christians were Roman Catholics. See Clifton E. Olmstead, *History of Religion in the United States* (Englewood Cliffs: Prentice-Hall, 1960), p. 408.

4 The first Negro priest to be ordained in this country was the Rev. Charles Uncles, S.S.J. He was ordained in the Baltimore Cathedral by Cardinal Gibbons in 1891. He spent most of his life as a professor at the Josephite seminary, and there he died in 1933.

Bishop Harold Perry, Auxiliary Bishop of New Orleans, is a graduate of the Bay St. Louis seminary. He is the only American Negro bishop in the twentieth century. Fr. James Healey of Portland, Maine, became the first American Negro bishop. He served in the episcopacy from 1875 to 1890.

[5] See the Annual Report of the Commission for Catholic Missions among the Colored People and the Indians, Washington, D.C., 1965. That estimate was 748,000, to which must be added an annual accession of about 30,000.

[6] Hubert Singleton, S.V.D., "The Catholic Church and the American Negro," in *Word in the World*, 1965, p. 176.

[7] Prepared by Charles D. Burns, S.V.D., Bay St. Louis, Mississippi.

[8] The latest accurate count was 64 in American major seminaries in 1962. See Hubert Singleton, S.V.D., "Negro Candidates for the Priesthood in the U.S.A.," *Divine Word Messenger*, April, 1962.

The best single and continuing source of information about Negro priests are the publications of S.V.D.: *The Divine Word Messenger,* and *The Word in the World.* See also *The Serran* for February-March, 1964; and *Sign,* November 1964, and the Annual Reports of the Commission for Catholic Missions among the Colored Peoples and the Indians.

[9] The same warning holds true for the Protestant churches. It is only the Negro communities in the ten largest cities in the United States which are predominantly Protestant.

[10] This is illustrated in recent months in the summary treatment given Catholic priests who have been strong civil rights leaders or who have been protesting foreign policy. The outraged reactions of many Catholic clergy and laity to this over-weening paternalism is indicative of a new type of Catholic protest against some clerical leadership.

[11] The National Baptist Convention of U.S.A., Inc.; the National Baptist Convention of America, the Progressive National Baptist Convention, Inc.; the African Methodist Episcopal; the African Methodist Episcopal Zion; the Christian Methodist Episcopal. By 1916 the wholesale withdrawal of Negroes into their denominations was finished, and 90 per cent of Negro Christians were in these denominations.

[12] It has only been within the last three years that the American Protestant churches and seminaries have taken an *outgoing* responsibility for seeking Negro seminarians. The best single reference article on this is "Crisis in Church Negro Leadership," by C. Shelby Rooks, *Theology Today,* October, 1965. Much of what he has to say is good homework for Catholic theological educators as well.

9

Fitly Joined Together:
An Ecumenical Reflection

The Catholic and Protestant Churches in the United States are in an enviable ecumenical environment. There is no religious establishment. There is no load of anti-clericalism. There is an ethos of ready cooperation. Even better, there is an astounding eagerness to go beyond cooperation to genuine ecumenical engagement. In 1870, Catholic Archbishop Purcell of Cincinnati declared, "All we want is a free field and no favor." Now there is a free field and a favoring wind.

In the Catholic seminaries, with very few exceptions, there is a readiness to talk, to visit, and to learn. With a charitable instinct which honors both parties, Protestants and Catholics increasingly feel in their souls, in a fashion still awkwardly expressed, the common affinity in Christ. This brotherhood is rooted in Christ and is not primarily a "hang together rather than separately" instinct prompted by the crises of the world. But insofar as a world hostile or indifferent to Christ serves to bring Christians together, then the members of Christ's Church are now ready to make the most of it.

The last fifty years of Protestant ecumenical activity[1] have washed out much of the dirt and accretions of Church history and have prepared Protestants for a refreshing and realistic relationship to a Roman Catholicism which, only in the past five years, has opened up with breathtaking ecumenical rapidity. *De Ecumenismo* is one fine flower of that development.

It is manifestly clear that seminarians who are educated for an ecumenical age will be the future priests and ministers who in their communities will be able to deal constructively with the challenges and opportunities of a more self-conscious Christian brotherhood. There are some seminaries, fewer and fewer each year, within the Catholic world, which have not faced up to ecumenical realities. The graduates of such schools will find it frustratingly hard to adjust to an ecumenical atmosphere. Such men will tend to become defensive or to hide behind the out-of-date moats and towers built during the nineteenth century. On the other hand, there are Catholic seminaries, particularly those with strong foreign missionary concerns and those (often religious orders) with lively theological and liturgical emphases, which are very much *au courant* in ecumenical affairs. If a generalization must be ventured, it appears that the diocesan seminaries are curiously lagging, though there are many heartening exceptions.

How can seminaries contribute their fair share to ecumenical advance?

There is a satisfying increase in the number of student-body interchanges. One form of this is the "floating seminar" which moves back and forth from Catholic seminary

X to Protestant seminary Y. Sometimes these are set up on a course-credit basis, meeting once a week. There is also the growing number of special lectures, colloquia, dinner meetings, and occasional gatherings on a set topic.

Protestant seminaries in the last twenty years have had a phenomenal growth in courses and departments of ecumenical studies. No field of subject-matter has grown faster.[2] This approach is now becoming more slowly evident in Catholic seminaries. One problem for the Catholic schools is that they find it more difficult unilaterally to change curriculum requirements.

Furthermore, and this ecumenicity comes through the back door of regular courses in theology, Bible, or history, a very impressive number of Catholic seminarians are acquainted with Protestant theologians, especially contemporary figures such as the Niebuhrs, Barth, Tillich. On balance, it is doubtful if as many Protestant seminarians are comparably acquainted with Bernard Haring, Schillebeeckx, Congar, Küng, or Rahner. A major ecumenical advance is in the making—whether or not it is thought of as "ecumenical" in the programmatic sense—as increasing numbers of Protestant and Catholic seminarians study theology and the Bible with serious and sustained attention paid to the best scholars in both camps. Protestants would be amazed and delighted to know how many of the most prominent Protestant biblical scholars are common class room names in so many Catholic seminaries.

The interchange of faculty is proceeding steadily. Yale, Harvard, and the University of Chicago divinity schools have recently engaged prominent Catholic scholars. Vanderbilt University is establishing a chair of Roman Catholic studies. There is a most promising inter-confessional involvement at the Graduate Theological Union in Berkeley. The Benedictine seminaries at Collegeville and St. Meinrad's are scenes of regular ecumenical dialogue. Kenrick Seminary in St. Louis invites Protestant theologians to lecture. There is a long list, of which the foregoing are only examples, of systematic faculty sharing and exchange. This type of professional courtesy will have many beneficial effects. One such benefit will be the disappearance of the old polemical apologetic: those dreary relics of the sixteenth and seventeenth centuries in which the teacher leveled the ranks of the opposition with a gatling gun made in a theological assembly line from pre-fabricated categories. This type of apologist, if Catholic, enjoyed nothing so much as dropping a 12-point Methodist on the dead run; or, if Protestant, drawing a bead on conspiring Purple Prelates. Nothing could be deader or more irrelevant to the new generation of seminarians than looking for fire in such old ashes.

The time has come for more sustained visitation of seminaries—i.e., a one-month "live-in" (one month to one semester) by Protestant seminarians who would be invited to share the daily schedule at a Catholic seminary, and *vice versa*. There is no better way to get inside the mind and heart of the other man than to live, study, eat, play, and pray with him for a time. This is not an ecumenical Trojan horse. It is asking Christians to take seriously all that was implied when Pope John XXIII said to the Jews, "I am Joseph, your brother." Such personal visitation would add incalculably to the manners and predisposition for ecumenical life in post-seminary pastorates.

Where seminaries of traditions are close together, they are able to experiment in ecumenical ventures of unusual promise. The hat should be doffed, for instance, to The Association of Theological Faculties in Iowa, Inc. This is a formal confederation of colleges and seminaries, both Protestant and Catholic, in the Dubuque-Iowa City area, for the purpose of 1) providing theological and philosophical interchange, 2) strengthening graduate programs, 3) sharing faculty resources, 4) common pursuit of ecumenical goals.

As the ecumenical impulse is conjoined with the academic attractions of the large university community, there will assuredly be a quick increase in the closer and closer affiliation of seminaries of various traditions. The demands of first-rank scholarship call for a supporting environment of adequate library resources, a diversified faculty, an ample supply of good students. These demands cannot be met in seminaries which are too isolated and withdrawn. The ecumenical movement has released transforming impulses which are frustrated when whole communities of Christians are kept incommunicado by ancient history and archaic institutionalization. Both the scholarly and the ecumenical momentum of our times will bring seminarians together. They in turn, as priests and ministers, will thus be able, over the years, to weave Protestant and Catholic threads into a more durable fabric.

Within the last year there have been two ecumenical projects launched in the United States which have enormous implications for Christian unity and theological education.[3] The first is the proposed Ecumenical Center for Roman Catholic Study in the City of Rome, described in detail in the first chapter of this volume. The second project was formally announced in January, 1966, and concerns the Institute for Higher Religious Studies at the University of Notre Dame. It is propitiously designed to fill a scholarly void, and, more significantly, it is being carried out under Roman Catholic initiative—a fact which should not pass unnoticed in the history of American Christianity.

The Notre Dame Institute will be located in an attractive building of its own and will be the gathering place for able scholars from various religious backgrounds. These persons will be residents, some permanent faculty, some annual visitors. They will have no formal teaching duties. They will be free to pursue research and to work together as they see fit. It will not be a graduate school for advanced-degree study, but a center for very promising younger post-doctoral students and for scholars with established reputations. The University of Notre Dame will provide over-all direction, but the policies of the Institute will be determined by the Governing Board, the membership of which will include Catholic and Protestant scholars on a parity basis. This Institute marks a necessary stage in the coming-of-age of ecumenical scholarship in the United States. It embodies the scholarly approach to religious study by providing a stage for completely free and critical conversation and writing. It upgrades theological study in general by establishing the highest possible standards. Any professional field needs such a stimulus; theology has lacked even one such in the United States, since the seminaries have been compromised as centers of "pure theological research" by the necessity for degree and professional work. Ecumenical statesmanship, given such an exciting opportunity as this, surely requires that Protestants especially rally round this Institute, support it financially, and not duplicate it.

Insufficient attention has been paid to the ways in which Protestant and Catholic theological seminaries may be more mutually helpful and even partially integrated. Seminaries in each tradition can now begin to plan much more systematically and hopefully about the future in ways which go beyond occasional exchange of teachers and students. In 1966 the School of Theology at Fordham University and the Union Theological Seminary announced a small but significant step in this direction, when a plan for systematic interchange and recognition of faculty was revealed. Another beginning step, in addition to the type of cooperation mentioned elsewhere in this chapter, would be for a selected group of Catholic students—perhaps accompanied by their own priest-supervisor—to spend a semester or a year at a Protestant seminary, and *vice versa.*

But the pace of ecumenical advance and scholarly coop-eration will very quickly go beyond such toe-in-the-water approaches to a resounding high dive in the deep water (with a splash heard 'round the world). As a mere test-case illustration, consider St. Optimus Seminary, an entirely fanciful, but not unrealistic model of what the future may hold by way of a more thoroughgoing integration of Protes-tant and Catholic seminary resources:

St. Optimus is a creation of four bishops who, in concert with their four existing diocesan seminary faculties, decided to respond affirmatively to the permissiveness and challenge of the Vatican II *Decree on Priestly Training*. St. Optimus is a new regional diocesan seminary. The four diocesan seminaries were closed and were moved to St. O's new campus, now enlarged to handle about 400 seminarians. St. O. is owned legally by the bishop of the diocese in which it is situated, although the other three bishops take *ex officio* two-year terms as presiding officer of the Board of Trustees. Each diocese contributes its fair share of the costs.

St. O. is in New Haven, Connecticut, immediately adja-cent to Yale University and Yale Divinity School.[4] The Yale Corporation had evidenced interest in attracting a first-rate Catholic scholarly community and had quietly let such bait dangle in the Catholic theological community (question: Which bishops nibbled?). Yale then made an attractive offer of land, and an agreement was concluded along the follow-ing lines:

1. St. Optimus retains final autonomy over its own destiny.

2. All entering seminarians must have the B.A. degree or its equivalent from a fully accredited college or university.

3. They must meet admissions standards commensurate with Yale's graduate schools.

4. The faculty, while chosen by St. Optimus, naturally will

be appointed according to the standards expected by an outstanding university. This is not a matter which is "policed" by Yale, but is the result of St. Optimus' own academic respectability.

5. St. Optimus will be a fully accredited member of the American Association of Theological Schools.[5]

6. All the libraries, facilities, classes, etc. of Yale are available for St. Optimus in return for a minimal financial consideration—and *vice versa* for Yale students doing work at St. Optimus.

7. Yale Divinity School and St. Optimus carry on mutual consultations regarding faculty appointments. St. Optimus, for example, has one of the world's leading scholars in Patristics; thus Yale Divinity School will use him rather than hiring a less able man of its own. Yale Divinity School, in turn, is furnishing St. Optimus with an exceptionally able Old Testament teacher. One result of these academic reciprocal trade agreements is that St. Optimus' entire faculty is about one half the size it would have to be were the seminary an independent and isolated one.

8. St. Optimus gives an S.T.D. degree for four years graduate professional training for the parish priesthood. The diploma bears both the Yale and the St. Optimus seal.

9. All Ph.D. degrees are granted solely by Yale, whose graduate faculties do the examining.

10. All courses, excepting those special ones (*sola Catholica*), which are required to meet the dogmatic requirements of the Holy See, are jointly planned by St. Optimus and Yale Divinity School.

A profile of the student body at St. Optimus reveals that

1. Two thirds have come from secular campuses, either public or private.

2. One third has come from Roman Catholic colleges and universities.

3. They have majored as undergraduates in a wide variety of disciplines.

4. More than half had entered college not definitely planning on the priesthood.

5. About 20 per cent drop out of seminary.

A profile of the St. Optimus faculty reveals that

1. About one half are lay scholars (including two women).
2. One Sister teaches on it.
3. All have the Ph.D. or its equivalent.
4. About one fourth did graduate work in Rome, the others mostly in the United States—a few in England, Germany, France, etc.
5. They are guaranteed the same sabbatical schedules, secretarial help, etc. as the majority of the Yale University faculty.
6. The faculty advances up the regular academic ranks (instructor to full professor). If an instructor or an assistant professor serves four years without being judged worthy of advance, he is dropped. In short, there is proper academic competition.

The strong Roman Catholic concern for spiritual formation will be maintained. While the schedule of a major secular university will not permit the same *horarium* found in most independent diocesan seminaries, there is no reason why a disciplined, liturgical, Eucharist-centered, communal life cannot be carried on. Undoubtedly, such a seminary as St. O. will interpret spiritual formation in a broader and more flexible pattern, giving more opportunity for student initiative and freedom, with less emphasis on rules, bells, and the military-manualistic type of formation. But one of the finest contributions of St. O. to the secular world of learning (and to Yale Divinity School) will be the presence of a dedicated worshipping community which defines its main purpose, in the words of the *Decree on Priestly Training,* "as living the Paschal mysteries."

The curriculum of St. Optimus will be characterized by these factors:

1. Fewer classes—perhaps three courses and two seminars per week. But in any event, not an overdose of routinized classroom hopping. Courses will be carried on at graduate level, with a maximum amount of independent and honors work.

2. During the first two years there will be a heavy concentration on biblical and theological matters.

3. Throughout the school year and during the summer there will be carefully supervised field-work (apostolic activity). Much of this can be correlated with the Yale Divinity School— especially the clinical training programs at the Yale Hospital and the Psychiatric Center.

4. During the last two years the seminarians will be permitted to move into areas of specialization.

5. There will be a maximum advantage taken of the many lectures, concerts, symposia, etc., of the University.

The Board of Trustees of St. O. will be a working Board. It will include a *majority* of competent laity. It will grant the Senior Faculty and Rector the right to determine academic policy, to elect its own Dean of the Faculty and its own "Committee on Committees." The Trustees will provide for regular visiting committees of prominent educators, both Catholic and non-Catholic, to criticize and to recommend.

In conclusion, this may be an "ideal" seminary, but there is nothing utopian about it. Its general form is in keeping with many types of graduate and professional schools. It would be no more expensive (probably less) than operating three or four small and weaker diocesan seminaries. The dogmatic requirements of the Church can be met, particularly if the bishops concerned are determined to take maximum advantage of the episcopal prerogatives granted by Vatican II. The greatest point of stress and strain, assuming the prior episcopal cooperation, probably would be with those who wish everything now taught in the philosophy years also to be taught at St. O. Even this is not an insuperable obstacle. It may be that a fifth year would have to be added—but hopefully not.

The key question is one which would have to be addressed to the Catholic hierarchy: "Can the Catholic vision of priestly training be carried out under such an inter-confessional scheme at a secular university?" *Far more than seminary education is involved in the answer!* For if the answer is affirmative, a whole new avenue of logic and action is opened up with Roman Catholicism.

From the Protestant side, while there would be stress and strain enough, it is *now* possible, given adequate financing, to integrate such an education. The Catholic response is far less certain. The uneasiness would not be due to a lack of ecumenical spirit or lack of charity, but to the deeply rooted assumptions about the "dogmatic protection" of seminarians and, secondly, to probing questions about spiritual formation. But leaders within both scholarly communities must continue to raise this possibility. What a breathtaking advance it would be if something like it could be tried!

The ecumenical possibilities emerging from a growing Catholic participation in the American Association of Theological Schools have been considered. Suffice it to say that this type of professional and scholarly fraternity is a perfect illustration of the goals of ecumenicity: the natural working together of Christians from varying backgrounds in a common effort to strengthen Christ's church.

The National Council of Churches of Christ in the United States is giving a growing and systematic attention to Roman Catholic affairs, some of which have direct implications for theological education. The Division of Christian Unity is in touch with Catholic ecumenical and theological leaders and follows closely seminary developments. The Department of Ministry and Parish Life sponsors regular contacts with Catholic seminary leaders and with those concerned with vocations. The Missionary Research Library of the National Council and the Maryknoll seminary are in frequent and beneficial touch with each other. These are but samples of what is bound to be an expanding rapprochement. It may be that the day is here when the National Council ought to establish a regular office for Roman Catholic matters.

On the Catholic side there is a veritable crescendo of ecumenical activities at the diocesan level. Unfortunately it does not fall within the purview of this book to go into parochial ecumenicity, but one thinks immediately of the work of Cardinal Shehan in Baltimore, of Cardinal Ritter in St. Louis, of Bishop Wright in Pittsburgh, and of Bishop Helmsing in Kansas City, as pleasing harbingers of what will undoubtedly become a normative pattern of Catholic life.

As one moves about among American Catholic and Protestant seminaries, the threshold of ecumenical expectation rises at a geometric rate of speed. It is at the seminary level that one can make the most accurate evaluation of what is and what is not possible, for here much of the ceremonial curtsying and ecumenical ritual is quickly dispensed with as students and faculty hurry forward to get at the facts of agreement and disagreement. There is little playing with the "you're nice, too" or "my religion is as good as yours" forms of pseudo-ecumenicity. Christian growth in unity is plagued by the "gee whiz" school of ecumenics which, having suddenly discovered long-lost Christian brothers, wants an ecclesiastical marriage without benefit of sober courtship. At the other extreme, genuine ecumenical advance has been agonizingly slow because of church leaders whose mind-set was formed by historical differences no longer relevant. The present generation of seminarians, given half a chance, will overtake and outrun all of us.

Dr. James Sylie, Professor of Church History at Union Theological Seminary, Richmond, Virginia, whose studies in the American setting for Roman Catholicism have made him one of the most competent Protestants in that field, has divided the history of Protestant-Catholic relations roughly into three periods: *The Monologue of Hostility* (c. 1750–1800); *The Debate of Distrust and Defense* (c. 1800–1890); *The Dialogue of Mutual Respect and Candor* (c. 1890–present).[1] Seminary communities are pace-setting in their ecumenical influence and potential. There is no excuse, under Christ, for any seminary with any ecumenical pretensions to continue to live in either of Dr. Smylie's first two eras. Indeed, another era in Protestant-Catholic relations has already dawned in certain circles, as it did some time ago within the larger circle of Protestant ecumenicity, namely, *The Era of Critical Unity*. This is a sizable step beyond mutual respect and candor, and it is meant to describe that deep companionship and affection which unites all Christians. It is a relationship which is forgetful of stylized ecumenical protocol, goes beyond comparative ecclesiologies, and is desperately eager to make a common witness without always stopping to ask, "Should I say this to my Catholic friend?" or "Will my Protestant colleague like this?" Things are said and done, painful or not, just because Christians must say them and do them. It is to this degree of critical unity that seminaries have much to offer. The spread of this *entente critical* among future clergy is as happy an ecumenical hope as one can imagine.

Notes

[1] A good one-volume survey of the ecumenical movement is Norman Goodall, *The Ecumenical Movement* (New York: Oxford University Press, 1961).

It is fascinating to observe that at the First Assembly of the World Council of Churches in Amsterdam in 1948 there was no Roman Catholic participation. At the Second Assembly at Evanston in 1954 there was more Catholic interest but still no official Catholic response (several Catholic priests had literally to be smuggled in, since Cardinal Stritch of Chicago had declared the Assembly off limits). By the time of New Delhi and the Third Assembly in 1961, there were official Catholic observers. At Vatican II the Protestant observers enjoyed a red carpet treatment, and now there are so many Protestant-Catholic ecumenical activities going on that it is impossible to keep count.

[2] For a more detailed analysis of this growth, see Keith Bridston and Walter D. Wagoner (eds.), *Unity in Mid-Career* (New York: The Macmillan Company, 1963), chapter 10.

[3] A third Protestant-Catholic-Orthodox graduate ecumenical study center, with location and financing still unsettled, is under discussion.

[4] Needless to say, this is pure fancy. I use Yale because it is the type of university (private, non-sectarian, and with a Protestant seminary) which would provide a fine setting for St. Optimus.

[5] The criteria for such membership may be found in the current literature of the A.A.T.S.

[6] "Phases in Protestant-Roman Catholic Relations in the United States," *Religion in Life,* Spring, 1965, p. 528 ff.

Appendix 1

Catholic Seminaries:
Logistics and Manpower

This appendix is written for the Protestant in particular, who will find the Catholic seminary system strange and difficult to understand. The Protestant system of theological education parallels the dominant pattern of American education: i.e., it is a graduate professional school which one enters after graduation from an accredited college or university. Most ministers are ordained after three years of such study and receive the B.D. degree. They are not called seminarians until they are admitted to such a professional school.

The Catholic educational preparation for ordination is more complicated. Originally imported from Europe in 1791 (the founding of St. Mary's Seminary, Baltimore, Md., the Catholic pattern thus conformed to seventeenth-century Sulpician models. Until recently these seminaries maintained a self-sufficient existence apart from the dominant American educational and accreditation patterns.

There are two types of Catholic seminaries: *major and minor:*

1. A *major* seminary (usually referred to as Major Theology) is a school preparing young men for the priesthood and which teaches all or any part of the last six years prior to ordination. The first two years of this are called *Philosophy,* the second four years are called *Theology.* Together, they include grades 15 through 20.

2. A *minor* seminary is a school training young men exclusively for the priesthood which teaches all or part of the first six years prior to major seminary. This includes high school and junior college years (grades 9–14).

In contrast to most Protestant ministers, the vast majority of Roman Catholic priests in the United States did not attend regular public or parochial high schools, followed by college or university, but began and continued their education within minor and/or major seminary systems.

Minor and major seminaries may be either *secular* or *religious.*[1] A diocesan seminary is operated by a bishop for the education of prospective secular clergy. A religious seminary is operated by a religious order for its prospective secular clergy. A religious seminary is operated by an order for its own prospective members. Occasionally a bishop will ask an order to educate both religious and secular. Under Canon Law each bishop has been expected, if at all possible, to operate both a minor and a major seminary.[2]

In the United States both minor and major seminaries are organized under either the "6–6" or the "4–4–4" plans.[3]

	"6–6"	
High School	— 4 years	
Junior College	— 2 years	Minor Seminary
Philosophy	— 2 years	
Theology	— 4 years	Major Seminary

	"4–4–4"
High School	— 4 years
Collegiate Seminary	— 4 years
Theology	— 4 years

It is not necessary that a seminarian begin his education in minor seminary, but the minimal length of the curriculum required for ordination was fixed by The Third Plenary Council of Baltimore (1884): "In all seminaries the course of study shall embrace not fewer than six years, two of which shall be devoted to the study of philosophy and four to that of theology."

Men desiring to enter a religious order take an additional one or two years of *novitiate* before entering the last four years of Theology.

A growing trend in the last fifteen years has been the number of seminaries shifting away from the old-style European "6–6" system to the "4–4–4" system which corresponds chronologically to the prevalent American educational pattern.

The curricular offerings at seminaries are largely determined by tradition and by the *Ordinationes* of the *Deus Scientiarum Dominus* and, more recently, by Vatican II decree *On Priestly Training*. Following the "4–4–4" plan, an entirely typical curriculum looks as follows:[4]

High School years:

Religion	Physics
Latin	Chemistry
Greek	Geography
English	History
Mathematics	Natural History

College years:

Logic	Theodicy
Cosmology	Ethics
Psychology	Natural Law
Epistemology	Philosophy
Ontology	

Theology years:

Fundamental Theology
Dogmatic and Sacramental Theology
Moral Theology
Scripture

Patristics
Christian Archeology
Canon Law

In addition, Hebrew, Greek, Liturgy, Ascetics, Oriental Theology, Sacred Music, Homiletics, are taught as supplementary courses with some options.

Statistical Analysis of Catholic Seminaries in the United States (*1965–66*) [5]

TABLE 1. NUMBER AND KINDS OF DIOCESAN AND RELIGIOUS SEMINARIES

MAJOR	Diocesan	Religious	Totals	Grand Total
Philosophy (Upper Division, College)	–	16	16	
Theology	9	57	66	
Philosophy and Theology	18	49	67	
	27	122		149
MINOR				
High School	33	90	123	
Junior College	6	30	36	
High School and Junior College	28	24	52	
Special Latin/Delayed Vocations	1	4	5	
	68	148		216
MAJOR-MINOR				
College	8	37	45	
High School and College	4	3	7	
High School and Philosophy	–	1	1	
High School and Theology	–	1	1	
High School, Jr. College, Theology	–	5	5	
Jr. College, Philosophy, Theology	1	1	2	
College and Theology	5	11	16	
12 Years	7	5	12	
	25	64		89
	120	334		454

All of these seminaries are staffed by 5036 clerical and lay faculty, including administrators and persons involved in the spiritual formation of candidates. A number of institutions share the faculty of a nearby high school, college, or seminary.

The total number of seminaries employing the 4–4–4 organization increased from 220 to 254 since 1963–64. This trend may be expected to continue.

More than 38 per cent of the total number of seminaries were founded after 1949, with 63 seminaries founded in the past five years.

TABLE 2.   CANDIDATES FOR THE PRIESTHOOD, 1965–66

	Diocesan	Religious	Uncommitted	Totals
High School	13,024	8,042	435	21,501
Junior College	5,392	3,162	6	8,560
Special Latin/Delayed Vocations	191	223	–	414
Novices	–	2,321	–	2,321
Total Minor	18,607	13,748	441	32,796
Philosophy	3,549	2,738	3	6,290
Theology	5,461	3,455	–	8,916
Scholastics	–	1,144	–	1,144
Candidates studying abroad (except in institutions already included)	319	492	–	811
Total Major	9,329	7,829	3	17,161
Grand Totals	27,936	21,577	444	49,957

Of the 45,681 seminarians in U.S. seminaries, 5937 diocesan candidates and 231 candidates for religious orders live at home and attend as day students. About 1100 of these seminarians are from abroad and will be returning home.

According to reports from diocesan chanceries and religious provincians, 1137 diocesan priests and 1122 religious priests were ordained during 1965.

Two thirds of the major seminaries have less than fifty students each.

The average faculty-student ratio is one to thirteen.

Twenty-four diocesan and 47 religious institutions plan accreditation in five years or less. Ninety-six institutions not accredited in their own names send their students to accredited institutions for all or part of their academic program. Forty-eight seminaries are departments or extensions of accredited institutions. A total of 36 seminaries are cooperating in the training of students.

TABLE 3. COMPARISON IN REGIONAL ACCREDITATION,
1963–64 and 1965–66

	Accredited Departments 1963–64	Accredited Departments 1965–66
High School	17	33
Junior College	8	8
Senior College or Philosophy	2	2
College	20	21
Theology	8	12
	55	76

In 1966 in the United States there were 36,419 secular priests and 22,774 religious priests.

Notes

1 *Secular clergy* are subject to a diocesan bishop and are devoted to ordinary parochial and administrative work. They are bound by celibacy and make a promise of obedience to their bishop. *Religious clergy* belong to a religious community or order and are immediately subject to a religious superior. They take vows of poverty, chastity, and obedience.

2 Canon 1354, § 2. (With episcopal approval, however, there is now a movement toward the regionalization of seminaries.)

3 A third possibility (which can be termed "other organization") is a variation of the 6-6 or 4-4-4; e.g., 6-2-4. Also, all Jesuit seminaries, with their unusually long pattern of study and teaching before ordination, would be classified as "other."

4 This curriculum outline is the one adhered to by the Pontifical Catholic University, Washington, D.C., in its own work and as a basis for affiliation requirement.

5 The data in this summary are taken from the annual survey questionnaires sent by the N.C.E.A. to all diocesan seminaries and religious houses of formation training candidates for the Catholic priesthood in the United States. The summary includes Mt. Carmel College in Ontario, the North American College in Rome, and the American College at Louvain, all of which train candidates for the United States exclusively.

Appendix 2

Rome for the Protestant Scholar

All of Rome is a University. From the Janiculum Hill to the Trevi Fountain, from the Vatican City to suburban Nemi, there is no other place in the world where, within a radius of ten miles, there is so much to be offered any scholar interested in the history, thought, art, and archeology of the Christian church.

Yet the Protestant scholars of America (indeed, of most of the world) scarcely have begun to mine the riches of Rome. There are several obvious reasons why this has been so, to our shame. Following the land-mark school of church history, aided by our distance from the Continent, Protestant scholars have neglected patristics and pre-reformation history. It also has been natural that Protestant scholars, as academic blood called unto confessional soil, followed the pilgrimage paths to Oxford and Cambridge, to Heidelberg and Marburg, to Geneva and Edinburgh. Graduate theological communities in the United States and Canada know well the faculties of such cities, the library collections, and under whom a dissertation is to be written. Finally, few Protestant students are equipped with ecclesiastical Latin and with Italian. The result has been that the monumental scholarly and esthetic riches of the Eternal City have been neglected beyond any excuse.

But we are now in a new era of church scholarship and theological inquiry—an era which will be characterized by increasing reciprocity between Roman Catholicism, Orthodoxy, Anglicanism, and Protestantism. This means that the American Protestant scholarly community must do more to encourage and prepare its graduate students and theological faculties to respond to a wider range of scholarly challenges, particularly those offered by Roman Catholicism and Orthodoxy. Response to such a challenge will mean that the City of Rome will be a prime center for such study, perhaps *the* center. One sure result of Vatican II, and it is already evident, is marked increase in the number of non-Roman Catholics desiring to study in Rome. No ecumenical evaluation, incidentally, of Vatican II should minimize the implication of this trend.

There are so many schools and libraries directly related to theological education in Rome that this chapter is offered as a guide to such students and faculty as may be interested. So far as is known, this chapter is the first attempt to summarize a few of the *whats, wheres,* and *hows* of study in Rome for non-Catholics.[1]

In addition to whatever help this chapter itself may provide, anyone planning to study in Rome should follow a few practical suggestions. If at all possible, talk with someone who has lived and studied in Rome. There are many Catholic priests who have spent from two to six years in Rome, and who have many insights to share. Scholars in other than theological areas can be of help also—men and women who have studied, for example, in such a place as the American Academy. Also, the Vatican City each year publishes the *Annuario Pontificio.* This is a Who's Who and What's Where of people and institutions and offices related to the Holy See. *The Foyer Unitas,* a Roman Catholic center near the Vatican, is a rendezvous of cordial hospitality and help for all scholars and visitors with serious ecumenical and research concerns. Protestants in particular should avail themselves of the good offices of the Waldensian. Theological Faculty, near the Piazza Cavour, less than a mile from St. Peter's. This Faculty is a knowledgeable group of Protestants (in close touch with the Secretariat for Promoting Christian Unity) which knows its way around Rome, has a good library, and which can save the novitiate scholar weeks of wasted time and motion. The Waldensian librarian has his diploma from the Vatican Library.

Beyond the Waldensian Faculty, the Vatican Library, and the University of Rome—heretofore the customary stops for Protesstant scholars—there is a whole other world of scholarly resources which has not been tapped by Protestants, scarcely even known to them. These are the libraries and schools referred to in the following pages. These are the scholarly and spiritual homes for Catholic clergy the world around. Most of these communities of scholars and these libraries will welcome visiting scholars of all faiths. In a letter dated July 17, 1961, Cardinal Ottaviani, Secretary of the Congregation of the Holy Office, wrote to Cardinal Pizzardo, Prefect of the Sacred Congregation of Seminaries and Universities of Study, concerning the criteria according to which non-Catholic students can be admitted to the various Roman Athenaea:

I. A non-Catholic scholar should have a letter of introduction from a Catholic bishop "Concerning his moral correctness and his benevolent disposition toward the Church."

II. All other things being equal, the Orthodox student will be favored over the Protestant, and the Protestant over the Jew.

III. Such non-Catholic students will be dismissed if they abuse the trust placed in them, especially if they should make anti-Catholic propaganda.

IV. Non-Catholic students who take degree courses, passing the examinations, etc. will receive the degree without being required to swear to the Confession of Faith. In doctoral diplomas for such students the name of the Roman Pontiff will not appear.

In most instances the letter from a bishop should be sent to the Sacred Congregation of Seminaries and Universities of Study, Vatican City, with a carbon going to the Rector of the school to which one wishes to be admitted. As a matter of fact, due to the constantly improving ecumenical ethos, on the basis of such a letter a non-Catholic can enter almost any ecclesiastical faculty and obtain any degree offered, provided, of course, he is scholastically prepared and can understand enough Latin. It is also possible, on the basis of individual negotiation, to attend lectures as an auditor.

Since a working knowledge of Latin and Italian is absolutely essential, no one should attempt serious study in Rome who either does not have those tongues under control or who is not prepared to spend at least three or four months prior to the beginning of study in the brushing up of them.

Tuition costs are astonishingly low. The average tuition for an entire year is less than $100.00. Anyone planning to study in Rome should write for the catalogues of the appropriate schools.

All Roman Catholic seminarians "live in"; all university students "live out." There are no dormitories for non-Catholic foreign students. Catholic university students generally live in special Houses belonging to their Orders or Dioceses: e.g., the North American College.

There is no intention in this article to evaluate various Roman Catholic Schools. American graduate students will certainly notice that the mass lecture, *memoritur* method, still prevails; that the faculty student-ratio is not very good; and the standards for dissertations will vary tremendously, with the general standard a good cut below that of the better American graduate schools. But, having said that, there are unrivaled resources to be worked at, an impressive number of world-famous scholars to sit under, and the great advantage not only of sustained acquaintance with the Roman Catholic community but also the unmatched satisfactions of living in the City of Rome for a prolonged period.

THE ROMAN ATHENAEA

I.   *The Pontifical Universities*[2]

Pontifical University of St. Thomas Aquinas
Founded 1580 (Dominican)
Address: Largo Angelicum 1, Roma

FACULTIES: Theology, Spirituality, Social Sciences.

At least 15 nationalities are represented among the professors, with the Spanish and Italian being the largest groups. The same is true of the 700 students. There is one layman on the teaching staff. The only students who live within the University are the Dominicans. All others live out, about 60 of them at the Convitto, a nearby hostel operated by the University.

The Institute of Spirituality, founded 1950, is within the Faculty of Theology. It has a twofold aim: the promotion of ascetic and mystical theology, and preparing students to become Spiritual Directors.

The Institute of Social Sciences, founded 1955, has the following aims: to instruct the students in the social sciences, that they may do further work in them and eventually teach them; to promote social work; to serve as a link between moral teaching and the social sciences of the present day, making the connection more manifest (based on St. Thomas, but taking note of the modern situation); to foster research on the international aspect of social questions as it bears on the union of peoples.

The degrees of Baccalaureate, Licentiate, and Doctorate are given in all Faculties except the Spirituality Institute, where a diploma is offered.

The library contains about 112,000 volumes and is open to the public. All Dominican authors must send the library a copy of their work. The Pre-Reformation and University History collections are of special importance.

Pontifical Gregorian University
Founded 1582 (Jesuit)
Address: Piazza della Pilotta, 4, Roma

FACULTIES: Theology, Canon Law, Philosophy, Ecclesiastical History, Missionology, Social Sciences, Spirituality.

The 150 professors come from many nations, with the Spanish, French, and Italian being the largest contingents. There are some laymen on the professorial staff. About 2,600 students represent almost every nation; Italian, American, and Spanish are the largest student groups numerically. All students live outside the school. The language of instruction is Latin, except for the Institute of Social Sciences, where Italian is used. (The Rector describes Latin as "a difficulty, not a problem.") Non-Catholic students are easily admitted.

The usual degrees of Baccalaureate, Licentiate, and Doctorate are offered. The required years to obtain each, per Faculty: Theology, 5, 4, 2; Canon Law, 3, 2, 4; Philosophy, 4, 3, 2; Ecclesiastical History and Missionology, Licentiate after 2, Doctorate after 3; Institute of Social Sciences, 4, 3, 2.

Between reviews and collections, there are some 14 publications sponsored.

The library, containing some 400,000 volumes, as it presently exists was founded only after 1870 (as with so many other religious libraries, it was confiscated in the 1870's and can be found today in the National Library), It is the best philosophical library in Rome and the strongest in modern theology. It is open to the public.

Pontifical Urban University
Founded 1627
Address: Via Urbana VIII, 16, Roma

(This is the former Pontifical Athenaeum "de Propaganda Fide.")

The some 60 professors are of at least eleven nationalities, with Italians being the largest group. There are a few laymen on the teaching staff. The 900 students represent some 60 nations, especially African and Asian. All of the students live outside the school. Latin is the language of instruction, and non-Catholics would not only be accepted for both study and degrees, but would be warmly welcomed.

The University has primarily a missionary orientation. Thus there is the special Missionary Institute, and a new (1960) Institute for the study of Atheism, which has a special section devoted to the study of Marxist atheism. With the exception of the latter, which offers only a diploma for the 2-year course, the usual three degrees (Baccalaureate, Licentiate, and Doctorate) are given. In Theology these degrees are offered after, respectively, 2,4, and 5 years minimum of study; in Philosophy, after 2,3, and 4; in the Missionary Institute, after

1,2, and 3. Within the Missionary Institute there are courses and degrees in Canon Law.

Publications of the school include the review *Euntes Docete* and at least seven series of scholarly works.

The library is divided into two sections, the Major and the Minor. The Major, founded in the XVII century, is located at the Sacred Congregation Propaganda Fide, and contains well over 100,000 volumes. It is wholly unique. The Minor library is in the University and contains some 50,000 volumes. There are a few manuscripts and incunabula and missions collections, but the general character of the library is theological.

Pontifical Lateran University
Founded 1773
Address: Piazza S. Giovanni in Laterano 4, Rome

FACULTIES: Theology, Canon Law, Civil Law, Philosophy, as well as the Chair of St. Thomas, the Medieval-Patristic Institute of John XXIII, the Pastoral Institute "Jesus Magister," and the Pontifical Institute Leoniano of High Literature.

The 150 professors are of many nationalities, but the Italians are by far the most numerous. More than half belong to various Orders. No other Pontifical University has such a spread. Some 20 laymen teach, especially in the Civil Law department. In the Faculties, the usual three degrees are offered, Baccalaureate, Licentiate, and Doctorate— per Faculty, respectively, after these minimum years of study: Philosophy: 2,3,4; Theology: 2,4,5; Canon Law: 1,2,3. The Institutes offer diplomas after 2 years, with the following exceptions:

Institute of Moral Theology: requires a Licentiate to enter and grants Doctorate in Moral Theology after 2 years; *"Jesus Magister."* 2 years to Baccalaureate and 2 more to Licentiate in Religious Sciences; *Literature Institute:* diploma after one year, which does not grant the capacity to teach; the *Chair of St. Thomas* does not offer degrees, being essentially a special series of lectures.

The students number about 1500, considerably over half of whom are Italians. Fifty nationalities are represented in all, with the Spaniards being second.

It would not be excluded for non-Catholics to follow courses, and perhaps even to take a degree. No student lives at the University. Latin is the language of instruction.

The reviews published by the University include: *Divinitas* (Theology), *Apollinaris* (Law), *Studia et Documenta* (Law), *Aquinas* (Philosophy), *Corona Lateranensis* (series of the best dissertations), *Biblioteca Sanctorum, Spiritualitas, Scrinium Patristicum,* and *Collectio Philosophica Lateranensis.*

The library contains about 250,000 volumes, 25 important incunabula, and at least 5 important medieval manuscripts (12th–15th centuries). The private libraries of Gregory XIII and Pius IX are among the collections. The library is especially strong in theology, philosophy, and canon law (best canon law library, especially for older volumes). The juridicial sections of the private library of Pius XII comprise a noteworthy collection. It is possible for non-students to use the library with special permission.

II. The Pontifical Athenaea

Pontifical Athenaeum St. Anselm
Founded 1687 (Benedictine)
Address: Via di Porta Lavernale 19, Roma

FACULTIES: Theology, Philosophy, Liturgy, and Monastic Studies.

At least eleven nationalities are represented among the professors, though the largest number are of the German language (Germans and Swiss). There are two laymen on the teaching staff. The 330 students represent 45 nations, and 90 are Benedictines. Only the Benedictine students live in the school. The language of teaching is Latin, except for courses in Archeology and the Esthetics of Gregorian Chant, which are done in Italian. The usual three degrees are given: Baccalaureate, Licentiate, and Doctorate. In Theology the degrees are awarded after, respectively, 2,4, and 5 years minimum of study; in Philosophy, after 2,3, and 4; in the Liturgical Institute the Master's diploma is given after 2 years' study, presupposing the usual training in theology and philosophy. Holders of the Licentiate can obtain a Doctorate in Theology with specialization in Liturgical Studies after 2 years. The last two observations are also true for the Monastic Institute. The Institute of Monastic Studies specializes in the history and spirit of monasticism, especially the Benedictine forms, giving the opportunity to study organically and systematically the sources of monastic spirituality, law, history, and modern developments. A Diploma is granted after 2 years. Non-Catholic students may follow any courses and obtain any degrees, with the notation that the Doctorate in Theology might be difficult. The Tridentine Confession would not be required of them.

The major publications include *Studia Anselmiana, Rerum Ecclesiasticarum Documenta,* and *Corpus Consuetudinum Monasticarum.*

The library was founded in 1887 and contains about 50,000 volumes. Its character is basically theological and liturgical. It is open to the public. Female readers must have the volumes taken to them in a separate room.

Pontifical Antonian Athenaeum

Founded 1933 (Friars Minor)

Address: Via Merulana 124-B, Roma

FACULTIES: Theology, Canon Law, Philosophy.

The students, mostly of the Order, live in the school, though a number live out. Secondary education plus two years of scholastic philosophy are required for entrance. The majority of the professors are Italians, though at least thirteen other nationalities are represented.

The national distribution of the students is the same, and they number between 150 and 200.

There are two courses in Theology, the Minor and the Major. The Minor is a 4 year course, leading to the Licentiate. The Major course is for those students who have studied in the provinces for 4 years, and come to Rome for a fifth year, obtaining also the Licentiate. A Baccalaureate is given, after two years, but it is considered to be an insignificant degree. After Licentiate in either Minor or Major course, the Doctorate requires two further years.

Non-Catholics may follow courses, and with special permission from the Sacred Congregation of Seminaries and Universities may take degrees. Latin is the language of instruction.

Connected with the Athenaeum is the *Studium Franciscanum Biblicum* in Jerusalem, where the Biblical section of the Theological Faculty is established. The students are sent there for three years.

Publications include the review *(Antonianum),* and four collections *(Spicilegium Pontificii Athenaei Antoniani, Bibliotheca Pontificii Athenaei Antoniani, Studia Antoniana,* and *Editiones Pontificii Athenaei Antoniani).*

The library was founded at the end of the nineteenth century, and contains about 180,000 volumes. It has doubled in size in the last decade. There are collections of incunabula and Franciscan literature, and it is described by the Rector as of only slightly less quality than the library of the Gregorian. It is open to the male public. Female students may use the books in a separate room.

Pontifical Salesian Athenaeum
Founded 1940 (Salesian)
Address: Via dell'Ateneo Salesiano 1118, Roma

FACULTIES: Theology, Canon Law, Philosophy, Pedagogy, and Advanced Latin.

Both the Superior Institutes of Pedagogy and of Latin are unique. The students and faculty in both are rather heavily non-Salesians and many are laymen. The Latin professors are drawn primarily from various important secular Italian universities. The language of teaching is Latin, except for the Institute of Pedagogy, where it is Italian. The usual degrees of Baccalaureate, Licentiate, and Doctorate are given. Six specializations are possible within Pedagogy: Historical, Methodological, Catechetic, Psychological, Didactic, and Sociological. The two approaches to Pedagogy, speculative and sytematic, are united.

Both professors and students are representative of many nations, with the numerically largest group being Italian. There are about 400 students, two thirds of whom are Salesians. The Salesian students live in the school, which has just moved to a new 14 building complex. Accommodations for 400 are available. Non-Catholic students may follow course in any Faculty or Institute; they may take Institute diplomas, but permission is required of the Sacred Congregation of Seminaries and University Studies for them to take degrees in any Faculty.

Two reviews are published: *Salesianum* and *Orientamenti Pedagogici*. Further, each Faculty has its own series of publications: monographs, texts, and studies. The publications of the Latin Institute are still being planned.

The library is divided into two sections, the General Library, containing some 100,000 volumes, and the Latin Library with some 10,000 volumes. The collection of reviews (about 800) is very extensive, and the pedagogical review collection is the best in Italy.

III. *Theological Faculties*

Marianum Theological Faculty
Founded 1398 (Servites)
Address: Viale 30 Aprile 6, Roma

FACULTIES: Theology, Mariological Institute.

Of the 188 students last year, about 50 lived in the school, all of them members of the Order. There were 21 nationalities represented, with Italian, Spanish, and Colombian being the three largest numerically. The 28 professors are mostly Italians, with two English and one Spaniard. Three professors are laymen, all teaching in the Course of Philosophy (two years) which is held in Florence.

The usual three degrees are given: Baccalaureate, Licentiate, and Doctorate; the latter including a Doctorate in Theology with Specialization in Mariology. Properly qualified non-Catholics follow courses and attain any degree except the straight Doctorate in Theology. Whether the Tridentine Confession of Faith and the *Giuramento Antimodernistico* would be required of non-Catholics at the presentation of degrees is a problem not yet solved.

The language of instruction is basically Latin, though Italian is used when convenient.

Aside from Doctoral dissertations, the publications include the review *Marianum* and a collection of *Scripta Professorum*.

The library continues the tradition of the library of the Gandavense College (1666), is open to the public, and is divided into two libraries. The General Library contains about 80,000 volumes, of which 60,000 are in actual use; the others are rare books incunabula, and collections of canonization and beatification processes, Councils, and Greek and Latin Fathers. The Mariological Library contains about 10,000 volumes, and is quite specialized. There is, further, the Archives of the Order.

Pontifical Theological Faculty "San Bonaventura"
Seraphicum
Founded 1587 (Conventual Friars Minor)
Address: Via del Serafico 1, Roma

The students are only those of the Order, though qualified non-Catholics can be admitted to study, but may not take degrees. The students are selected by the Provinces of the Order, each Province sending the two or three best students they have. They number slightly over one hundred and are of many nations. The professors are predominantly Italian and include no laymen at the present. The students live in the school. Entrance requirements are a secondary education and two years of philosophy. The Baccalaureate degree is given after two years, the Licentiate after four, and the Doctorate after five. The language of instruction is Latin.

The publications of the Faculty include a review (*Miscellanea Francescana*), *Special Editions* (studies by professors), the collection *Selecta Seraphica,* and the printed doctoral dissertations.

The library contains about 50,000 volumes, with a capacity of 250,000. It was founded in 1587, and is theological. Special collections exist in the fields of Patristics, Councils, Canon Law, and Ecclesiastical History. The library is open to the male public. Female applicants for use of the library must study in another part of the building.

Pontifical Theological Faculty of Saints Teresa of Jesus and John of the Cross
Founded 1935 (Discalced Carmelites)
Address: Piazza San Pancrazio 5-A, Roma

FACULTIES: Theology and Spirituality.

The Institute of Spirituality is for students both of the Order of Discalced Carmelites and for the secular and religious clergy, as well as for religious and lay people who have completed secondary studies.

The degrees offered in the Faculty of Theology are the usual: Baccalaureate, Licentiate, and Doctorate. The first is awarded at the end of the second year of study, the Licentiate after the fifth, and the Doctorate after the sixth or seventh. The Institute of Spirituality awards a Master's Diploma after two years, which presupposes the usual courses of theology and philosophy prescribed by the Code of Canon Law and enables the holder to teach in ordinary ecclesiastical schools. Students not taking the Master's degree can obtain a lesser certificate of proficiency, which does not allow them to teach. Further, the Theological Faculty grants the Doctorate in the Spiritual Institute after two years of study. The Faculty students number about 85, while in the Institute they are slightly over one hundred (12 of the Order, and about 90 others, mostly religious, but also lay school teachers interested in higher spiritual formation). Entrance requirements for the Faculty are a secondary education plus two or three years of philosophy and theology. Non-Catholics are permitted to follow courses only in the Institute and, with permission from the Sacred Congregation of Seminaries and Universities, would be allowed to take degrees.

The principal material in the teaching of the Institute is as follows: Spiritual Theology; Biblical and Liturgical Spiritual Theology; Religious Psychology; Dogmatic-Spiritual Questions; History of Spirituality; the Spiritual Doctrine of St. Teresa of Jesus and St. John of the Cross. The secondary material includes: The Madonna in Our Spiritual Life; Mystic Phenomena; Spiritual Direction; Spiritual Exercises; the Spiritual Doctrine of the Teresian School; Methods of Prayer; the Main Spiritual Currents of Our Time; and Comparative Spirituality.

The publications of the school are of two types, periodicals and collections. The two periodicals are *Ephemerides Carmeliticae* and *Archivum Bibliographicum Carmelitarum*. The collections include the *Bibliotheca Carmelitica* (three series: *Textus, Studia,* and *Subsidia*) and "Fiamma Viva," a collection of conferences and studies of spiritual life.

The library contains about 100,000 volumes, mainly theological. There are special collections of the Church Fathers and on the Carmelite Order. It is open to the public.

IV. Institutes and Schools

Institute of Roman Studies
Founded 1925
Address: Piazza Cavalieri di Malta 2, Roma

The fundamental scope is to cultivate and contribute to the study of Roman history. There are 100 members of the Institute. The Institute works through publications, conferences and lectures, visits to historical sites, and the *Review*. There is an International Concourse of Latin Prose, with prizes given on Capitoline Hill, to promote the knowledge and use of Latin. A series of lessons (Superior Courses) is given each year. Anyone can become an Associate Member of the Institute, thus receiving the Review, admission to the Superior Courses, and many other benefits: purchase of publications at reduced prices, admission to any city museum or ruin in Italy, and other advantages to the student of Roman history. While this Institute is a non-ecclesiastical one, it is of considerable importance and certainly must be reckoned as one of the important scholarly centers in Rome.

Pontifical Institute of Oriental Studies
Founded 1917 (affiliated with the Gregorian University)
Address: Piazza Santa Maria Maggiore 7, Roma

Of the 37 professors, 23 come from Western Europe, 13 from Eastern

Europe, and one from India. Of the 103 students last year, 45 were regular students, 37 were guests, and 21 were preparing theses while not frequenting lessons. They represented 25 countries. Of the 103, 23 were Italians most of whom were guests (i.e., students of other institutions following selected courses) rather than regular students. There were six Orthodox students. Qualified non-Catholics, males only, may study here.

Latin is the language of instruction.

The usual degrees (Baccalaureate, Licentiate, Doctorate) are offered, one degree at the end of each of three years.

The publications of the institute include: *Orientalia Christiana Analecta, Orientalia Christiana Periodica, Anaphorae Syricae,* and *Concilium Florentinum.*

The library, founded in 1926, contains 86,200 volumes, and is mostly Oriental-Ecclesiastical in character. There are several collections of rare periodicals, especially complete sets of reviews unavailable outside Russia (collected by purchase when the communist Russian government sold them to raise money in their early years, collected by the Holy See and later deposited in this library). It is open to the public.

Pontifical Biblical Institute
Founded 1909
Address: Piazza della Pilotta 25, Roma

This Institute, like the Institute of Oriental Studies, is affiliated with the Pontifical Gregorian University.

The Biblical Institute has two faculties: one in Biblical Studies, the other in Ancient Oriental Studies. The total faculty is twenty-nine, including two professors at the division in Jerusalem.

In 1966 there were 292 students registered. The degrees offered are the Baccalaureate, Licentiate (or Master's) and Doctorate. The great majority of the students are in the Biblical Faculty. Latin is the language of instruction.

Qualified Protestants (and others) may study and/or audit the courses. Degree study under the Biblical Faculty entails the Licentiate in Roman Catholic Theology as a prerequisite.

The Institute publishes three periodicals:

Biblica: Quarterly devoted to scientific study of the Bible, with articles in English, German, French, Spanish, Italian, and Latin. Its annual supplement, *Elenchus Bibliographicus Biblicus,* is the most complete Biblical bibliography.

Orientalia: Quarterly devoted to scientific study of the ancient Near East. Includes as supplements *Keilschriftbibliographie* and *Bibliographie copte. Verbum Domini:* Bi-monthly. Non-technical Biblical review intended for the Catholic clergy. Latin.

The Institute also publishes books in various languages and certain series, such as *Analecta Biblica, Analecta Orientalia, Biblica* and *Orientalia.*

The library numbers about 160,000 volumes, over one third of which consists of the periodicals collection. The holdings in MSS. and incunabula are insignificant.

Pontifical Institute of Christian Archeology
Founded 1925
Address: Via Napoleone III 1, Roma

This school is open to any student, regardless of religion, and re-quires a Doctorate (in Theology, Letters, History, Canon Law, for example) as entrance requirement. A special course of Introduction to Christian Antiquities is open to those with secondary education, and is presented in English, French, and Italian. An examination may be taken at the end of the course and a diploma given.

The ordinary course of the Institute is three years in length, leading after each year respectively to the degree of Baccalaureate, Licentiate, and Doctorate. The language of instruction is Italian.

The three goals of the school are: (1) to form teachers and specialists in Christian Archeology, (2) to promote research by publication, and (3) to be the best scholarly center in the field by concentrating all possible instruments of study.

The usual number of students in any given year is about fifteen. The special introductory course draws about one hundred. At the present there are nine professors (2 French, 4 Italian, and one each Belgian, Canadian, and Brazilian.)

The publications of the school are particularly important. There are five collections: (1) *Monumenti dell Antichità Cristiana,* in two series, (a) *Monumenta epigraphica christiana saeculo XIII antiquiora, quae in Italiae finibus Adhuc exstant, iussu Pii XII edita,* and (b) *Corpus Basilicarum Christianarum Romae;* (2) *Roma Sotteranea Cristiana;* (3) *Inscriptiones Christianae;* (4) *Sussidi allo Studio delle Antichità Cristiana;* and (5) *Studi di Antichità Cristiana.* There is also the im-portant *Rivista di Archeologia Cristiana.*

The library is the leading one in the world on the subject. It was begun in 1925 by Monsignor Kirsch and it contains about 38,000 volumes. Among collections of special interest are the Wilbert aquarels of catacomb paintings, collections of excavation photographs, and the Vatican Copy of the Index of Christian Art of Princeton University.

Pontifical Institute of Sacred Music
Founded 1911
Address: Piazza S. Agostino 20-A, Roma

Lay students seem to have no difficulty in being admitted. Only in exceptional cases are non-Catholics admitted. Item 5 of the rules for students, contained in the catalogue of the school, reads: "The students who do not observe their duties or who render themselves guilty with regard to Catholic faith and morals, are liable to expulsion." Lay students must have completed classical Liceo and have done some previous musical study; those students working toward degrees must not be enrolled in any other Ateneo or Institute during the time of their musical studies.

Academic degrees offered: Baccalaureate, Licentiate, Master, Doctorate. There are seven basic courses: (1) Fundamental Course, 3 years, leading to Baccalaureate; this Course is prerequisite for all others; (2) Course of Gregorian Chant, 2 years, leading to Licentiate after first and Master after second; (3) Course of Sacred Composition, 4 years, leading to Licentiate after second, Master after fourth; (4) Musicology Course, 2 years, leading to Licentiate after first and Master after second; (5) Principal Organ Course, 4 years, leading to Licentiate after third and Master after fourth; (6) Liturgical Organ Course, 3 years, leading to certificate of proficiency; (7) Course of Perfection in Organ, six months, presupposing grade of Master of Organ. Doctorate in any field presupposes the Master's degree.

The school's strong point is organ study. According to the Secretary, similar opportunities are found in no other school.

In the year 1963–64 (last year in which statistics were available), there were 59 degree and 25 non-degree students, from many nations. The 16 professors for the year 1965–66 are predominantly Italian, with two each French and Spanish, and one German.

The library was begun in 1911, but systematic development started only with the arrival of the present President in 1947. There is no estimate available as to the number of volumes. The library is strong in Musicology and in periodicals (in at least seven languages—Latin,

English, Italian, Dutch, German, Spanish, and French—the best in Italy). There are sets of the *Opera Omnia* of many composers.

Vatican School of Paleography and Document Study
Founded 1884
Address: Vatican City

This school gives scientific preparation in the disciplines mentioned, leading to diploma of Paleographist-Archivist, which is recognized also by the Concordat with Italy. The school costs nothing to the students, who must have a doctorate—or very nearly so—to enroll. The course is two years. Three hours per week, with personal research in addition. The students number 30–40.

The *Corso Archivistico,* which is a one-year, four-hours-a-week course, also free, is for professional archivists, and grants a diploma. Secondary education is all that is required for admission.

V.   Seminaries in Rome

Major Pontifical Roman Seminary: Piazza S. Giovannin in Laterano, 4.
Minor Pontifical Roman Seminary: Viale Vaticano, 42.
Roman Pontifical Seminary for Juridic Studies: Piazza S. Appollinare, 49.
French Seminary (Pontifical): Via di S. Chiara, 42.
Lombard Seminary of SS. Ambrose and Charles (Pontifical): Piazza S. Maria Maggiore, 5.

VI.   National Colleges in Rome

There are more than thirty such colleges in and around Rome. A complete listing, with mailing addresses, can be found in *The Official Catholic Directory.* These colleges are essentially dormitories for visiting priests and seminarians attending the various schools of the Roman Athenaea. Some of the colleges have fine libraries, and a few of them conduct their own courses of study.

The North American College on the Janiculum Hill deserves special attention. This college was established by the bishops of the United States for the purpose of training and housing selected seminarians and graduate students in the Roman tradition. It was opened in 1858, and it was granted pontifical status in 1884. Most of the students attend the Pontifical Gregorian University. The college also offers its own special and supplementary courses. It is directed by an American Rector and staff.

VII. Waldensian Theological Faculty

Founded 1855
Address: Via Pietro Cossa 42, Roma

Dr. Waldo Vinay, Dean, Chair of Ecclesiastical History and Practical Theology

Dr. Bruno Corsani, Chair of New Testament

Dr. Alberto Soggin, Chair of Old Testament

Dr. Vittorio Subilia, Chair of Systematic Theology

The courses for 1965-66 included:

Old Testament: Hebrew Grammar, Old Testament Introduction, Old Testament Exegesis, History of Israel

New Testament: Biblical Greek, New Testament Introduction, New Testament Exegesis

Church History: Contemporary Catholicism, Waldensian History, Christian Archeology

Systematic Theology: New Testament Theology, History of Dogma, Dogmatics, History of Philosophy

Practical Theology: Pastoral Theology, Formal Homiletics, Church Law, Sacred Music

The students number about 30, some of whom are in residence abroad for their third year of study. The entrance requirement is a secondary education. The course lasts four years, with a fifth year obligatory at a theological faculty of either the English or German language. The degree granted, after examinations, thesis, and foreign study, is the Licentiate.

It should be noted also that the bookstore in the Waldensian building is the best place in Rome at which to buy non-Catholic writings.

LIBRARIES

This list contains the libraries in Rome and the Vatican which are of particular interest to scholars in the field of theological education and related disciplines. It is a selective list. The *Annuario Delle Biblioteche Italiane* lists more than two hundred libraries in Rome which are of higher quality than popular libraries.

Unless otherwise stated, each of the libraries is either open to the public or can be visited by a scholar armed with permission, which is usually easy to get. With suitable introductions and perseverance most scholars can get access even to those libraries which are here indicated as *reserved*.

One of the great scholarly deficiencies in Rome is that, even among the Roman Catholic libraries, there is no union catalogue. The Victor Emmanuel National Library is attempting such a catalogue for a few of the libraries, but after eight years and three volumes it is not even finished with the letter "A."

It is most important to call attention of Protestant and Catholic scholars to the *Biblioteca Della Facolta' Valdese Di Theologia* (Via Pietro Cossa 42). Founded in 1855, it contains 30,000 volumes and 10 incunabula. *It is the only academic library of Protestant theology in Italy today.*

In addition to the libraries listed here, readers should take note of the brief description of the libraries of the various Roman Athenea and Pontifical Universities, as previously mentioned in this chapter.

Vatican Libraries

Biblioteca Apostolica Vaticana (Citta del Vaticano, Cortiledi Belvedere) 900,000 vols., 8,000 inc., 62,000 mss. This is the Papal Library. Its history is very long and complicated. It is a library of universal culture, extremely rich in indispensable material for the study of codexes written in the most diverse languages and epochs. For patristic, liturgical, philological, and humanistic studies, it offers, as perhaps no other library in the world, copious and rare study materials. Rather rigorous admission requirements must be met (normally a doctor's degree is required—though this is an elastic requirement—as well as an introduction by an academic or scientific authority). Nothing is ever loaned, under pain of excommunication. Among the other priceless materials conserved there, the Codex B (Codex Vaticanus) of the New Testament must be mentioned. There are in use some 34 catalogues of its manuscripts and numerous catalogues of printed books.

Biblioteca della Basilica di S. Paolo (Via Ostiense 180) 80,000 vols., 54 inc., many mss. Important library for ecclesiastical and liturgical studies. It is reserved.

Biblioteca del Pontificio Collegio Russo di S. Teresa del Bambin Gesu' (Via Carlo Cattaneo 2) 10,000 vols. Theology, philosophy, and literature. Especially rich in Russian works not easily obtained today. Reserved to the personnel of the College.

Biblioteca del Römisches Institut der Gorres Gesellschaft (Citta del Vaticano, Via della Sagrestia 17) Unstated number of volumes. Especially rich library for Christian Archeology, ecclesiastical history (particularly the history of the Councils and of the Vatican Secretariat of State).

Non-Vatican Roman Libraries

Biblioteca Angelica (Piazza S. Agostino 8) 153,056 vols., 1041 inc., 2664 mss. Founded in 1614. Has collections of note, such as a Dante collection, and collections of laws of confraternities and pious works. There are numerous mss. from the Middle Ages. Prevailing character: ecclesiastical, theological, historical, philological, and literary.

Biblioteca Bertini Frassoni (Via dell'Anima 16) 40,000 vols., unstated number of mss. An old library specializing in heraldry and geneology. It is reserved.

Biblioteca Britannica (Via Quattro Fontane 20) 24,000 vols. A library of general culture.

Biblioteca Capranicense (Piazza Capranica 98) 20,000 vols., 9 inc., 4 mss. A library of general culture, though works of ecclesiastical culture predominate. It is reserved to the Capranica College.

Biblioteca Casanatense (Via S. Ignazio 52) 307,700 vols., 2035 inc., 5612 mss. Very rich in material of historical and theological nature, and religious thought in general. Other collections of note: music, theater, etchings, and poetry. The manuscript collection is of great value, as is that dealing with Rome and the Pontifical State. There are 13 catalogues.

Biblioteca d'arte Beato Angelico (Piazza della Minerva 42) 6,500 vols. Founded 1943; has a strictly scientific character in the interests of serving scholars of the history of art. Dedicated especially to medieval and modern art, both Italian and foreign, with special attention to sacred art in general, the art of the Christian East, and miniatures.

Biblioteca Dei Redentoristi Presso Il Collegio S. Alfonso (Via Merulana 31) 130,000 vols. Founded 1855. Important in the fields of religious culture, theology, morality, dogmatics, ascetics, and patristics, especially of the XVII and XVIII centuries. Reserved to the Fathers of the College, but accessible to scholars.

Biblioteca Dei Servizi Informazioni e della Proprieta' Letteraria Artistica e Scientifica della Presidenza del Consiglio del Ministri (Via Buoncompagni 15) 190,000 vols. Founded 1934. General culture library, with a collection of about 20,000 vols. in the fields of sociology and politics.

Biblioteca del Centro Culturale Francese (Piazza Campitelli 3) 28,000 vols. In existence since 1946. French literature.

Biblioteca del Centro Studi Saint Louis (Piazza S. Luigi dei Francesi 22) 10,000 vols. Founded 1943 to offer the scholar, especially the international ecclesiastical scholar, books and reviews useful for religious sciences, especially for the preparation of doctoral theses.

Biblioteca del Collegio Americano del Nord (Via Gianicolo 14) 10,000 vols. Philosophy, theology, Greek and Latin Classics. Reserved to the College.

Biblioteca del Collegio Belga (Via del Quirinale 26) 12,000 vols. Founded 1844, deals with the ecclesiastical sciences, and is reserved for students of the College.

Biblioteca del Collegio di S. Clemente Dei Domenicani Irlandesi (Via S. Giovanni in Laterano, Basilica di S. Clemente; Via Labicana 95) 5,300 vols., 20 inc., 10 mss. Founded 1677. Contains noteworthy collections of theological, philosophical, Biblical, and juridical works. A reserved library which can be frequented by scholars with permission.

Biblioteca del Collegio di S. Girolamo degli Illirici (Croati) (Piazza Augusto Imperatore 4) 7,500 vols. Founded 1901. Specializes in scientific works on the various ecclesiastical disciplines (theology, canon law, church history, Bible) and books in the Croatian and Slavian languages on history, philology, and general culture.

Biblioteca del Collegio dis S. Isidoro (Via degli Artisti 6) 25,000 vols., 20 inc., 300 mss. Founded 1625, has primarily an ecclesiastical and Franciscan character. A Franciscan Archive is annexed. Open with permission.

Biblioteca del Collegio di S. Lorenzo da Brindisi e dell'Istituto Storico Dei Minori Cappuccini (Via Sicilia 159; Via Boncompagni 71) 105,000 vols. Founded 1894. Contains works of ecclesiastical culture (theology, sacred scripture, canon law, history, philosophy), especially with reference to Franciscans and Cappuccins. Contains the largest collection of Cappuccin writings in the world (every Cappuccin writer sends in his work). Among the richest libraries dealing with Franciscan history and doctrine. The library is reserved.

Biblioteca della Camera Dei Deputati (Via della Missione 8) 500,000 vols. Founded 1848. General library, with special collections in history, politics, economics, and law. Open to members of the Italian parliament, others if accompanied.

Biblioteca della Casa di Dante (Piazza Sonnino 5) 7,500 vols., 20 incs., 4 mss. Founded 1920, a specialized Dante library. Open to scholars upon request.

Biblioteca dell'Accademia Americana (Via Angelo Massina 5) 63,000 vols. Founded by combining libraries founded in 1895 and 1905. Its main collections are in archaeology, classics, arts, and history. Open to members of the Academy and other scholars.

Biblioteca dell'Accademia Belga (Via Omero 8, Valle Giulia) 50,000 vols. Founded 1939 by combining libraries founded in 1904 and 1930. Medieval history, Belgian and Lowland history.

Biblioteca dell'Accademia Britannica (Via Gramsci 61, Valle Giulia) 45,000 vols. Founded 1901, specialized in archaeology, history, and the arts. Open by request.

Biblioteca dell'Accademia Dei Lincei e Corsiniana (Via della Lungara 10) 335,220 vols., 2,293 inc., 3,505 mss. Founded 1730. Islamic studies, archaeology, general culture.

Biblioteca dell'Accademia Filarmonica Romana (Via S. Pantaleo 66) 1500 vols., 275 musical mss., 650 printed scores, 4,200 assorted other musical works. Founded 1822. Of special note: collection of motets and madrigals 1552–1566. There are also about 6,000 loose sheets.

Biblioteca della Civilta' Cattolica (Via di Porta Pinciana 1) 286,000 vols., 20 inc. Founded 1850. General culture, with emphases on theology, philosophy, history, sociology, economy, literature, and art. The library is private, and only persons known to the Fathers or who have an introduction are admitted.

Biblioteca della Fondazione Marco Besso (Largo di Torre Argentina 11) 58,000 vols., 8 inc., 90 mss. Concerns especially Roman studies.

Biblioteca della Keats-Shelly Memorial Association (Piazza di Spagna 26) 7,000 vols. Best library in the world for the study of these poets, plus Lord Byron, and their friends.

Biblioteca della Pontificia Abbazia di S. Girolamo in Urbe (Via di Torre Rossa 1) 25,000 vols. Founded 1933. The primary scope of this Abbey is the revision and emendation of the text of the Vulgate. They are preparing a critical edition of the work. The library has a general character, but prevails in material necessary for the described studies, and further works of theology, ecclesiastical and monastic history, and religious sciences. It is not open to the public.

Biblioteca dell'Archivo di Stato e Archivi della Republica (Corso del Rinascimento 40) 20,000 vols., 496 mss. The manuscripts deal mostly with the Popes, the ecclesiastical institutions, and the city of Rome.

Biblioteca della Scuola Francese (Piazza Farnese, Palazzo Farnese) 140,000 vols. One of the richest libraries of foreign institutes in Rome. Has a special archeological and historical character.

Biblioteca della Societa' Filologica Romana (Piazza dell' Orologio 4) 8,000 vols. Strictly philological library, reserved to members or scholars presented by members.

Biblioteca dell'Associazione Archeologica Romana (Piazza Cenci 56) 10,000 vols. History, archeology, art history. Reserved for members.

Biblioteca dell'Istituto Archeologico Germanico (Via Sardegna 79) 70,000 vols. Founded 1830. Character: Ecclesiastic, theological; historical, juridical, philological, art. Independently of the Library there is a photographic collection containing 120,000 negatives and photographs of ancient works of art.

Biblioteca dell'Istituto Austriaco di Cultura (Viale Bruno Buozzi 113) 10,000 vols. History and art.

Biblioteca dell'Istituto Centrale del Restauro (Piazza S. Francesco di Paola) 9,400 vols. Specialized in books and articles regarding the restoration and conservation of works of art, art history, and the sources of art.

Biblioteca dell'Istituto di Pedagogio della Facolta' di Magistero dell'-Universita' (Via delle Terme di Diocleziano 10) 11,000 vols. Pedagogy.

Biblioteca dell'Istituto di Studi Orientali dell'Universita' (Città Universitaria, Palazzo Centrale) 23,000 vols. Oriental studies, Semitic languages, Sanskrit, etc.

Biblioteca dell'Istituto di Studi Romani (Piazza dei Cavalieri di Malta 2) 15,000 vols. Roman studies. There is also a photograph library, containing a collection of great importance of slides and negatives on Roman subjects. Also very noteworthy is the Central Catalogue of Roman bibliography, which has over 640,000 entries, listing works in libraries in all countries.

Biblioteca dell'Istituto Italiano di Studi Germanica (Via Calandrelli 25) 30,000 vols. Founded 1932. History, literature (also Nordic), philology, philosophy, pedagogy, art.

Biblioteca dell'Istituto per il Medio ed Estermo Oriente (Via Merulana 248, Palazzo Brancaccio) 15,000 vols. Founded 1933. Middle and Far Eastern history, literature, art, archeology, and religion. Over half the books are in Oriental languages. The sections dealing with China and Japan are especially rich.

Biblioteca dell'Istituto per l'Oriente (Viale Lubin 2—Villa Borghese) 12,000 vols. Founded 1921. Works relevant to the study of the Islamic Near East. Collections in European languages, and Arabic, Persian, Turkish, and Hebrew, which are not easily available in other libraries.

Biblioteca dell'Istituto Storico Germanico (Corso Vittorio Emanuele 209) 35,000 vols. Founded 1888. Scientific German literature on the Middle Ages, and modern times until 1800.

Biblioteca dell'Istituto Storico Italiano per il Medio Evo (Piazza dell'Orologia 4) 28,000 vols. Founded 1887. Medieval studies. Strong on Italy 500–1500.

Biblioteca dell'Istituto Storico Olandese (Via Omero 10–12) 17,000 vols. Founded 1904. National and artistic history of the Lowlands, their relations with Italy, and works on Rome by Lowlands authors.

Biblioteca dell'Istituto Svedese di Studi Classici (Via Omero 14) 16,231 vols. Founded 1926. Archaeological, classical, art history, ancient history, and classical philological studies.

Biblioteca dello Studentato Internazionale Dei Missionari Oblati di Maria Immacolta (Via Vittorino da Feltre 5) 25,000 vols. Ecclesiastical sciences; reserved.

Biblioteca del Museo Preistorico Etnografico Luigi Pigorini (Via del Collegio Romano 26) 25,000 vols. Specialized in studies of prehistory, paleoethnology and ethnology. Founded 1875.

Biblioteca del Pontificio Collegio Armeno (Via S. Nicolò da Tolentino 17) 5,000 vols. A small library, but rich in Armenian religious literature. Founded 1883. Reserved.

Biblioteca del Pontificio Collegio Germanico e Ungarico (Via S. Nicolò da Tolentino 13) 45,000 vols. Philosophy and theology.

Biblioteca del Pontificio Collegio Greco di S. Anastasio (Via del Babuino 149) 25,000 vols., 3 inc., unstated number of mss. Founded 1557. Particularly important collection of Greek liturgical works.

Biblioteca di Archeologia e Storia Dell'Arte (Piazza Venezia 3) 166,874 vols., 14 inc., 483 mss. Founded 1922. Archeology and art history. There are seven catalogues.

Biblioteca di Storia Moderna e Contemporantea (Via Michelangelo Ceatani 32) 98,000 vols. Founded 1923. Modern and contemporary history.

Biblioteca Hertziana (Max-Planck-Institut) (Via Gregoriana 28) 50,000 vols. History of medieval art especially.

Biblioteca Musicale di S. Cecilia (Via dei Greci 18) 146,000 vols., 5 inc., 6,707 mss. Founded 1584. Important musical library, with at least five catalogues.

Biblioteca Nazionale Centrale Vittorio Emanuele II (Via del Collegio Romano 27) 2,000,000 vols., 1876 inc., 5,667 mss. The library was founded at the unification of Italy, and the major element in its foundation seems to have been the confiscation of the libraries—at least 69 of them—of Roman religious orders which were suppressed in 1873. It has been further enlarged by the donation of many large collections, and today receives by a law a copy of every work edited in Italy, which accounts for its greatest present growth. There are 18 catalogues in use. Due to the presence of confiscated religious libraries, this Biblioteca has a special importance for ecclesiastical studies.

Biblioteca Romana (Piazza della Chiesa Nuova 18) 60,000 vols., 3 inc., 102 mss. Devoted entirely to Roman studies.

Biblioteca Romana A. Sarti (Piazza dell'Accademia di S. Luca 77) 33,115 vols., 174 mss. Founded 1877. Rich in the fields of art, architecture, and archeology.

Biblioteca Universitaria Alessandrina (Città Universitaria, Piazzale delle Scienze 7—Palazzo del Rettorato) 747,383 vols., 663 inc., 366 mss. Founded 1661. A general library, addressed primarily to the needs of students in the fields of literature, history, philology, philosophy, law, and the social and economic sciences. Receives a copy of everything printed in the province, and collects also many doctoral dissertations published by foreign universities. Nine catalogues are in use.

Biblioteca Vallicelliana (Piazza della Chiesa Nuova 18) 84,500 vols., 444 inc., 2,928 mss. The effective foundation of the library was in 1581, though it is in fact older. A library specialized in history in general and the history of the Catholic Church in particular.

Entrusted to the Vallicelliana is also the Biblioteca Romana di Storia Patria (40,000 vols., included in the number listed for the Vallicelliana above.) This is primarily a historical library for Roman-

Italian studies. Between the two collections, there are 14 catalogues in use.

Notes

1 No academic Baedekker, no ready handbook exists.

2 The title "Pontifical" means that the school is under the direct control of the Sacred Congregation of Seminaries and Universities and that it is canonically entitled to award degrees in the name of the Pope. In the United States there are four pontifical universities: De Paul University, Chicago; Georgetown University, Washington, D.C.; Niagara University, Niagara Falls, N.Y.; and the Catholic University of America, Washington, D.C.

Appendix 3

The Vatican II Decree
on Priestly Training

When the passage of time has given perspective on Vatican II it will, of course, be found that some of its documents received much more publicity than was warranted. Everyone at the Council had causes to forward and lobbying to do on favorite projects. Everyone naturally will evaluate the Council according to the attention given pet hopes and long nourished ambitions. The decree *On Priestly Training*, promulgated October 28, 1965, while it most certainly did not receive much public attention, will have a much more definitive impact on the shaping of the Catholic Church than is generally realized. A conciliar *decree* does not have the theological authority of a *constitution*, such as *De Ecclesia*, but it carries more canonical weight than a conciliar *declaration*—those three being the categories into which most Vatican II decisions were divided. As a decree, this document on priestly training takes precedence over, at any points where there may be differences, both *Sedes Sapientiae* and *Deus Scientarum Dominus*. Thus the Catholic-seminary enterprise around the world will be, or should be, directly and immediately affected by this decree. Furthermore, consonant with a basic thesis of this entire volume, the long-range nature and effectiveness of the Catholic Church, as of all churches, is very, very substantially prefigured in the patterns of theological education. Thus, in this decree one finds, for better or worse, crucial clues not only about the future shape of the Church, but also about how fast it will be able to move toward seminary reforms.

By far the most intriguing aspect of the decree is its permissiveness with regard to the educational autonomy of national episcopacies. Since Trent the custom has been to set the seminary styles from Rome. The seminaries in the United States, until quite recently, thus have been heavily influenced by Roman guidance working through seventeenth- and eighteenth-century Irish and French Sulpician models. But there is too much cultural and educational diversity in the world, too much necessity for a flexible correlation with prevailing national educational systems (the "6–6" system, for example, presents all kinds of hazards for American Catholic theological educators). Furthermore, neither S.C.S.U.S. nor any other Vatican authority has enough wisdom to regulate seminary systems, country by country, beyond the most elementary and dogmatic guidelines. S.C.S.U.S. can be and certainly will continue to be a key nerve center, clearing house, and help to seminaries; but this new national freedom is much to be applauded. One could argue, of course, that such freedom might permit a worse situation to develop in certain countries. On the whole, however, and most certainly in the United States, this green light for episcopal leadership is a boon. The American bishops—O'Boyle, Cody, and Lanke—who were on the Preparatory Commission for this decree, will now have a chance, in concert with a special commission of their American episcopal colleagues, to give pioneering leadership. It would be grievously disappointing if this commission did not take advantage of the writing and thinking about theological education now so apparent in faculty and administrative circles. The questions raised elsewhere in this book about the need for educational and administrative initiative *vis à vis* the episcopal control of seminaries now faces a classic test case. Bishops are harassed and overburdened men; they do not alway work as a team (one priest remarked, "We have bishops, but not hierarchy"), and most bishops in the United States are stronger in administrative and chancery matters than in educational and conceptualizing realms. If the American episcopacy will realize the exciting opportunity which is now theirs and, most especially, will openly solicit ideas and reforming procedures from their professional theological educators, and if they somehow will cooperate in national planning, it is fair to say that American Catholic theological education would soon set the pace for the entire Catholic seminary world. In any event, the *Decree on Priestly Training* removes any last and lingering excuse for not developing a strong and indigenous American seminary system.

The decree is encouraging in its open-ended approach to the place of St. Thomas Aquinas and scholasticism. There is no knowing, until such a day as the minutes of the preparatory commission may be published, what struggles went on about the normative role of the Angelic Doctor and the perennial philosophy. To the outsider it appears that Aquinas was given one curtain call and a medium-sized bouquet. Or, in another figure, he appears to have been a ping-pong ball which has been badly dented as a result of so much battering back and forth over the net of debate. In effect, the decree does not tie down a seminary curriculum to too much preoccupation with Aquinas, and it does urge that contemporary and relevant philosophies be cultivated. This non-doctrinaire note about Aquinas will be cheered by those educators who are eager to experiment with a closer integration of philosophy, theology, and biblical studies.

It is apparent, too, that the decree has been responsive to the current agitation for more seminary attention to modern psychology and the dynamics of human maturation. This has been a notoriously weak point in Catholic curriculums (due in part to the myopia about Freud).

This observer is quite pleased to note the leeway given to the age of ordination, encouraging with episcopal approval the postponing of ordination until well after the age of twenty-four. This suggestion is bound to help those seminarians who otherwise may decide too soon for celibacy and ordination.

Item by item, taken one at a time, there is little to argue with and much to praise.

But what judgement should be ventured about the *Decree on Priestly Training* as a whole? This sympathetic critic must say that it is only fair to good. It is not a great or monumental decree. It lacks the dimensions achieved by *De Ecclesia, De Ecumenismo,* by the Vatican II documents on religious liberty and on the liturgy. It is difficult, however, to see how thirty bishops and twenty-five *periti,* working four years (and more), could not have come up with a decree which more radically thinks through the nature of theological education in the twentieth century. The decree, of course, does not stand alone. It is supported and complemented by the documents on Christian education, on the priesthood, and by *De Ecclesia.* It is understandable that the preparatory commission was reluctant to legislate untried experiments or passing fads. It is a middle-of-the-road document. It is permissive and suggestive. It has all the appearance of too much patchwork and paste (Cardinal X wants this, and Bishop Y wants that). The decree does not appear to have been written by a first-rate educational theorist; it betrays no final pen held in the hand of an outstanding mind. Its permissiveness, it is true, will help bishops here and rectors there who do have imagination and courage, but its lack of challenge, of declarative majesty, weakens it to the status of helpful, but rather bland writing.

More specifically, it is disappointing in its silence about celibacy. No assumptions are questioned. This silence is the more curious since the decree was in final form before the Pope publically put the quietus on the conciliar debate on celibacy. Nor does the decree say anything new about the nature of spiritual formation and the methodology behind its achievement. Surely

Catholic concepts of spirituality, so central to seminary life, deserved a more thorough, even ruthless, re-examination. Also, the decree seems to go along with the prevailing assumptions about minor seminaries, encouraging more flexibility and openness, to be sure, but not giving the reader a sense of critical appraisal. The decree is alarmingly remiss in its lack of treatment of the "professionalization" of seminaries.

This *Decree on Priestly Training* was issued under a *vacatio legis,* with the understanding that any attempt to enforce it before June, 1966, was impractical. The American hierarchy probably will not be in a position to implement the decree much before the school year 1967–68.

The most haunting reflection deriving from this decree comes when one realizes that it is not a document commensurate with the significance and accomplishments of Vatican II. The Council of Trent set in motion monumentally effective forces because of what it said about seminaries. Vatican I, which adjourned prematurely, said nothing about seminaries. This Vatican II decree, while of encouraging potential, reached only about half the distance it should have covered.

The translation which follows was prepared by the National Catholic Welfare Conference, Washington, D.C.

DECREE ON
PRIESTLY TRAINING

INTRODUCTION

Animated by the spirit of Christ, this Sacred Synod is fully aware that the desired renewal of the whole Church depends to a great extent on the ministry of its priests.[1] It proclaims the extreme importance of priestly training and lays down certain basic principles by which those regulations may be strengthened which long use has shown to be sound and by which those new elements can be added which correspond to the constitutions and decrees of this Sacred Council and to the changed conditions of our times. Because of the very unity of the Catholic priesthood this priestly formation is necessary for all priests, diocesan and Religious and of every rite. Wherefore, while these prescriptions directly concern the diocesan clergy, they are to be appropriately adapted to all.

I.   The Program of Priestly Training to be Undertaken by Each Country

1. Since only general laws can be made where there exists a wide variety of nations and regions, a special "program of priestly training" is to be undertaken by each country or rite. It must be set up by the episcopal conference,[2] revised from time to time and approved by the Apostolic See. In this way will the universal laws be adapted to the particular circumstances of the times and localities so that the priestly training will always be in tune with the pastoral needs of those regions in which the ministry is to be exercised.

II.   The Urgent Fostering of Priestly Vocations

2. The duty of fostering vocations[3] pertains to the whole Christian community, which should exercise it above all by a fully Christian life. The principal contributors to this are the families which, animated by the spirit of faith and love and by the sense of duty, become a kind of initial seminary, and the parishes in whose rich life the young people take part. Teachers and all those who are in any way in charge of the training of boys and young men, especially Catholic associations, should carefully guide the young people entrusted to them so that these will recognize and freely accept a divine vocation. All priests especially are to manifest an apostolic zeal in fostering vocations and are to attract the interest of youths to the priesthood by their own life lived in a humble and industrious manner and in a happy spirit as well as by mutual priestly charity and fraternal sharing of labor.

Bishops on the other hand are to encourage their flock to promote vocations and should be concerned with coordinating all forces in a united effort to this end. As fathers, moreover, they must assist without stint those whom they have judged to be called to the Lord's work.

The effective union of the whole People of God in fostering vocations is the proper response to the action of Divine Providence which confers the fitting gifts on those men divinely chosen to participate in the hierarchical priesthood of Christ and helps them by His grace. Moreover, this same Providence charges the legitimate ministers of the Church to call forward and to consecrate with the sign of the Holy Spirit to the worship of God and to the service of the Church those candidates whose fitness has been acknowledged and who have sought so great an office with the right intention and with full freedom.[4]

The Sacred Synod commends first of all the traditional means of common effort, such as urgent prayer, Christian penance and a constantly more intensive training of the faithful by preaching, by catechetical instructions or by the many media of social communication that will show forth the need, the nature and the importance of the priestly vocation. The Synod moreover orders that the entire pastoral activity of fostering vocations be methodically and coherently planned and, with equal prudence and zeal, fostered by those organizations for promoting vocations which, in accord with the appropriate pontifical documents, have already been or will be set up in the territory of individual dioceses, regions or countries. Also no opportune aids are to be overlooked which modern psychological and sociological research has brought to light.[5]

The work of fostering vocations should, in a spirit of openness, transcend the limits of individual dioceses, countries, religious families and rites. Looking to the needs of the Universal Church it should provide aid particularly for those regions in which workers for the Lord's vineyard are being requested more urgently.

3. In minor seminaries erected to develop the seeds of vocations the students should be prepared by special religious formation, particularly through appropriate spiritual direction, to follow Christ the Redeemer with generosity of spirit and purity

of heart. Under the fatherly direction of the superiors, and with the proper cooperation of the parents, their daily routine should be in accord with the age, the character and the stage of development of adolescents and fully adapted to the norms of a healthy psychology. Nor should the fitting opportunity be lacking for social and cultural contacts and for contact with one's own family.[6] Moreover, whatever is decreed in the following paragraphs about major seminaries is also to be adapted to the minor seminary to the extent that it is in accord with its purpose and structure. Also, studies undertaken by the students should be so arranged that they can easily continue them elsewhere should they choose a different state of life.

With equal concern the seeds of vocations among adolescents and young men are also to be fostered in those special institutes which, in accord with the local circumstances, serve the purpose of a minor seminary as well as among those who are trained in other schools or by other educational means. Finally, those institutions and other schools initiated for those with a belated vocation are to be carefully developed.

III. The Setting Up of Major Seminaries

4. Major seminaries are necessary for priestly formation. Here the entire training of the students should be oriented to the formation of true shepherds of souls after the model of our Lord Jesus Christ, teacher, priest, and shepherd.[7] They are therefore to be prepared for the ministry of the word: that they might understand ever more perfectly the revealed word of God; that, meditating on it they might possess it more firmly, and that they might express it in words and in example; for the ministry of worship and of sanctification: that through their prayers and their carrying out of the sacred liturgical celebrations they might perfect the work of salvation through the Eucharistic sacrifice and the sacraments; for the ministry of the parish: that they might know how to make Christ present to men, He who did not "come to be served but to serve and to give His life as a ransom for many" (*Mark* 10,45; cf. *John* 13,1–17), and that,

having become the servants of all, they might win over all the more (cf. *1 Cor.* 9,19).

Therefore, all the forms of training, spiritual, intellectual, disciplinary, are to be ordered with concerted effort toward this pastoral end, and to attain it all the administrators and teachers are to work zealously and harmoniously together, faithfully obedient to the authority of the bishop.

5. Since the training of students depends both on wise laws and, most of all, on qualified educators, the administrators and teachers of seminaries are to be selected from the best men,[8] and are to be carefully prepared in sound doctrine, suitable pastoral experience and special spiritual and pedagogical training. Institutes, therefore, should be set up to attain this end. Or at least courses are to be arranged with a proper program, and the meetings of seminary directors are to take place at specified times.

Administrators, however, and teachers must be keenly aware of how much the success of the students' formation depends on their manner of thinking and acting. Under the rector's leadership they are to form a very closely knit community both in spirit and in activity and they are to constitute among themselves and with the students that kind of family that will answer to the Lord's prayer "that they be one" (cf. *John* 17,11) and that will develop in the students a deep joy in their own vocation. The bishop, on the other hand, should, with a constant and loving solicitude, encourage those who labor in the seminary and prove himself a true father in Christ to the students themselves. Finally, all priests are to look on the seminary as the heart of the diocese and are to offer willingly their own helpful service.[9]

6. With watchful concern for the age of each and for his stage of progress an inquiry should be made into the candidate's proper intention and freedom of choice, into his spiritual, moral and intellectual qualifications, into his appropriate physical and psychic health—taking into consideration also possible hereditary deficiences. Also to be considered is the ability of the candidate to bear the priestly burdens and exercise the pastoral offices.[10]

In the entire process of selecting and testing students, however, a due firmness is to be adopted, even if a deplorable lack of priests should exist,[11] since God will not allow His Church to want for ministers if those who are worthy are promoted and those not qualified are, at an early date, guided in a fatherly way to undertake other tasks. The latter should also be given sufficient direction so that, conscious of their vocation as Christians, they might eagerly embrace the lay apostolate.

7. Where individual dioceses are unable to institute their own seminaries properly, seminaries for many dioceses or for an entire region or for a country are to be set up and developed, so that the sound training of the students, which must be considered the supreme law in this matter, can be taken care of in a more effective manner. These seminaries, if they are regional or national, are to be regulated according to directives set down by the bishops[12] concerned and approved by the Apostolic See.

In these seminaries, however, where there are many students, while retaining a unity of direction and of scientific training, the students should be conveniently divided into smaller groups so that a better provision is had for the personal formation of each.

IV. The Careful Development of the Spiritual Training

8. The spiritual training should be closely connected with the doctrinal and pastoral, and, with the special help of the spiritual director,[13] should be imparted in such a way that the students might learn to live in an intimate and unceasing union with the Father through His Son Jesus Christ in the Holy Spirit. Conformed to Christ the Priest through their sacred ordination they should be accustomed to adhere to Him as friends, in an intimate companionship, their whole life through.[14] They should so live His paschal mystery themselves that they can initiate into it the flock committed to them. They should be taught to seek Christ in the faithful meditation on God's word, in the active participation in the sacred mysteries of the Church, especially in the Eucharist and in the divine office,[15] in the bishop who sends them and in the people to whom they are sent, especially the poor, the children, the sick, the sinners and the unbelievers.

They should love and venerate with a filial trust the most blessed Virgin Mary, who was given as mother to the disciple by Christ Jesus as He was dying on the cross.

Those practices of piety that are commended by the long usage of the Church should be zealously cultivated; but care should be taken lest the spiritual formation consist in them alone or lest it develop only a religious affectation. The students should learn to live according to the Gospel ideal, to be strengthened in faith, hope and charity, so that, in the exercise of these practices, they may acquire the spirit of prayer,[16] learn to defend and strengthen their vocation, obtain an increase of other virtues and grow in the zeal to gain all men for Christ.

9. The students should be so saturated with the mystery of the Church, especially as described by this Sacred Synod, that, bound to the Vicar of Christ in a humble and trusting charity and, once ordained priests, adhering to their own bishop as faithful helpers and engaging in a common effort with their fellow-priests, they bear witness to that unity that attracts men to Christ.[17] They should learn to take part with a generous heart in the life of the whole Church in accord with what St. Augustine wrote: "to the extent that one loves the Church of Christ, to that extent does he possess the Holy Spirit."[18] The students should understand most clearly that they are not destined for domination or for honors but are given over totally to the service of God and to the pastoral ministry. With a particular concern they should be so formed in priestly obedience, in a simple way of life and in the spirit of self-denial[19] that they are accustomed to giving up willingly even those things which are permitted but are not expedient, and to conform themselves to Christ crucified.

The students are to be made clearly aware of the burdens they will be undertaking, and no problem of the priestly life is to be concealed from them. This is to be done, however, not that they should be almost solely concerned with the notion of danger in their future labors, but rather that they might be more readily conformed to a spiritual life which more than in any other way is actually strengthened by the very pastoral work they do.

10. Students who follow the venerable tradition of celibacy

according to the holy and fixed laws of their own rite are to be educated to this state with great care. For renouncing thereby the companionship of marriage for the sake of the Kingdom of Heaven (cf. *Matt.* 19, 12) they embrace the Lord with an undivided love[20] altogether befitting the new covenant, bear witness to the resurrection of the world to come (cf. *Luke* 20,36),[21] and obtain a most suitable aid for the continual exercise of that perfect charity whereby they can become all things to all men in their priestly ministry.[22] Let them deeply realize how gratefully that state ought to be received, not, indeed, only as commanded by ecclesiastical law, but as a precious gift of God for which they should humbly pray. Through the inspiration and help of the grace of the Holy Spirit let them freely and generously hasten to respond to this gift.

Students ought rightly to acknowledge the duties and dignity of Christian matrimony, which is a sign of the love between Christ and the Church (cf. *Eph.* 5,32 ff.). Let them recognize, however, the surpassing excellence of virginity[23] consecrated to Christ, so that with a maturely deliberate and generous choice they may consecrate themselves to the Lord by a complete gift of body and soul.

They are to be warned of the dangers that threaten their chastity especially in present-day society.[24] Aided by suitable safeguards, both divine and human, let them learn to integrate their renunciation of marriage in such a way that they may suffer in their lives and work not only no harm from celibacy but rather acquire a deeper mastery of soul and body and a fuller maturity, and more perfectly receive the blessedness spoken of in the Gospel.

11. The norms of Christian education are to be religiously observed and properly complemented by the newer findings of sound psychology and pedagogy. Therefore by a wisely planned training there is also to be developed in the students a due human maturity. This will be made especially evident in stability of mind, in an ability to make weighty decisions, and in a sound evaluation of men and events. The students should be accustomed to work properly at their own development. They are to

be formed in strength of character, and, in general, they are to learn to esteem those virtues which are held in high regard by men and which recommend a minister of Christ.[25] Such virtues are sincerity of mind, a constant concern for justice, fidelity to one's promises, refinement in manners, modesty in speech coupled with charity.

The discipline of seminary life is to be reckoned not only as a strong safeguard of community life and of charity but also as a necessary part of the whole training formation. For thereby self-mastery is acquired, solid presonal maturity is promoted, and the other dispositions of mind are developed which very greatly aid the ordered and fruitful activity of the Church. Seminary discipline should be so maintained, however, that the students acquire an internal attitude whereby they accept the authority of superiors from personal conviction, that is to say, from a motive of conscience (cf. *Rom.* 13,5), and for supernatural reasons. The norms of discipline are to be applied according to the age of the students so that they themselves, as they gradually learn self-mastery, may become accustomed to use freedom wisely, to act spontaneously and energetically,[26] and to work together harmoniously with their fellows and with the laity.

The whole pattern of seminary life, permeated with a desire for piety and silence and a careful concern for mutual help must be so arranged that it provides, in a certain sense, an initiation into the future life which the priest shall lead.

12. In order that the spiritual training rest upon a more solid basis and that the students embrace their vocation with a fully deliberate choice, it will be the prerogative of the bishops to establish a fitting period of time for a more intense introduction to the spiritual life. It will also be their charge to determine the opportuness of providing for a certain interruption in the studies or of establishing a suitable introduction to pastoral work, in order that they may more satisfactorily test the fitness of candidates for the priesthood. In accordance with the conditions of individual regions it will also be the bishops' responsibility to make a decision about extending the age beyond that demanded at present by common law for the reception of sacred orders,

and of deliberating whether it be opportune to rule that students, at the end of their course in theology, exercise the order of deacon for a fitting period of time before being promoted to the priesthood.

V.   The Revision of Ecclesiastical Studies

13. Before beginning specifically ecclesiastical subjects seminarians should be equipped with that humanistic and scientific training which young men in their own countries are wont to have as a foundation for higher studies. Moreover they are to acquire a knowledge of Latin which will enable them to understand and make use of the sources of so many sciences and of the documents of the Church.[27] The study of the liturgical language proper to each rite should be considered necessary; a suitable knowledge of the languages of the Bible and of tradition should be greatly encouraged.

14. In revising ecclesiastical studies the aim should first of all be that the philosophical and theological disciplines be more suitably aligned and that they harmoniously work toward opening more and more the minds of the students to the mystery of Christ. For it is this mystery which affects the whole history of the human race, continually influences the Church, and is especially at work in the priestly ministry.[28]

That this vision be communicated to the students from the outset of their training, ecclesiastical studies are to be begun with an introductory course which should last for an appropriate length of time. In this initiation to ecclesiastical studies the mystery of salvation should be so proposed that the students perceive the meaning, order, and pastoral end of their studies. At the same time they should be helped to establish and penetrate their own entire lives with faith and be strengthened in embracing their vocation with a personal dedication and a joyful heart.

15. The philosophical disciplines are to be taught in such a way that the students are first of all led to acquire a solid and coherent knowledge of man, the world, and of God, relying on

a philosophical patrimony which is perennially valid[29] and taking into account the philosophical investigations of later ages. This is especially true of those investigations which exercise a greater influence in their own nations. Account should also be taken of the more recent progress of the sciences. The net result should be that the students, correctly understanding the characteristics of the contemporary mind, will be duly prepared for dialogue with men of their time.[30]

The history of philosophy should be so taught that the students, while reaching the ultimate principles of the various systems, will hold on to what is proven to be true therein and will be able to detect the roots of errors and to refute them.

In the very manner of teaching there should be stirred up in the students a love of rigorously searching for the truth and of maintaining and demonstrating it, together with an honest recognition of the limits of human knowledge. Attention must be carefully drawn to the necessary connection between philosophy and the true problems of life, as well as the questions which preoccupy the minds of the students. Likewise students should be helped to perceive the links between the subject-matter of philosophy and the mysteries of salvation which are considered in theology under the higher light of faith.

16. The theological disciplines, in the light of faith and under the guidance of the magisterium of the Church,[31] should be so taught that the students will correctly draw out Catholic doctrine from divine revelation, profoundly penetrate it, make it the food of their own spiritual lives,[32] and be enabled to proclaim, explain, and protect it in their priestly ministry.

The students are to be formed with particular care in the study of the Bible, which ought to be, as it were, the soul of all theology.[33] After a suitable introduction they are to be initiated carefully into the method of exegesis; and they are to see the great themes of divine revelation and to receive from their daily reading of and meditating on the sacred books inspiration and nourishment.[34]

Dogmatic theology should be so arranged that these biblical themes are proposed first of all. Next there should be opened up to the students what the Fathers of the Eastern and Western Church have contributed to the faithful transmission and development of the individual truths of revelation.[35] The further history of dogma should also be presented, account being taken of its relation to the general history of the Church. Next, in order that they may illumine the mysteries of salvation as completely as possible, the students should learn to penetrate them more deeply with the help of speculation, under the guidance of St. Thomas, and to perceive their interconnections.[36] They should be taught to recognize these same mysteries as present and working in liturgical actions[37] and in the entire life of the Church. They should learn to seek the solutions to human problems under the light of revelation, to apply the eternal truths of revelation to the changeable conditions of human affairs and to communicate them in a way suited to men of our day.[38]

Likewise let the other theological disciplines be renewed through a more living contact with the mystery of Christ and the history of salvation. Special care must be given to the perfecting of moral theology. Its scientific exposition, nourished more on the teaching of the Bible, should shed light on the loftiness of the calling of the faithful in Christ and the obligation that is theirs of bearing fruit in charity for the life of the world. Similarly the teaching of canon law and of Church history should take into account the mystery of the Church, according to the dogmatic constitution De Ecclesia promulgated by this Sacred Synod. Sacred liturgy, which is to be considered as the primary and indispensable source of the truly Christian spirit, should be taught according to the mind of articles 15 and 16 of the Constitution on the Sacred Liturgy.[39]

The circumstances of various regions being duly considered, students are to be brought to a fuller understanding of the churches and ecclesial communities separated from the Apostolic Roman See, so that they may be able to contribute to the work of re-establishing unity among all Christians according to the prescriptions of this Holy Synod.[40]

Let them also be introduced to a knowledge of other religions which are more widespread in individual regions, so that they may acknowledge more correctly what truth and goodness these religions, in God's province, possess, and so that they may learn to refute their errors and be able to communicate the full light of truth to those who do not have it.

17. But since doctrinal training ought to tend not to a mere communication of ideas but to a true and intimate formation of the students, teaching methods are to be revised both as regards lectures, discussions, and seminars and also the development of study on the part of the students, whether done privately or in small groups. Unity and soundness of the entire training is carefully to be provided for by avoiding an excessive multiplication of courses and lectures and by the omission of those questions which scarcely retain any importance or which ought to be referred to higher academic studies.

18. It will be the bishops' concern that young men suited by temperament, virtue, and ability be sent to special institutes, faculties, or universities so that priests may be trained at a higher scientific level in the sacred sciences and in other fields which may be judged opportune. Thus they will be able to meet the various needs of the apostolate. The spiritual and pastoral training of these men, however, especially if they are not yet ordained as priests, is in no way to be neglected.

VI. The Promotion of Strictly Pastoral Training

19. That pastoral concern which ought to permeate thoroughly the entire training of the students[41] also demands that they be diligently instructed in those matters which are particularly linked to the sacred ministry, especially in catechesis and preaching, in liturgical worship and the administration of the sacraments, in works of charity, in assisting the erring and the unbelieving, and in the other pastoral functions. They are to be carefully instructed in the art of directing souls, whereby they will be able to bring all the sons of the Church first of all to a fully conscious and apostolic Christian life and to the fulfillment of the duties of their state of life. Let them learn to help, with equal solicitude, Religious men and women that they may per-

severe in the grace of their vocations and may make progress according to the spirit of their various institutes.[42]

In general, those capabilities are to be developed in the students which especially contribute to dialogue with men, such as the ability to listen to others and to open their hearts and minds in the spirit of charity to the various circumstances and needs of men.[43]

20. They should also be taught to use the aids which the disciplines of pedagogy, psychology, and sociology can provide,[44] according to correct methodology and the norms of ecclesiastical authority. Likewise let them be properly instructed in inspiring and fostering the apostolic activity of the laity[45] and in promoting the various and more effective forms of the apostolate. Let them also be imbued with that truly Catholic spirit which will accustom them to transcend the limits of their own diocese, nation, or rite, and to help the needs of the whole Church, prepared in spirit to preach the Gospel everywhere.[46]

21. But since it is necessary for the students to learn the art of exercising the apostolate not only theoretically but also practically, and to be able to act both on their own responsibility and in harmonious conjunction with others, they should be initiated into pastoral work, both during their course of studies and also during the time of vacations, by opportune practical projects. These should be carried out in accordance with the age of the students and local conditions, and with the prudent judgment of the bishops, methodically and under the leadership of men skilled in pastoral work, the surpassing power of supernatural means being always remembered.[47]

VII.   Training to Be Achieved After the Course of Studies

22. Since priestly training, because of the circumstances particularly of contemporary society, must be pursued and perfected even after the completion of the course of studies in seminaries,[48] it will be the responsibility of episcopal conferences in individual

nations to employ suitable means to this end. Such would be pastoral institutes working together with suitably chosen parishes, meetings held at stated times, and appropriate projects whereby the younger clergy would be gradually introduced into the priestly life and apostolic activity, under its spiritual, intellectual, and pastoral aspects, and would be able, day by day, to renew and foster them more effectively.

Conclusion

The Fathers of this Holy Synod have pursued the work begun by the Council of Trent. While they confidently entrust to seminary administrators and teachers the task of forming the future priests of Christ in the spirit of the renewal promoted by this Sacred Synod, they earnestly exhort those who are preparing for the priestly ministry to realize that the hope of the Church and the salvation of souls is being committed to them. They urge them also to receive the norms of this Decree willingly and thus to bring forth most abundant fruit which will always remain.

The entire text and all the individual elements which have been set forth in this Decree have pleased the Fathers. And by the Apostolic power conferred on us by Christ, we, together with the Venerable Fathers, in the Holy Spirit, approve, decree and enact them; and we order that what has been thus enacted in Council be promulgated, to the glory of God.

Rome, at St. Peter's, 28 October 1965.

I, PAUL, Bishop of the Catholic Church

There follow the signatures of the Fathers.

Notes

1 That progress among all the People of God primarily depends on the will of Christ Himself and the ministry of priests is clear from the words by which the Lord established His Apostles and their successors and cooperators, heralds of the Gospel, leaders of the new chosen people and dispensers of

the mysteries of God; it is likewise confirmed by the utterances of the Fathers and saints and repeatedly in documents of the supreme pontiffs. Cf. especially: St. Pius X, exhortation to the clergy, *Haerent Animo*, Aug. 4, 1908: *St. Pius X Acts IV*, pp. 237–264. Pius XI, encyclical *Ad Catholici Sacerdotii*, Dec. 20, 1935: *A.A.S.* 28 (1936), especially pp. 37–52. Pius XII, apostolic exhortation *Menti Nostrae*, Sept. 23, 1950: *A.A.S.* 42 (1950), pp. 657–702. John XXIII, encyclical *Sacerdotii Nostri Primordia*, Aug. 1, 1959: *A.A.S.* 51 (1959), pp. 545–579. Paul VI, apostolic letter *Summi Dei Verbum*, Nov. 4, 1963: *A.A.S.* 55 (1963), pp. 979–995.

2 The entire sacerdotal institution—that is, the establishment of a seminary, the spiritual institution, the course of studies, the common life and discipline of students, pastoral practices—all are to be accommodated to the needs of the various localities. This accommodation, especially in its fundamental principles, is to be made according to common norms set down by the episcopal conferences as far as secular priests are concerned, and for suitable reasons by competent superiors in the case of Religious clergy. Cf. general statutes attached to the apostolic constitution *Sedes Sapientiae*, article 19.

3 Among the main afflictions troubling the Church today, the shortage of vocations predominates virtually everywhere. Cf. Pius XII, apostolic exhortation *Menti Nostrae:* ". . . the number of priests both in Catholic regions and mission territories is in most cases insufficient to the growing needs." *A.A.S.* 42 (1950), p. 682. John XXIII: "The problem of ecclesiastical and Religious vocations is the daily preoccupation of the Pope . . . It is the yearning of his prayer, the ardent aspiration of his soul." From the allocution to the First International Congress on Vocations to the State of Perfection, Dec. 16, 1961: *L'Osservatore Romano*, Dec. 17, 1961.

4 Pius XII, apostolic constitution *Sedes Sapientiae*, May 31, 1956: *A.A.S.* 48 (1956), p. 357; Paul VI, apostolic letter *Summi Dei Verbum*, Nov. 4, 1963: *A.A.S.* 55 (1963), pp. 984 ff.

5 Cf. especially: Pius XII, motu proprio *Cum Nobis* ("Concerning the establishment of the Pontifical Society for Priestly Vocations under the direction of the Sacred Congregation of Seminaries and Universities of Studies"), Nov. 4, 1941: *A.A.S.* 33 (1941), p. 479; with the related norms and statutes promulgated Sept. 8, 1943, by the same Sacred Congregation; motu proprio *Cum Supremae* ("Concerning the Pontifical Society for Religious Vocations"), Feb. 11, 1955: *A.A.S.* 47 (1955), p. 266; with the related norms and statutes promulgated by the Sacred Congregation of Religious, *ibid.*, pp. 298–301; Second Vatican Council Decree *On the Renovation of the Religious Life*, No. 24; Decree *On the Pastoral Duties of Bishops*, no. 15.

6 Cf. Pius XII, apostolic exhortation *Menti Nostrae*, Sept. 23, 1950: *A.A.S.* 42 (1950), p. 685.

7 Cf. Second Vatican Council, Dogmatic Constitution *On the Church*, no. 28: *A.A.S.* 57 (1965), p. 34.

8 Cf. Pius XI, encyclical *Ad Catholici Sacerdotii*, Dec. 20, 1935; *A.A.S.* 28

(1936), p. 37. "Especially diligent must be the selection of moderators and teachers . . . Assign to sacred colleges of this kind priests endowed with the highest virtue; and charge them to withdraw from assignments, especially those more burdensome, which cannot be compared with this duty of capital importance, whose place no other can take." This principle of selecting the best is again inculcated by Pius XII in his apostolic letter to the Ordinaries of Brazil of April 23, 1947, *Discourses and Radio Messages* IX, pp. 579–580.

9 Concerning the common duty of supporting zealously the work in seminaries, cf. Paul VI, apostolic letter *Summi Dei Verbum*, Nov. 4, 1963: *A.A.S.* 53 (1963), p. 984.

10 Cf Pius XII, apostolic exhortation *Menti Nostrae*, Sept. 23, 1950: *A.A.S.* 42 (1950), p. 684; and cf. Sacred Congregation of Sacraments, circular letter *Magna equidem* to local Ordinaries, Dec. 27, 1935, n. 10. For Religious cf. *Statuta Generalia* attached to the apostolic constitution *Sedes Sapientiae* of May 31, 1956, art 33 [and] Paul VI, apostolic letter *Summi Dei Verbum*, Nov. 4, 1963: *A.A.S.* 55 (1963), p. 987 ff.

11 Cf. Pius XI, encyclical *Ad Catholici Sacerdotii*, Dec. 20, 1935: *A.A.S.* 28 (1936), p. 41.

12 It is established by statute that in determining the statutes of regional or national seminaries all interested bishops take part, despite the prescription of Canon 1357, part 4 of the Code of Canon Law.

13 Cf. Pius XII, apostolic exhortation *Menti Nostrae*, Sept. 23, 1950: *A.A.S.* 42 (1950), p. 674; Sacred Congregation of Seminaries and Universities of Studies, *The Spiritual Formation of the Candidate for the Priesthood*, Vatican City, 1965.

14 Cf. St. Pius X, exhortation to the Catholic clergy, *Haerent Animo*, Aug. 4, 1908: St. Pius X Acts IV, pp. 242–244; Pius XII apostolic exhortation *Menti Nostrae*, Sept. 23, 1950: *A.A.S.* 42 (1950), pp. 659–661: John XXIII, encyclical *Sacerdotii Nostri Primordia*, Aug. 1, 1959: *A.A.S.* 51 (1959), p. 550 ff.

15 Cf. Pius XII, encyclical *Mediator Dei*, Nov. 20, 1947: *A.A.S.* 39 (1947), pp. 547 ff. and 572 ff., John XXIII, apostolic exhortation *Sacrae Laudis*, Jan. 6, 1962: *A.A.S.* 54 (1962), p. 69; Second Vatican Council Constitution *On the Sacred Liturgy*, art. 16 and 17: *A.A.S.* 56 (1964), p. 104 ff.; Sacred Congregation of Rites, *Instruction for the Correct Implementation of the Constitution on the Sacred Liturgy*, Sept. 26, 1964, no. 14–17: *A.A.S.* 56 (1964), p. 880 ff.

16 Cf. John XXIII, encyclical *Sacerdotii Nostri Primordia*: *A.A.S.* 51 (1959), p. 559 ff.

17 Cf. Second Vatican Council Dogmatic Constitution *On the Church*, no. 28: *A.A.S.* 57 (1965), p. 35 ff.

18 St. Augustine, *Tract on John*, 32, 8: PL 35, 1646.

19 Cf. Pius XII, apostolic exhortation *Menti Nostrae*: *A.A.S.* 42 (1950), pp. 662 ff., 685, 690; John XXIII, encyclical *Sacerdotii Nostri Primordia*: *A.A.S.* 51 (1959), pp. 551, 553, 556 ff.; Paul VI, encyclical *Ecclesiam Suam*, Aug. 6,

1964: *A.A.S.* 56 (1964), p. 634 ff.; Second Vatican Council, Dogmatic Constitution *On the Church*, especially no. 8: *A.A.S.* 57 (1965), p. 12.

20 Cf. Pius XII, encyclical *Sacra Virginitas*, March 25, 1954: *A.A.S.* 46 (1954), pp. 165 ff.

21 Cf. St. Cyprian, *De Habitu Virginum*, no. 22: PL 4, 475; St. Ambrose, *De Virginibus*, I, 8, 52: PL 16, 202 ff.

22 Cf. Pius XII, apostolic exhortation *Menti Nostrae: A.A.S.* 42 (1950), p. 663.

23 Cf. Pius XII, encyclical *Sacra Virginitas*, 1. c., pp. 170–174.

24 Cf. Pius XII, apostolic exhortation *Menti Nostrae*, 1. c., pp. 664 and 690 ff.

25 Cf. Paul VI, apostolic letter *Summi Dei Verbum*, Nov. 4, 1963: *A.A.S.* 55 (1963), p. 991.

26 Cf. Pius XII, apostolic exhortation *Menti Nostrae*, 1. c., p. 686.

27 Cf. Paul VI, apostolic letter *Summi Dei Verbum*, 1. c., p. 993.

28 Cf. Second Vatican Council, Dogmatic Constitution *On the Church*, no. 7 and 28: *A.A.S.* 57 (1965), pp. 9–11, 33 ff.

29 Cf. Pius XII, encyclical *Humani Generis*, Aug. 12, 1950: *A.A.S.* (1950), pp. 571–575.

30 Cf. Paul VI, encyclical *Ecclesiam Suam*, Aug. 6, 1964: *A.A.S.* 56 (1964), pp. 637 ff.

31 Cf. Pius XII, encyclical *Humani Generis*, Aug. 12, 1950: *A.A.S.* 42 (1950), pp. 567–569; allocution *Si Diligis*, May 31, 1954: *A.A.S.* 46 (1954). p. 314 ff.; Paul VI, allocution given at Pontifical Gregorian University, March 12, 1964: *A.A.S.* 56 (1964), p. 364 ff.; Second Vatican Council Dogmatic Constitution *On the Church*, no. 25: *A.A.S.* 57 (1965), pp. 29–31.

32 Cf. St. Bonaventure, *Itinerarium Mentis in Deum*, Prol., no. 4: "[No one] believes that reading suffices of itself without unction, speculation without devotion, investigation without wonder, circumspection without exultation, conscientiousness without piety, knowledge without charity, intelligence without humility, zeal without divine grace, observation without wisdom divinely inspired" (St. Bonaventure, *Complete Works* V, Quaracchi 1891, p. 296),

33 Cf. Leo XIII, encyclical *Providentissimus Deus*, Nov. 18, 1893: *A.A.S.* 26 (1893–1894), p. 283.

34 Cf. Pontifical Biblical Commission, *Instruction on the Correct Teaching of Sacred Scripture*, May 13, 1950: *A.A.S.* 42 (1950), p. 502.

35 Cf. Pius XII, encyclical *Humani Generis*, Aug. 12, 1950: *A.A.S.* 42 (1950), p. 568 ff.: ". . . sacred disciplines always find rejuvenation in the study of the sacred fonts; while on the other hand that speculation becomes sterile which neglects deeper inquiry into the sacred deposit in order to provide knowledge from experience."

36 Cf. Pius XII, sermon to seminarians, June 24, 1939: *A.A.S.* 31 (1939), p. 247: Emulation . . . in seeking and propagating the truth is not suppressed by commending the doctrine of St. Thomas, but rather stimulated and thoroughly directed. Paul VI, allocution given at the Pontifical Gregorian

University, March 12, 1964: *A.A.S.* 56 (1964), p. 365: "[Teachers]—should reverently listen to the voice of the Church's Doctors, among whom Aquinas holds a special place; such is the power of the Angelic Doctor's genius and such his sincere love of truth; so great his wisdom in investigating the highest truths, in demonstrating and linking them with the most appropriate bonds of unity that as a result his doctrine becomes a most efficacious instrument not only for gathering the fundamental aspects of the faith into a unified whole, but also for attaining usefully and securely the fruits of a healthy progression." Cf. also the allocution addressed to the Sixth International Thomastic Congress, Sept. 10, 1965.

37 Cf. Second Vatican Council, Constitution *On the Sacred Liturgy*, no. 7 and 16: *A.A.S.* 56 (1964), pp. 100 ff. and 104 ff.

38 Cf Paul VI, encyclical *Ecclesiam Suam*, Aug. 6, 1964: *A.A.S.* 56 (1964), p. 640 ff.; Second Vatican Council, schema of the Pastoral Constitution *On the Church in the Modern World* (1965).

39 Second Vatican Council, Constitution *On the Sacred Liturgy*, no. 10, 14, 15, 16; Sacred Congregation of Rites, *Instruction for the Correct Implementation of the Constitution on the Sacred Liturgy*, Sept. 26, 1964, no. 11 and 12: *A.A.S.* 56 (1964), p. 879 ff.

40 Second Vatican Council, Decree *On Ecumenism*, no. 1, 9, 10: *A.A.S.* 57 (1965), pp. 90 and 98 ff.

41 The ideal of the pastorate can be deduced from documents of recent pontiffs which treat distinctly of the life, qualifications and institution of priests; cf. especially: St. Pius X, exhortation to the clergy *Haerent Animo*, St. Pius X Acts IV, pp. 237 ff. Pius XI, encyclical *Ad Catholici Sacerdotii: A.A.S.* 28 (1936), pp. 5 ff. Pius XII, apostolic exhortation *Menti Nostrae: A.A.S.* 42 (1950), pp. 657 ff. John XXIII, encyclical *Sacerdotii Nostri Primordia: A.A.S.* 51 (1959), pp. 545 ff. Paul VI, apostolic letter *Summi Dei Verbum: A.A.S.* 55 (1963), pp. 979 ff. Much concerning pastoral formation can be found also in the encyclicals *Mystici Corporis* (1943), *Mediator Dei* (1947), *Evangelii Praecones* (1951), *Sacra Virginitas* (1954), *Musicae Sacrae Disciplina* (1955), *Princeps Pastorum* (1959), and in the apostolic constitution *Sedes Sapientiae* (1956) for Religious. Pius XII, John XXIII and Paul VI have often illustrated the ideal of the good pastor in their allocutions to seminarians and priests as well.

42 Concerning the importance of the state characterized by the profession of the evangelical counsels, cf. Second Vatican Council, Dogmatic Constitution *On the Church*, Ch. VI: *A.A.S.* 57 (1965), pp. 49–53; Decree *On the Renovation of the Religious Life*.

43 Cf. Paul VI, encyclical *Ecclesiam Suam*, Aug. 6, 1964: *A.A.S.* 56 (1964) in several places throughout, especially pp. 635 ff. and 640 ff.: Second Vatican Council Schema of the Pastoral Constitution *On the Church in the Modern World* (1965).

44 Cf. especially John XXIII, encyclical *Mater et Magistra*, May 15, 1961: *A.A.S.* 53 (1961), pp. 401 ff.

45 Cf. in particular Second Vatican Council, schema of the Decree *On the Lay Apostolate* (1965) no. 25 and 30, pp. 54, 62.

46 Cf. Second Vatican Council, Dogmatic Constitution *On the Church*, no. 17: *A.A.S.* 57 (1965), p. 20 ff.; schema of the Decree *On the Church's Missionary Activity* (1965), especially no. 36 and 37, p. 25 ff.

47 Several pontifical documents warn against the danger in pastoral action of neglecting the supernatural goal and considering supernatural aids of little value at least in practice; cf. especially the documents cited in note 41.

48 More recent documents of the Holy See urge particular concern for newly ordained priests; especially noteworthy are Pius XII, motu proprio *Quandoquidem*, April 2, 1949: *A.A.S.* 41 (1949), pp. 165–167; apostolic exhortation *Menti Nostrae*, Sept. 23, 1950: *A.A.S.* 42 (1950); apostolic constitution (for Religious) *Sedes Sapientiae*, May 31, 1956 and related general statutes; allocution to priests, *Convictus Barcinonensis*, June 14, 1957, *Discourses and Radio Messages* XIX, pp. 271–273; Paul VI, allocution to priests of the Gian Matteo Giberti Institute in the diocese of Verona, Italy, March 11, 1964.

Appendix 4

Selected Bibliography

These few references are only to recent books and periodicals of a general nature. There are hundreds of valuable and more specialized articles in learned journals. But with these writings as a start, following footnote leads, the interested reader quickly can compile his own more thorough bibliography.

Roman Catholic Seminaries:

Burns, James, S.S., *Bibliography of Recent Periodicals and Books Dealing with Seminaries: 1960–65*, St. Mary's Seminary, Baltimore.

Keller, James, and Armstrong, Richard (editors), *Apostolic Renewal in the Seminaries* (New York: The Christophers, 1965).

Lee, James M., and Putz, Louis J., C.S.C. (editors), *Seminary Education in a Time of Change* (Notre Dame: Fides Publishers, 1965).

Miller, Francis Joseph, *A History of the Athenaeum of Ohio: 1829–1960*, unpublished doctoral dissertation, University of Cincinnati, 1964. This is a scholarly study of the historical development of a typical seminary.

Poole, Stafford, C.M., *Seminary in Crisis*, Herder & Herder, New York, 1965.

The annual *Bulletin*, National Catholic Educational Association, Washington, D.C.

Seminarium, quarterly journal, Sacred Congregation of Seminaries and Universities, Vatican City.

Protestant Seminaries:

Bainton, Roland H., *Yale and the Ministry* (New York: Harper & Row, 1957). A fine developmental study of one outstanding Protestant seminary.

Bridston, Keith R., and Culver, Dwight W. (editors), *The Making of Ministers* (Minneapolis: Augsburg Publishing House, 1964, and *Pre-Seminary Education*, Augsburg, 1965).

Niebuhr, H. Richard, Williams, Daniel D., and Gustafson, James M. (editors), *The Advancement of Theological Education* (New York: Harper & Row, 1957).

Wagoner, Walter D., *Bachelor of Divinity* (New York: Association Press, 1963).

Theological Education, quarterly journal, The American Association of Theological Schools, Dayton, Ohio.

Protestant and Catholic Seminaries:

Allen, Yorke Jr., *A Seminary Survey* (New York: Harper & Row, 1960).

Appendix 5

Persons and Institutions
Cooperating in This Study

Following is a list of those persons whom the author visited and interviewed and whose unfailing help was of both informational and inspirational value in the preparation of this book.

THE UNITED STATES

Aquinas Foundation, Princeton University
    The Rev. Robert Murray
Aquinas Institute of Philosophy and Theology, River Forest, Illinois
    The Very Reverend Benedict M. Ashley, O.P.
    The Rev. William H. Crilly, O.P.
Catholic University, Washington, D.C.
    The Very Rev. Walter J. Schmitz, S.S.
    The Rev. Roland Murphy, O.Carm.
Divine Word Seminary, Bay St. Louis, Mississippi
    The Rev. Charles Burns, S.V.D.

Episcopal Seminary of the Southwest, Austin, Texas
    Professor Frederick Pope
Kendrick Seminary, St. Louis, Missouri
    The Most Rev. Robert C. Coerver, S.M.
Maryknoll Fathers, Ossining, New York
    The Rev. Edward F. Malone, M.M.
    The Rev. William McCarthy, M.M.
Moreau Seminary, Notre Dame, Indiana
    The Rev. Donald Draine, C.S.C.
Mt. St. Agnes College, Baltimore, Maryland
    Professor Arthur G. Madden
National Catholic Educational Association, Washington, D.C.
    The Rt. Rev. Frederick Hochwalt
    Mr. and Mrs. John Cermak
Priory of St. Rose of Lima, Dubuque, Iowa
    The Rev. Kevin D. O'Rourke, O.P.
Seton Institute, Baltimore, Maryland
    Dr. Leo Barteimier
Saint John's University, Collegeville, Minnesota
    The Rev. Colman J. Barry, O.S.B.
    The Rev. Paschal Botz, O.S.B.
    The Rev. Godfrey Diekmann, O.S.B.
St. Charles Borromeo Seminary, Overbrook, Pennsylvania
    The Rev. William K. Leahy
    The Rev. Philip A. Farley
    The Rev. Anthony T. Massimini
St. Joseph's College, Princeton, New Jersey
    The Rev. John V. Newman, C.M.
    The Rev. John J. Hodnett, C.M.
St. Mary's Seminary, Baltimore, Maryland
    The Very Rev. John R. Sullivan, S.S.
    The Rev. Daniel C. Maguire, S.S.
St. Mary's Seminary, Perryville, Missouri
    The Rev. Stafford Poole, C.M.
St. Meinrad Seminary, St. Meinrad, Indiana
    The Rev. Adrian Fuerst, O.S.B.

The Rev. Kiernan Conley, O.S.B.
The Rev. Hilary Ottensmeyer, O.S.B.
St. Patrick's College, Menlo Park, California
The Very Rev. Paul Purta, S.S.
St. Paul Minor Seminary, Saginaw, Michigan
The Rt. Rev. James A. Hickey
Stanford University
Professor Robert McAfee Brown
Professor Michael Novak
The Conference of Major Superiors of Men, U.S.A., Inc., Washington, D.C.
The Rev. Boniface Wittenbrink, O.M.I.
Woodstock College, Woodstock, Maryland
The Rev. Terence J. Toland, S.J.
The Rev. Joseph A. Fitzmeyer, S.J.
University of Notre Dame, Notre Dame, Indiana
Dr. George Shuster

CITY OF ROME

Pontifical University of St. Thomas Aquinas (Angelicum)
His Eminence, Michael Cardinal Browne, O.P. Rector
  Magnificent
The Rev. Conleto Kearns, O.P., Rector
The Rev. P.M. Said, O.P.
The Rev. P.F. Giardini, O.P.
The Rev. P.S. Carlson, O.P.
Pontifical Gregorian University
The Rev. Francis A. Sullivan, S.J.
The Rev. William Van Roo, S.J.
The Rev. Renatus Latourelle, S.J.
Pontifical Urban University
The Rev. Stefanus Virgulin, Secretary General
Pontifical Lateran University
The Rev. Giuseppe Lastovica, Secretary
Pontifical Athenaeum St. Anselm

The Most Rev. Agostinus Mayer, O.S.B., Rector Magnificent
Pontifical Antonianum Athenaeum
The Most Rev. Damiano Van Den Eynde, O.F.M. Rector
Magnificent
Pontifical Salesian Athenaeum
The Most Rev. Alfonso Stickler, S.D.B., Rector Magnificent
Theological Faculty Marianum
The Rev. Licinius Peretto, O.S.M., Secretary
Pontifical Faculty "San Bonaventura" Seraphicum
The Rev. Giovanni Odoardi, O.F.M. conv., Secretary
Pontifical Institute of Oriental Studies
The Most Rev. Joseph Gill, S.J., Rector
Pontifical Biblical Institute
The Most Rev. Roderick MacKenzie, S.J. Rector
The Rev. Francis S. Devine, S.J.
The Rev. Francis McCool, S.J.
The Rev. Luis Alonso Schoekel, S.J.
Pontifical Institute of Christian Archeology
The Rev. Felice D. Darsy, O.P., Rector
Pontifical Institute of Sacred Music
The Rev. Angelo Coan, O.Carm., Rector
Vatican School of Paleography and Document Study
Professor Guilia Battelli, Director
Apostolic Vatican Library
Dr. Nello Vian, Secretary
Sacred Congregation of Seminaries and Universities
The Rt. Rev. Pietro Pavon
The Rev. Luigi Ferrari
The Rev. Antonio Romeo
Pontifical Office for Religious Vocations
The Rev. Godfrey Poage, C.P.
Secretariat for Promoting Christian Unity
The Rev. Thomas S. Stransky, C.S.P.
Convento San' Onofrio
The Rev. Germanius Tomanio, S.A.
The White Fathers
The Rev. A. V. DeMeeren, W.F.

Divine Word Seminary (Nemi)
  The Rev. Francis Mihalic, S.V.D.
The Waldensian Faculty
  Professor Alberto Soggin
  Professor Vittorio Subilia
  Professor Valdo Vinay
National Federation of the Evangelical Churches of Italy
  The Rev. and Mrs. Thurlow Weed

BELGIUM

Mission de Scheut, Namur
  The Rev. Edmund E. Veillesse, C.I.C.M.
Lumen Vitae, Brussels
  The Rev. Georges Delcuve, S.J.
  The Rev. P. Watte, S.J.
University of Louvain, Louvain
  The Rev. Gustav Thils
  The Rev. Albert Houssiau
Séminaire John XXIII, Louvain
  The Rev. Herman Servotte
Archdiocese, Malines
  The Rev. René Cueppens
Heverlee
  The Rev. Peter F. Fransen, S.J.

FRANCE

Séminaire St. Sulpice
  The Rev. Pierre Girard, S.S.
  The Rev. Michael Child, S.S.

HOLLAND

The Rev. Henri Nouwee, Utrecht

ENGLAND

Downside Abbey
  Abbot Butler
St. Edmund's College
  The Rev. Charles Davis
Cambridge University
  The Rev. Kenelm Foster, O.P.
  The Rev. James Burtchaell, C.S.C.
London:
  Mr. Neil Middleton, Sheed and Ward
  Mr. John Todd, Darton, Longman and Todd
Ushaw
  The Rev. John McHugh